POLAND THE UNEXPLORED

BY THE SAME AUTHOR

Flags

Heroes of Liberty

Illinois, The Story of
the Prairie State

Stories of Our Great
Inventions

Women in American
History

The main gateway of Krakow

POLAND
THE UNEXPLORED

By Grace Humphrey

Illustrated

Indianapolis

THE BOBBS-MERRILL COMPANY

Publishers

To
SOPHIE HART
IN GRATITUDE FOR ENGLISH SIX
AT WELLESLEY

CONTENTS

ILLUSTRATIONS

ILLUSTRATIONS—*Continued*

POLAND THE UNEXPLORED

POLAND THE UNEXPLORED
CHAPTER I
I'M GOING TO POLAND!

"To POLAND!"

"You're going to Poland!!"

"Poland—well!!!"

My friends were thunderstruck at my announcement.

Why in the world was I going off there? What was I going to do in Poland? Was there anything to see in Poland? Did I know anybody? But only one person, and she was a little old lady in black silk, asked if it was safe for me to go to Poland.

"I want to see the country and the people. No, I haven't any friends there—no acquaintances even."

"But why do you want to go? Whatever put it into your head?"

Before my eyes flashed a picture of myself at nine, reading some book—I have no idea what book it was—and coming across the word *Poland*. Half an hour later my mother found me in the library, perched on the arm of a chair, with books all around me, and every book open at a map.

"Child, what are you hunting for?"

"For Poland. I can't find it on the map."

"No, you won't find it."

"But, Mother, I saw it in a book and it sounds like the

[13]

name of a real country; it doesn't sound like a fairy place. Isn't there a Poland?"

"There was—once. Come and sit by me while I'm sewing, and I'll tell you."

Once upon a time, she began, Poland was a large country, one of the very important countries in Europe. But strong greedy neighbors made war upon her, under one excuse and another, and took her land. Once, twice, three times they did this, and then—there was nothing left. Poland simply vanished from the map. She showed me where it used to be—Austria took some, Germany some, Russia the biggest part; she thought we could find, in one of father's books, a map that would show the old Poland. When did all that happen? The last Partition was— she looked to make sure—in the seventeen-nineties.

"Then, Mother, there isn't any Poland now?" I asked with a catch in my breath. Even then it seemed a dreadful thing, wiping a country off the map—as if a nation were drawn on the blackboard and just erased.

"Yes," and often since I've wondered how she knew this, "yes, there is a Poland now, a hundred years after. Poland lives in the hearts of her people. A man born in the Russian part of Poland never says, 'I am a Russian,' but always proudly, 'I am a Pole!' And in the west, the part that's now under Germany, the people say they're Poles, not Germans. The children have to learn German at school, but secretly at home the mothers teach them Polish. In Austrian Poland the same. All these years they've hoped, they've dreamed and kept on hoping that some day Poland would come back on to the map, that they could have their country once more.''

Was it then and there I resolved that some day, some time I'd go over to Poland and get acquainted with these people who could not give their country up, who proudly announced that they were her citizens when there was no Poland? But school and college, writing books and making talks filled the years; whenever I was in Europe Poland seemed too far away—off the beaten path, almost off the map.

But I could not forget. The very word had a strange fascination for me. I read the little there was to read. To my surprise I found myself writing something about Poland. I put Kosciuszko and Sobieski into a book of hero stories. Doing a brief life of Catherine the Great, I read for more than a week on the Partitions of Poland, read till I exhausted the New York Library, though I had to condense it into two paragraphs. And ''The Third of May,'' a tale of the famous Constitution of 1791, was one of the chapters I liked best in *Stories of the World's Holidays*.

Did any one in the whole United States read Wilson's thirteenth point (that there must be a Poland, with access to the sea) with more of a thrill, or follow with greater interest the Versailles discussions of boundaries, or become more excited when finally an atlas appeared, showing the new Europe with Poland back on the map once more? A hundred and twenty-four years and Poland was born anew.

It needed a suggestion, from just the right person, to start me on my journey to this new-old country. It came while I was writing *Flags,* working on a story called "The White Eagle." I wanted to check up a date and get a fuller account of the legendary Lech who saw a white eagle against the sunset sky and there built the first town in Poland, and ask about the king's flag of red and white; so I betook me to the Consulate and was sent in to talk with——

I've never been christened nor had a godmother, and I never supposed that to make up for this loss I'd be given a fairy godmother. But I'm sure she waved her wand that morning, and she was seldom absent during all my months of adventuring in Poland.

"Some time ago," explained this young man, "a little boy wrote in and asked about the Polish flag. I spent a lot of time getting all the facts together. I'll show you the duplicate of my letter, that'll answer your questions."

But he didn't know the boy's name, or where he lived, or the date, so the poor clerk had to go through the files and I had to wait. Would he tell me about the president's flag? Did it have a crown?

"Yes—a crown like this," and he slipped off his seal ring and passed it over for me to examine the design. What title did his family have, I wondered, and to myself called him the prince. He began talking about Poland and I listened, as spellbound as when I first heard the story from my mother. Old churches and palaces; how the knights were armed, the crests of eagles' feathers,

[16]

how they charged, two rows together, in battle; he acted it out, with a paper-knife for a lance, with Tartars just beyond his desk. Peasant arts; Marshal Pilsudski; wall hangings woven with threads of gold and silver; and a tiny bit of his own story, born in St. Petersburg where his parents were exiles after the last insurrection, Poles burning with patriotism.

"Why," he turned on me suddenly, "why don't you go to Poland?"

"I will."

"Please let me know when. Would you like some introductions? My father and mother live in Warsaw now, and I have a cousin in one of the ministries—he has an American wife. They might be able to help you."

Out on the streets of New York again I looked around, surprised to find everything just as usual, when for me the world was altered completely—I was going to Poland!

But making plans and getting ready were entirely different from the preparations for any other trip to Europe. To my dismay I found no Baedeker for Poland, no Blue Guide. I went to half a dozen travel agencies, hoping their booklets and folders would give me numerous suggestions; nowhere could they give me anything on Poland. Oh, yes, plenty of literature on Czechoslovakia, on Norway, even one tour announced for Russia; but Poland? Nothing whatever. Why, nobody goes to Poland.

With results no better I tried the Public Library. A few histories, one of them coming down to 1924; pam-

phlets published at the end of the war, debating boundaries and plebiscites and minorities; one volume telling
a Red Cross worker's experiences, and a fat one of sta-
tistics on the relief work of the Hoover Commission. Of
travel books, telling what towns to see and what tourists
must not miss in Poland, the newest was written by an
Englishman, there in 1912! Could I start with no more of
an itinerary than the names of four cities?

Just then a Polish professor who'd been in this country
lecturing returned to New York and some one put me in
touch with him before he sailed. "Yes, yes," he glanced
at my list, "and you must go to——" He pulled a sheet
of paper toward him, and began writing out my whole
itinerary, marking towns one day or three, or a week.

"A month for Warsaw," I remarked, "and a month for
Krakow."

"What!" He put down his pen and stared at me. "Do
you mean to say you're planning to stay as long in Krakow as at Warsaw?"

"Yes."

"H—m. Most of our English and American visitors
go to Warsaw because it's the capital, stay till their time's
nearly up, and then run down to Krakow and want me to
show it all in one or two days. Why, Krakow has six
times as much to see as Warsaw!"

I didn't know he came from Krakow, so I was perfectly
innocent; but that chance remark enlisted his friendly
help. He planned short excursions—to the salt mines
half an hour from Krakow, to a lake if I went to Wilno,

to Sobieski's summer palace near Warsaw. He drew a rough sketch of Poland showing where these places were. I thanked him and started to go.

"Wait a moment. You must have some introductions to people who speak English. Let me see—at Gdynia (Ge-deen′ya) I know no one, but stay at this hotel. To-run—the Princess R. Warsaw—Mme. G. and Professor A." Right through the list he went, writing names of hotels and pensions, addresses of friends, without ever looking up a number or the spelling of puzzling names. Counting his sister-in-law's address in Krakow, in case he should be away when I arrived (and he was!), I had sixteen introductions. More than anything else they gave me courage when I realized that I was starting off alone to a new country where I couldn't speak the language.

If I couldn't "read up" on Poland, I must have contacts with interesting people there, and in my last busy days in New York I set out to get a second sixteen. The American Minister in Warsaw was a Philadelphia man, so I begged an acquaintance in that city to get me an introduction to him and to his wife. I wrote a dozen letters telling my plans and asking if by some lucky chance my friends knew anybody in Poland. Some brought no answer. Some said no. Two were prizes.

"I have no contacts in Poland," read one reply, "but a guest here for the week-end has a Cornell friend who was there under Hoover. You'll hear from him direct, for I made Jack sit down at my desk and write him at once."

[19]

Three introductions (and splendid ones they proved to be) arrived in due time from the friend's friend's friend. The second letter—but that's a story by itself.

I consulted my list and found I had no one in Czestochowa, and two paragraphs in the Englishman's book made me sure that if I went there at all, I wanted to do and see far more than he had. By this time I was quite shameless in asking. What was the largest Polish church in or near New York? St. Stanislas, on Seventh Street? I raced down there to see the priest and demanded breathlessly, "Do you know some one at Czestochowa?"

"Yes, the bishop."

"Could you give me a letter to him? It wouldn't in any way embarrass you? You know, that's one place where I must have special help, since I don't speak Polish."

He smiled.

"The Bishop of Czestochowa was my guest when he came to America two years ago, and stayed at my house. He will do whatever I ask, whatever you ask too. Now, what else? Would you like a letter to the Mother Superior of a convent where the nuns are cloistered? You could never get in by yourself, but perhaps you'd like to see such a place; you don't have many here in America."

"One more to come, a note to the head of the Anaconda Copper Company in Poland," I announced, gloating over my substitute for Baedeker, "and then my contacts will cover everything—except the Jews. But there are so many Jews—isn't it one man out of nine? I feel as if

I ought to meet some of them, see how they live, talk to them. How go about it?"

"Ask your friend, Doctor Wise," some one suggested, "and Mrs. B. could help you."

A letter to a Jewish lawyer, to the head of a school, one typed in the Russian alphabet, to the head of a relief committee, and a fourth, written in Hebrew, commending me to all the worthy rabbis of Poland. Now I was ready to start.

How did one get there? I studied the map. Land at a French port, there'd be a long train trip, with three extra visas. Wasn't there some way of going straight to Poland? The Gdynia-America Line sailing from Brooklyn, around the north of Scotland and up the Baltic, would land me at Gdynia, the new port Poland was making—making out of nothing but a stretch of beach. Where there had been only a cluster of fishermen's huts is a town of nearly thirty thousand. It sounded so romantic, I decided at once to go on that line.

A wise decision that, for on the *Polonia* I met Poles—indeed I was the sole American passenger, not counting the Americans of Polish descent—talked with them constantly, and learned my first words in their difficult language. I'd learned to count in half a dozen tongues, but never before did it take me five mornings to get up to ten. In Italian some words remind you of Latin or French, but counting in Polish you just have to memorize strange-sounding words that don't tie up with anything—*jeden, dwa, chee, tairy, peench*—it sounded, well, something like that; how amazed I was to find later that four is spelled *cztery!* Then I mastered "good morning," "how much does it cost," "please," and "thank you"—these last two I needed constantly in Poland.

How did I get along without knowing Polish? Of course I missed a great deal—that I was conscious of every day; but I did get along, using gestures when French or German words failed me. I found that German was the language to try in shops and when I asked my way on the street, that French would always help me out socially, especially in the large cities; but I soon learned to be wary of telling Poles that I knew French, for they speak it even more rapidly than Frenchmen. But it's amazing how many, many Poles speak English, men as well as women. Like all the Slavs they're good linguists, and where an American laboriously learns one language, they master four, five, six, eight.

But they realize that Polish is difficult, some of them say it's harder than Russian. You know how the French are; everybody ought to know French, and if you can't speak it and understand it when they run the words together, they feel sorry for you, and that's that. The Poles, on the contrary, don't expect you to know their language. Almost the first question at a tea is, "What shall we speak to-day?" Don't think that implies the slightest contempt for Polish, it's thoughtfulness for a guest.

For Poles are enormously proud of their language and—I learned this to my amazement—actually think it beautiful. American ears are slow to grow accustomed to the strange sounds and combinations of letters, but it gets easier after a bit, when you learn that *chrz* is like our *sh* and the barred *l* something like *w*. As is frequently the case in Poland, this devotion to their language is partly a question of patriotism. The Germans and the Russians made many attempts to stamp it out: letters addressed in Polish were delayed and then charged a translation fee before the German post-office would deliver them; Marshal Pilsudski was one of many boys expelled from a Russian school for speaking Polish in the classroom; and some Americans have not forgotten the horror with which they read of the Polish school children at Wrzesnia, whipped by the Prussian teacher for refusing to say the Lord's Prayer in German. Every attempt failed and only made the Poles hold their language the dearer, as one loves passionately the thing one suffers for, makes great sacrifices for. I could pay them no greater compliment than to say, however haltingly, a few words of Polish; and an American woman in Warsaw said, "Do you want to win their hearts? Just say casually, 'I can't go to-morrow, I'm taking a Polish lesson.'" When in December I added to an English letter the Polish words for "Merry Christmas!", copying them painstakingly from a gay peasant card on my desk, the man wrote back and congratulated me on getting them exactly right and said I was making good progress in Polish.

The very word "Slav" tells the story, Panna Helena

[23]

explained to me. The stem originally meant "a word" and the Poles called Slavs all the people who used words, whereas their queer word for Germans, *Niemcy,* means dumb. No, she went on quickly, not stupid; what was our slang word for it—dumb-bell; but just dumb. To the Poles they were men who could not talk, because they didn't speak Polish.

"Like the Athenians," I suggested, "calling all the Asiatics barbarians, because their words sounded like bar-bar?"

"I'd never thought of that comparison, but it fits to a T."

Still, with all my introductions, with a few words of Polish mastered, and the ability to count up to ten, I confess that it was with many doubts and misgivings I landed at Gdynia, for a stay of four months—five at the most. I stayed fifteen and didn't want to leave then, and in all that time I had not one unpleasant incident to mar my happy journeyings, I met with nothing but the most beautiful courtesy from all classes of people, I found friendly help at every turn. I was never once short-changed, and that's more than I can say for the rest of Europe.

I traveled to the four corners of Poland and over nearly all the country in between. I saw great plains, the rich farm lands of a nation two-thirds (or is it three-fourths?) agricultural. I saw also forests and mountains, seacoast, oil-fields, mining district and factory towns. I went by train—first-class, second, third—by boat and motor-bus and tramway, in automobiles and carriages and twice in a peasant's cart. Never once did I ask directions, ask any question, and find people too busy to stop and help me. Railroad conductors and porters, taxi drivers, hotel clerks, telephone operators, street-car men—all went out of their way to assist a foreigner. I had constantly the feeling that I was a guest, and a very special guest. The Poles were very curious as to where I came from, but instead of keeping still and letting them wonder I'd tell, for I soon learned that *Amerikanka* was a magic word and would get me almost anything.

Witness the morning I got on the wrong car in Warsaw and the conductor wouldn't let me pay my fare, but helped me off and explained to a man waiting at the tram-stop what car he was to put me on. And once as I gave the man my two-and-a-half cents I said (in English), "Will you tell me when to get off? Ulica Lwowska, please," hoping my voice would interpret the question. He spoke only Polish, but clapped his hands for attention and called out something that must have been, "Can somebody help this poor lady?" Up came three passengers asking in German, in French, in English where I wanted to go, and could they be of any service? I gave them a once-over and took my choice—the elderly man in a frock coat.

"I will show you the way, madam. Your street is just around the corner from the tram-stop."

We walked a few steps together, I thanked him, he lifted his hat and started back, following the tram.

"Oh," I cried, "you weren't really getting off here?

(Tram-stops are very far apart in Warsaw, and in all Polish towns.) You did this just for me?"

"Madam, it is nothing. It is always a pleasure, I assure you, to be of some slight service to an American. We can never forget how much we owe to your country. Good-by, madam."

And yet, and yet I must not give you the impression that fifteen months in Poland was always a bed of roses. There were times when I longed for something to read, besides the guide-books that took all the luggage space I could give to books. How many *zlotys* I'd have given for a magazine or a newspaper that day I waited from four-thirty in the morning till noon in a railroad station! There were times when I felt starved for American food, for our kind of coffee, for salads and more fresh fruit (though I greatly enjoyed Polish meals and thrived on them, coming back to the States many pounds heavier than when I left).

There were times when I couldn't make them understand in a restaurant, and could only point to the next table and gesture, "Bring me that—and that." It worked all right if my neighbors had what I happened to want, but it limited my ordering. One hot July night I motioned to the waitress and made her understand that she was to bring me a bowl of sour milk and new potatoes, a favorite supper dish for summer, of which I was very fond; sour milk in Poland is wholly different from ours that's been pasteurized. I was still hungry and thinking that I knew the word for cakes, said to the girl, *"Prosze* (please), *shustka.*" (I've no idea how to spell it, but it sounded something like that.)

"*Shustka?*" she repeated, looking blank.

"*Tak, tak* (yes—Poles never say yes once, but two or three or four times, very fast), *shustka.*"

She called two waitresses and consulted them, trying to find out what in the world I wanted. At not one table in the room was any one eating cakes. At last the head-waitress came, they all talked volubly in Polish, and some one had an idea. Let me show them out in the serving-room, and I was led by the hand through the restaurant, and by gestures told to point to this mysterious *shustka.* There was a glass case with plate after plate of the delicious cakes you get all over Poland.

"Here it is," I cried triumphantly in English, "here—*shustka!*"

The four of them stared at one another, at me, at the cakes, and burst out laughing. When they could get the words out, they exclaimed, "*Shustka*—the Amerikanka ordered *shustka* for *shastka.* Listen, madam, *shastka, shastka!*" And they all laughed again. I memorized *shastka,* cakes, that evening, and learned from experience that I must say my Polish words exactly right or no one could understand me; one vowel wrong, a sound incorrect, the accent in the wrong place, and I was helpless.

But generally, if I was patient, things worked out somehow. For example, just before I left Warsaw, I wanted to see the tomb of Adam Czartoryski, "the uncrowned king of Poland" after the Partitions, head of a family so important that it was often referred to as The Family. I'd been to Holy Cross Church to see the urn with Chopin's heart and its touching inscription in honor of the composer whose body lies in Paris, "To Frederic Chopin, our countryman. Where your treasure is, there shall your heart be also." I'd found the new tablet above the heart of Reymont. But how could I find unaided the Czartoryski tomb, when a chance paragraph I'd come across said it was made of black marble, with no name at all, to insure it against Russian orders of removal? Twice I went and found services going on. The third time I asked person after person, but no one could understand me. A last attempt, and I found a priest who spoke English—from the church of St. Stanislas in New York!—and he took me at once to the right chapel, pointed out the plain, black marble tomb, and proved this was the right spot from the Czartoryski arms above it.

"Why couldn't I find it before?" I consulted an American woman when I'd told her of my ultimate success. "I knew the word for monument—*pomnik*, isn't it?—and I said very distinctly, '*Prosze, pomnik* Adam Czartoryski?' And every one stared at me and said in Polish, 'I don't understand you, lady.'"

"But every word has seven endings in Polish, and if you get your ending wrong of course they haven't the slightest idea what you're trying to say. You should have asked, '*Prosze, pomnik Adama*—accent on the second syllable—*pomnik Adama Czartoryskiego*,' and they'd have taken you right to it."

TRAIN SERVICE

No, it wasn't always easy in Poland. I lived for ten days in a hotel where no one in the office spoke English or French or German; when I wanted them to look up a train or translate a telegram, I must wait till a guest happened along who knew some language I did.

I took trains at impossible hours, frequently starting at eleven or midnight, once at two A.M., changing at four or five-thirty, arriving at seven; and sometimes no sleeping-car. For train service in Poland isn't scheduled as yet for the convenience of tourists; it's planned to get Poles to a town early in the morning, give them the whole day and evening there, and start them back at night, thus avoiding hotel bills; for most of the people are poor and count their *zlotys;* moreover they can sleep anywhere, any time. With much practise I learned to sleep sitting on a bench in a station, with my head on my luggage, or in a railroad compartment, in the corner seat if I went early and was lucky enough to get it, yes, even with the light shining in my eyes, because some selfish man wanted to read a rustly newspaper after midnight. But I knew beforehand that if I went off the beaten track, I must make up my mind to get along as best I could and not grumble; all that was part of the adventure. In large cities, I hasten to add, I was perfectly comfortable; but in Poland, as everywhere in Europe, Americans must remember that comfort and luxury are not identical.

Why did I stay so long? There were so many fascinating things to see and to do; regulation touristy-Baedekery things such as visitors do in many lands—a royal palace,

[29]

an art gallery, monuments, cathedral and chapel, city walls—and specially Polish things besides—like the pilgrimage to Czestochowa, and climbing to the top of a great mound raised in memory of some hero or some great event, or hearing a Polish opera and watching the marvelous dancing, or going at dusk on the first day of November to a cemetery glowing with the light of thousands of candles, in honor of the dead.

Of course my itinerary had to be elastic so that I could do unexpected things. I could not foresee that my wanderings would take me to a mill town like Fall River or Manchester; to the oil-fields; to a virgin forest, the largest one left in Europe, kept inviolate for centuries as the hunting-ground of Polish kings and later of the czars, and to-day a carefully guarded forest reserve; to a boys' camp in the mountains where the Y.M.C.A. director, an American, and a hundred and twenty Polish boys from twelve to eighteen vied with one another to make my visit memorable, giving in my honor a circus of their own making, and a Charlie Chaplin picture and a film of camp life; to a fox hunt where the beaters enclosed a great circle of forest land with a rope with gay streamers every few yards, which moved in the wind and drove Master Fox back—our party got two that morning; to the mining country of Upper Silesia, with so many, such rich coal mines, lead mines, zinc mines, such forests of shafts and chimneys that in ten minutes I understood, as no reading could make me understand, why Germany tried hard to keep this province; for a visit with a family who used to own a mountain range that's now a national park, who took me on a raft down the Dunajec River, the most romantic excursion in Poland; for a few days in a country house, on a farm of eighteen thousand acres; for a trip through the badly named "Polish Corridor"; to the government salt mines; to dinner in seventeenth-century palaces and in a peasant's cottage; and—and—and—— Oh, there's no monotony in a journey through Poland!

I learned enough Polish to get around by myself, but the guide-books I could read were all too meager; it's necessary to go with a Pole. They'll take any amount of time and trouble to go with you, to share their treasures, once they find you're interested in Poland. I defy any cultured Americans to read up on their country, to see a little of Poland, and not get deeply, keenly interested. You learn Polish history on the spot, for they put color and life into palace and monument, into market-place and church. Think of being taken into a sacristy and shown vestments made from embroidered Turkish tents captured by King John Sobieski at Vienna; or hearing the story of a knight, suddenly healed as he prayed before this Madonna, who gave the picture a "dress" of gold and silver, that covers every inch of the canvas except face and hands; or reading a story of three sieges at Lwów where Turkish and Swedish and Ukrainian cannon-balls are embedded in the cathedral walls.

Just walking along the street may be as exciting as sightseeing if you keep your eyes open. Here's a peasant family driving to market, with one little horse hitched

[31]

on the left side; the ends of the cart are plaited of willow; two pigs to sell, a jar of sour cream, wooden spoons and toys, a long string of mushrooms. You pass a smart young officer in khaki who stops to salute a white-haired man in blue, with "1863" in silver on his left shoulder (a veteran of the last insurrection); then a line of school children with their bags strapped on their backs in the most approved modern way; barefoot monks in brown, or black and white; some nuns in wide, stiff head-dresses reaching far out to the sides, or far in front; and university students in their club caps; or somebody's maid carrying home two live chickens or a piece of ice, if it's a hot day; and winter and summer a peasant woman in a heavy shawl, plaid or striped, in which she dexterously wraps herself and her baby.

At the corner stand two Jews in their long black coats with greasy sleeves, in the tiny caps that give them a grotesque appearance; always Jews talking with Jews, and Poles with Poles. There's a group of peasants in their best clothes, come with a priest to some shrine— gay headkerchiefs with roses in the center of the pattern, flowered skirts, black jackets trimmed with sequins and tiny white buttons, showing a white blouse with embroidery on the sleeves. Wait, there may be a religious procession with lighted candles and many banners.

Or you may meet a funeral. Every one stands quietly while it goes slowly by—a little boy who is cross-bearer (perhaps with sport hose showing below his white surplice); one or two or several priests; the open hearse with

[32]

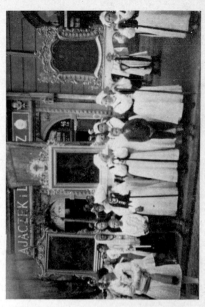

Photo by Polskie Tow, Krajoznawcze

My program was elastic, to give time for a trip on a raft, a fox hunt, for loitering in the market-place and waiting for a procession to start

Photo by Jan Bulhak, Wilno

I spent hours exploring in queer little streets and byways where the sky-line
was often broken by a church

men walking alongside, dressed in black coats with silver trimming, carrying lighted torches on black and silver poles; then the family, always in the deepest mourning, always on foot; and friends. How shocked they were when I said we go to funerals in motors!

"That would not be showing fitting respect to the dead. The least we can do is to walk beside them for a last time. A long distance to the cemetery? Yes, often a very long way. But it is good for people to get thoroughly tired, for when your body is tired it numbs your grief."

After all, interesting as sightseeing and street-loitering are in Poland, my greatest joy was in knowing Poles. They are the most courteous people I've ever met, with the most beautiful manners. I don't mean that I noticed this among the aristocracy only; I don't mean that I myself met always with such politeness, from all classes of people. They're courteous to each other—the men take off their hats to other men, a woman shakes hands with a roomful of women guests at afternoon tea, a child of four or five speaks to all the children and all the nurses when he leaves a group in the park.

And along with their courtesy they're hospitable to the *nth* degree. The slightest excuse and they invite you to dinner or tea, or to stay at their homes. I could have spent another fifteen months in Poland if I'd accepted all my invitations. In one little town I expected to stay three or four hours, just between trains, but found my hostess had made plans for four days. When I spoke of leaving a country house on Thursday, the niece exclaimed,

"Thursday! But you've just come! My aunt expects you to stay a fortnight, if not a month. I'm here for a month, and some of the guests for two." They've made hospitality a fine art; they thank you for coming till you half feel you're doing the favor instead of receiving it.

I think one reason they are model hosts is because Poles are modest. My introductions told, of course, something about me, but alas! they told me little or nothing about my hosts. Often and often I wished I didn't have to ask so many questions, that they'd voluntarily tell me more. Eight months after I'd been her guest, I happened to learn that my first hostess had been a pupil of Mme. Curie-Sklodowska in Paris, her most promising pupil, the discoverer of radium said; again that she'd done some notable work in mathematics; it was only because it came up in another connection that she casually referred to her translation of Shakespeare's sonnets (into Polish!). If you had such records and a foreign guest, would you keep absolutely still about your achievements?

Nor was she an exception to the rule. I arrived in Warsaw to find that a friend had arranged for me to live in a Polish household, Pani L.'s. (Pani means Mrs. and Pan Mr. as nearly as I can put it in English.) I had a pleasant talk with her and answered her questions about my writing and my plans for Poland; of herself not a word. But when later in the day I gave this address at the bank and the American Embassy and to half a dozen persons, they asked, "Is it Suzanna L.? Are you living in the house of the Pani L. who writes poetry as well as novels?" And I was, though I had to ask her point-blank to confirm it.

When one host met me at the station, I sensed at once that he was somebody of importance, how important I learned by very slow degrees—that he'd gone to Paris to speak for Poland before the treaty-makers, that the League of Nations had given him an important appointment, that he'd been one of the three Poles who distributed the Hoover supplies, that he's president of a bank, head of a landowners' association, and various other things. Not one item of this incomplete list did he give me.

They're modest too about what they've done for Poland. They keep still about what they did during the war, what they suffered under the Russians or Germans or Austrians; it was like pulling teeth to get them to talk. You must ask a Pole's best friend if you want to learn something about him. An American schoolboy whom I met had for a year and a half a Polish roommate. Something was said about teeth and Robert commented, "So many Poles have bad teeth. Why, look at Ladislas!"

"Have you shared a room with him for so long," asked Robert's mother, "and he's never told you?"

"Told me—what? We've never mentioned teeth. I just took it for granted, but his are worse than the average. What happened?"

"Only this: the Russians tried to make him answer their questions and he refused to speak, lest he betray some Poles; and at each refusal they knocked out a tooth, or knocked it crooked. It's like him not to have told the story, isn't it?''

It was somebody else who explained to me, when I was going to spend the day, that the family were living very simply indeed, because in 1920 they sold their large estate and poured the money into the treasury of the new Poland. For unlike Czechoslovakia and some other new nations, Poland began without a treasury—began with nothing but memories and hopes.

They're almost as modest about their country. You know how French people are; they take you to see, say, the church where the signal for St. Bartholomew's was given, and if every detail isn't fresh in your mind, why, you don't know history at all. Now the Poles don't take it for granted that you're perfectly familiar with their story. They stop before a great canvas by Matejko and tell you of this king, his Italian queen, the lad in red who grew up to be a king too, and the painter's own portrait in the corner, before they give any artistic comments. In front of the tomb of the Unknown Soldier they stand by the statue of Jozef Poniatowski, and tell you it was made by Thorwaldsen, and do you know about this nephew of the last king of Poland, general of the Polish armies and marshal of France?

Not that Poles aren't as pleased as Punch if you do know something of their history. I used to spread out my scanty scraps and make the most of them, and my friends were touchingly surprised. Once a woman asked if I would be at home the next afternoon, and could she bring her father to call on me. An old soldier, she added.

"Eighteen-sixty-three?" I asked.

"Yes, eighteen-sixty-three." Then she turned to me and inquired earnestly, "How did you know that is a special date, a tragic year in Polish history?"

"Isn't that right? The last insurrection against Russia?"

"Yes, yes, yes. But generally visitors know only vaguely about the Partitions. All our later history is just a blank. Pray, tell me, how did you know about eighteen-sixty-three?"

And lastly, Americans like Poles for their courage; that appeals to us particularly, for it has the same quality as the courage of our pioneer ancestors. We hear little of the devastation in Poland in comparison with losses in Belgium and France, but in those western lands one side at least spared towns and farms and villages; in Poland every army—German, Russian, Austrian, Lithuanian—was an enemy, marching back and forth, destroying what they couldn't take away, devastating two-thirds of the land. And the war lasted two years longer than on the western front.

There was everything to do: bridges and stations to rebuild before trains could run, a housing shortage that even now is not adequately met, schools to open, every detail of a national government to start, and no money, no capital, for a while no credit. Look at the huge sums we've loaned to France and Belgium, to Italy, even to Germany, and the small amount to Poland. The country's like a man who is down, struggling to get to his feet, and doing it with almost no help from outside. I take off my hat to Poland for the amazing amount she's accomplished in a decade. That's Polish courage!

Which is the greater miracle—the nation divided into three parts, that could not lose the Polish spirit, in spite of oppression and censorship and persecution, or the new Poland that has at last come back to the map of Europe?

CHAPTER II

The Lady Isn't Doing This for Herself

"But you can't! It's impossible!" cried the prince at the Consulate when I calmly announced that I wanted to spend a week in a Polish village and live in a peasant's house.

"Nothing's impossible for an American. You're afraid I wouldn't be comfortable? I could stand things for a bit, it'd just be part of my job. You still shake your head? Why can't I?"

"You'll see enough of peasants in market-places and railroad stations and on the streets and at mass. That's not enough to satisfy you? You want to see their houses and eat their food and talk with them? Well, then, go to some village for a day, but take your own food with you. No, you can't possibly stay overnight, for peasant houses have two or three rooms, and I don't suppose there's one in Poland with an extra bed. But remember, I've warned you."

It sounded discouraging, and seeing Polish peasants in their homes was one of the things I'd particularly set my heart on. Surely there must be some way.

"What you want is a reason for going," advised a friend. "You could pick out your village, walk up and down its street a livelong day, and never see more than the outside of the houses. You must have an excuse that'll get you an invitation into a real peasant home. Let me think——"

After many telephone calls to people busy in social service, she put me in touch with a Polish case—the father in Brooklyn, his old mother, his wife and children, his brother and sisters all in Poland. It wasn't one of the tragic stories of a separated family, they said in the Charities office when I'd read the case history and all the letters from the Warsaw worker who'd spent ten months in locating this man's relatives. They were getting along all right in Poland, and he had a steady job here and a little money in the bank. But if what I wanted was an excuse to visit a peasant family, they could make one—no letters had come for months. Here was the address, and good luck!

Toward the end of June I saved a day for this trip from Warsaw to my village. I telephoned the social service woman to ask the best way to go, but she was out of town. Well, with the full address—village, community, post-office—I could scarcely go wrong; so cock-sure, with a package of lunch, I started off at half past eight, in case this should prove to be not an adventure, but merely a tedious waste of time.

A long tram ride to the railroad station on the very outskirts of Warsaw. The building was crowded, packed, jammed with people. Every working man was traveling somewhere with his family. No one had told me it was a holiday. The lines at the ticket windows stretched two and three times across the room, moving up by inches. A friendly policeman asked somebody to buy my ticket; second-class, lady? Oh, no, third-class; wasn't I going to a peasant's house? then I'd better travel with them.

But the throng in the station was nothing to the throng in the little train. I was early, and lucky enough to find a place. The wooden bench was marked "for 4 persons," but two more crowded in, plus their impedimenta— bundles of food, pillow-cases used as knapsacks, packages awkwardly tied together, cheap bags and suitcases. The opposite bench had six too, and I thought our compartment was full up. Not at all, for this was a holiday. More came and more and more, till we had fourteen standees, to say nothing of those out in the corridor.

Not a glimpse of the Polish landscape could I see in that subway jam, so I studied the faces of my traveling companions, picked out the man in the corner seat, and presently accosted him. Yes, he could speak German; he knew where my post-office was, but not the village; I explained why I was going; he would ask; some one in the compartment would be sure to know. He stood up and made a long speech, and all the peasants answered, staring at me, and passing from hand to hand the paper with the address and the list of Smigielski's relatives.

Finally he sat down and translated: he was getting off at the next stop, and so couldn't go with me; no one knew this family, indeed, no one knew where the village was; a holiday, so I couldn't inquire at the post-office; but putting all their suggestions together, he'd thought of a way—in the town was a Protestant church (that means Lutheran in Poland), with a priest who could speak German; he would know, he would help me. It was a long way from the station to the priest's house, I must take a doroshka and it would cost one *zloty* (eleven cents); would the lady pay so much? Yes. But I mustn't pay more than one *zloty* (a caution I was to receive many times in Poland), and I promised I would not.

The train stopped, the standees piled off with their luggage, and I began to window-gaze when in came a sailor, bowed before me and asked, ''May I speak with you, please, lady? I heard what they all said, standing out in the corridor. Now, I'm going to Nowy Dwór and I'll make the inquiries and show you the way. Then you won't have to spend any time going to the priest's house, and you'll save one *zloty*.''

''That's very kind of you, to help an American who's all alone in Poland. But—have you the time? It may take several minutes.''

He was going to spend the day with his mother and could see her later. It would never do for the Amerikanka to go the wrong way, and not find the family she wished to help. My conscience pricked violently—was I going to straighten out a separated family or to see a real peasant house?

After an hour's ride we reached Nowy Dwór, a most unattractive town of just over ten thousand, said my sailor; nine thousand Jews, one thousand Poles, a couple of hundred Germans. All the shops were shut up tight. I was glad when we left the town, and walked along a country road, across fields, up a hill, down to a river. Suddenly my guide gave a loud halloo, waved his arm, cried, "Come, come quickly!" and down the hill we dashed. There was a boat with its sails up and eleven peasants aboard, evidently waiting for the twelfth passenger. They made room for me and we started at once, the sailor calling out that some one must tell me where to go and help me, because I wasn't doing it for my own pleasure at all. (Wasn't I?)

One of the passengers, a boy of sixteen or so, who could speak a little German, offered himself as my guide. First of all, when did the boat go back? Not till eight o'clock in the evening. Panicky, I looked at my time-table; a train at ten-forty; why, I'd get home at midnight! Nothing to do but go on, and now there was no need to hurry.

We landed, and the boy and I started up the road, down a lovely lane, between long rows of willows. In perhaps an hour we came to a broad paved street; not a man nor a wagon in sight; only one house to be seen, a thatched cottage with a tidy garden, gay with flowers. With a few words and many gestures I was made to understand that he turned off here, I must wait till two o'clock (it was then twelve-forty) when a motor-bus would come along; no, no, it would pass me, turn around a short distance farther on, and come back; I must run out to the middle of the road and wigwag vigorously for it to stop; did I understand everything? I said it over in the simplest German words I knew, and thanked him in my best Polish.

I'd just started my lunch when I heard the honk-honk of a motor-bus. An extra for the holiday? Was my lad wrong? No matter, I rolled the food into my skirt, picked it up like an apron, and ran out to the middle of the road, signaled as hard as I could, and clambered aboard the bus. A whole hour saved.

It was slow work finishing my lunch, for I had to answer questions from the conductor and his one passenger, a pretty young school-teacher. Where was I going? Why? All alone? Where was my husband? How old was I? Where did I come from? Oh, then I had relatives in Poland? No, neither of them knew the family I was seeking, but we went near that village; they'd show me, but it was a long ride (it proved to be nearly an hour) and would cost a great deal (twenty-two cents!).

"Is it true," demanded the conductor, "that in your America people can be good friends if one's a Catholic and the other a Protestant?"

"That is true, absolutely true," I said firmly.

"How can such things be?" he began in a puzzled way when the school-teacher interrupted with, "I understand. If you belong to the intelligentsia it makes no difference what you believe or where you go to church. But if you're a peasant it makes—oh, the greatest difference in the world!"

When the bus stopped for me, they explained that I must walk back to the wayside cross and turn to the left. That group of trees and houses off on the horizon was my village. I went along a narrow footpath bordered by fields of wheat which would be ready to cut in a fortnight. At the first house the people spoke only Polish. A child ran next door to bring some one who knew German.

(I found out later the reason for my good fortune in being able to get along with German. The village had been started by a little colony of Germans, settled there before the Partitions, and now the most loyal of Poles. How much colonizing there was in central Europe! You get constant reminders of it in Poland. And how this mixing of peoples complicates every question!)

"Pani Justyna Smigielska," I began. "I met her husband in America."

A crowd gathered, staring. Excited talk in Polish, with a murmur of voices that somehow told me I'd made a mistake. They pointed out the Smigielski house, about two-thirds of the way along the one street of the village. I counted twenty-six houses.

"Pani Justyna Smigielska," I said as I neared a group of seven or eight people.

They stared. No one answered. I felt something sinister in the air.

"Jozef," I tried again, consulting my list, "Jozef, the brother of Antoni Smigielski in Brooklyn?"

"I am Jozef." And a man of thirty-odd took a step forward, then stopped doubtfully.

"I have come from America," I began, but could get no farther.

"Come in, come in, lady."

He motioned to the nearest cottage, then angrily turned

to the group and shouted something in Polish—perhaps to tell them not to follow. His wife introduced herself, threw open the door, and I entered my first peasant house. White plastered walls, a low roof of thatch. A tiny square hall, one room to the right, one to the left.

My first impression was that the room was crowded. It was kitchen and dining-room, bedroom and living-room for three persons, for the old mother lived with this married son. A low, white tile stove served for cooking and heating. Two beds, our three-quarter size; one had a pile of the fat square pillows that make an important part of every Polish girl's equipment for marriage. A corner cupboard with dishes and odds and ends, a table under the casement window, a broken mirror. On the wall a large crucifix, pictures of Christ and of the Virgin, of Jozef and his wife on their wedding-day, crayon portraits of her parents—all this I catalogued mentally while we talked; not one thing there was particularly Polish, not one gave any hint of beauty or peasant art.

All of Antoni's relatives came in and as they were introduced I tried to make out who they were from my list—his sister and her husband, with their new baby; a brother, two little nieces; several others; at last the old mother, seventy-two, but she seemed far older.

"Oh," she cried in a quavering voice, but in the best German of any of the family, "you have come all the way from America. You have seen my son, my Antoni, and now—now I can not see your face."

I looked at her sharply and caught my breath. Even

my untrained eyes could read the truth—a complete cataract over one eye and the other half veiled.

"You have seen my son," she repeated, "and I can not see your face," and the tears ran down her cheeks.

"Oh yes, you can," I tried to speak cheerfully in spite of the lump in my throat, "just feel. My hair is short, it's as white as yours. My face——" I could not go on, I could only have her touch my forehead and chin while the tears spilled over and ran down my face and splashed on her wrinkled hand.

"Tell us about Antoni—he is sick, very sick."

"Sick? But I saw him just before I sailed, he was well then and doing his regular work."

"He's sick in the head. He said we must send our answer to the hospital, and so he must be very sick. We did not write again."

"But you don't understand. It was some years ago he was sick, and the hospital took good care of him and got him well again, and he's worked there ever since."

"What does he do?" they asked doubtfully.

"He polishes the floors."

"Is it a big house?"

I wondered what they would call big.

"Yes, three hundred people can stay there at a time."

"Oh," cried the sister-in-law in horror, "such a big house! Poor Antoni must be worked to death!"

"Not at all," I reassured her, "he doesn't do the floors the way you do in Poland. He has an electric machine."

"How much does he get, at the end of a whole month?"

"His room and his meals, and some money besides. I don't know how much. (I was glad I didn't know.) But when you change dollars into *zlotys* you must always remember that things cost more in America. You can ride on the tram in Warsaw four times for one *zloty*; in Brooklyn only twice. How much did you pay for"—I looked about for something I could compare, something they would understand; a cloth coat, about the same color as mine, was hanging near the door—"for that coat? Fifty-five *zlotys*? Mine was more than two hundred. Food and clothes and rent, everything nearly costs more than in Poland."

Presently Mrs. Jozef cleared one end of the table and brought a plate and cup. It was about half past two when I arrived. Their dinner was long since over. But hospitality in Poland, in cottage or palace, requires that a guest must be fed, and a young girl appeared with my dinner. She'd built up a fire in the next house, so that the room where we sat wouldn't be hot and uncomfortable. Numberless flies came in at the open window. Some curious neighbor left the door ajar and a flock of chickens came in too. Could I eat anything in that peasant household? Wouldn't I offend them if I refused? I could almost hear the prince's voice saying, "Take your own food. Remember, I warned you."

This is what they gave me to eat—yes, all for me—tea, so strong it was almost black, with very coarse, grayish sugar; and how amazed they were when I asked for hot water and diluted it; eight eggs, which proved to be soft-boiled and lukewarm; and fourteen slabs of black bread, over an inch thick and about ten inches across, with sad lines that made great streaks of dark across them. Of all the bread I saw in Poland, that was the worst. It was sour, so sour that one bite made me feel sick. I wondered if I could possibly swallow it and keep it down. I sipped the tea and tried one of the eggs, talking hard and pretending to eat.

"What," I kept saying over and over to myself, "what more could any hostess do than give me her best, in the most generous amount? Don't be squeamish, because this is the best of a Polish peasant."

I thought of an excuse to push back the dishes and asked Jozef to show me just how he addressed a letter to his brother in America. He searched for a scrap of paper and toiled laboriously over the long address. It would have taken an unusually clever and efficient decipherer in the New York post-office to have made it out, and sent it to that hospital in Brooklyn, for words that belonged together were widely scattered. I'd taken along half a dozen envelopes and proceeded to address them in our fashion with my fountain-pen. They all watched me with big eyes, I wrote so fast, with a pen that didn't have to be dipped into the ink. Then I stamped the envelopes and made them promise to write on Sunday.

I had supposed that every Polish family had an enormous number of children, but Mrs. Jozef told me they'd had only one little girl who died. I thought I'd see some beautiful peasant costumes, especially as it was a holiday;

everybody had on the most ordinary clothes, store clothes, minus any touch of embroidery. Why, I might have been talking to country people in New England or the Middle West.

I'd taken it for granted that, being peasants, the Smigielskis would own a tiny piece of land and farm it, or else work on a big estate with the dream of owning a few acres at some distant day. But no, they were—how shall I put it?—they were textile workers. Jozef took me into the other room of the cottage—as large as the living-room, as crowded, as dirty and disorderly. There were huge gunnysacks of wool, spilling over on to the floor. There were piles of sheepskin coats. There were two knitting machines, run by foot-power, with a complicated arrangement of threads and bobbins and wires.

"We both work," he answered my many questions, "but it's a seasonal job lasting five, six, eight months; it depends on how cold the winter is and how much money peasants have. The machines came from Germany and cost seven thousand *zlotys*—yes, for one. What do we make on them? Why, the knitted part of sheepskin coats. We buy the wool from the Jews and then we sell the finished coats to these same Jews; they come around every week and take what we have on hand. If we both work, oh, very long hours, we can do twenty in a day. Then just before warm weather comes they suddenly give notice: 'Next time we buy what's ready—and then no more.' "

"And how do you manage then?"

"We buy no meat. We are careful about every *zloty*."

[50]

Meanwhile Mrs. Jozef had slipped away, washed up, brushed her straight bobbed hair, and changed the dirty knitted dress of light blue for one of green silk with two scalloped flounces on the skirt. I scarcely recognized her and reminded myself that I'd come unannounced and mustn't be too critical if I'd arrived when they weren't "spruced up" for visitors. I seized the opportunity for a little talk with her.

"Tell me about the old lady's eyes."

"They've been wrong for a long, long time, getting worse and worse. We had the doctor come all the way from Nowy Dwór and he thinks an operation would make her see, but he couldn't do it, and it would cost a great deal of money—maybe thousands of *zlotys*—to take her all the way to Warsaw and ask a doctor there. We wrote to Antoni, but he didn't send the money. Yes, she can see a little with one eye—just enough to know if something comes between her and the window.

"Will you tell Antoni?" she appealed to me. "If you tell him he will send the money, and then she can see again. She could even help a little about the house, she'd be happier with something to do, for now her days are endlessly long."

I agreed to go to see Antoni when I returned to America, but as that would not be for a good many months I'd write him. She seemed to feel it was as good as done, almost as if to-morrow the cataract would be removed and the old lady busy with reading and sewing and cooking, such confidence she had in the lady from America.

Hesitating, I asked her about Antoni's wife. She made no secret of what had happened, but told the bare facts of the tragedy with no attempt to dress them up or to minimize them.

"She ran away, soon after we came back from Russia. You know, our whole village was ordered to leave when the czar's army retreated. Oh, that was a dreadful time, the years we lived in Russia—it was a sort of camp, with not enough to eat and no fields of our own to work in. When the war was over we came back and found everything in a dreadful way. We were all so poor and there weren't any jobs to be had. Antoni's wife ran away— with another man. Don't think I excuse her—no, not for one minute. What she did was a great sin, a very great sin. We begged the lady from Warsaw not to write it to America. She took Antoni's daughter along with her and said she was going to Germany to look for work. You won't tell him—oh, say you won't tell him! It will only make his heart ache more and it will do no good. Antoni's boy? Why, he's grown up to be a big fellow by this time. He's away doing his military service. Here's his picture. You must tell Antoni I showed it to you."

With husband and wife I set out to see the village. We passed the new school, an attractive brick building; there are forty-some children, but some of them come a long distance. We stopped at a new house, nearly finished. To my amazement it was their house. Five rooms; two were plastered, they'd finish the other three next year when they had more money. It cost about sixteen hundred dollars. They would move in in three weeks more. See, what a big light room for the two machines; and the kitchen had a trap-door to the cellar where they could keep supplies; not double windows—only rich people had those; the old mother would have the little room; and there was a good sunny space for a garden.

"Would I," I asked myself as we inspected every detail of the new house, "keep the old one in apple-pie order if we were getting ready to move, and spending what time we could helping the carpenters? I'm sure I'd do just what these peasants are doing—let things slide at the old house. Don't blame them if it wasn't tidy."

We paid a call on Antoni's best friend, the man through whom the Warsaw social worker had finally made connections with the Smigielskis. He lived in a larger, better furnished house, the most attractive in the village, I thought. I explained all over again who I was and why I'd come, and answered questions about America and Antoni and Hoover. The daughter brought in food, and every one sat down at the table. Did I have to eat again? The bread was buttered and was really good; there were two platters of meat, a sort of bologna home-made, sliced thin; and a tall bottle of honey mead which we drank from tiny glasses. I was hungry!

They were astonished to hear how I had found their village and said there was an easier way to go back, if I could walk three kilometers. Jozef and his wife in her store dress and I started out, single file along a narrow path, with a wheat-field on one side and rye on the other.

Polish farms have no fences, even along the highroad, even between two peasants' holdings; when they plow they leave ten or twelve inches at the side of a field and this space serves as a path. At last we came to the road and far in the distance could see some object they said was a motor-bus.

"You won't lose your way, lady?"

"Oh, no. Will this bus take me all the way to Warsaw? Is it a long trip?"

"One *zloty*. You don't need to hurry. It doesn't start till there are passengers enough."

"What do you do about letters?"

"The nearest post-office is Nowy Dwór—the place you got off the train. They send us word when some one's coming our way, and I go to fetch it, or my husband goes, whichever can take the time off. It's a full half-day, there and back."

"And when you want to send a letter?"

"We walk to the bus and pay the chauffeur to buy a stamp in Warsaw and post it there."

(If he doesn't leave it forgotten in his pocket, or keep the money and throw the letter away. Small wonder one hears so often that letters get no answer!)

I reached the bus in due time and waited nearly an hour. Passengers came, one by one. No one in Poland watches the clock. No one's in a hurry. At last three young officers made up the required number and we set off on a jolty ride to the capital city. The tram took me almost to my door. It was nine o'clock!

Later on I made inquiries and sent the Smigielskis the address of a clinic in Warsaw where the operation on the old mother's eyes would be well done and the charge would depend on their income. Did they have to lose a day's work to fetch the letter? Did they consult the surgeons at the clinic? Can the old woman see?

The next day I dined at a Polish house, built in the seventeenth century. The street floor was vaulted in stone. The tapestries in the reception-rooms were as fine as those I'd seen in the royal palace. There were crowns on the napkins. We were six at table, with three butlers who wore white cotton gloves. So many glasses at my place, so much silver, heavy with a raised crest, so many courses I lost count. But the most lavish host could do no more than my peasants—give their best.

CHAPTER III
HETMAN TRADITION AND MODERN WAYS

"Lwów, then a day in Lublin. Here's a thing you mustn't miss," a Warsaw banker urged as we looked over my itinerary. "Stop off at Zamosc (Za-mosh). It's about half-way between those two towns. By all means, you must have an hour or two in Zamosc!"

"And why should I take the time for Zamosc? What is there to see?"

"Something you'll not find anywhere else in Poland, and maybe not anywhere else in all Europe. Zamosc has a medieval market-place, arcaded clear around. No one's ever dared to 'restore' one building in any other type of architecture. It's as lovely as when it was first planned. It's just about perfect," he added with an enthusiasm that was surely contagious.

For I not only interpolated Zamosc between Lwów and Lublin, but stuck to my determination even when I found that it was most decidedly off the beaten track and this must be my schedule: leave Lwów at eleven-twenty at night, no sleeper; get to some little junction at five, wait till six-twelve, arrive at six-thirty. Was it worth it?

The conductor on the train moved me into a compartment where there was only one other passenger, a young woman going all the way to Warsaw. (Even for a long journey, say eight or nine hours, Poles often take local

trains because the tickets are less than for express trains.
Saving three *zlotys* is far more important than saving two
hours; for time means nothing to a Pole, and three *zlotys*
is indeed something!) He put up a sign, *Ladies only.*
That nice woman showed me the trick of pulling out the
upholstered seat, section by section, to make a wider bed,
and to my surprise I fell asleep and slept till she wakened
me at the junction and summoned a porter.

Soldiers and peasants were dozing in the airless little
station, so I sat outside in the sunshine and opened a
French guide-book to see what it had to say about Zamosc.
Perhaps it was better than nothing, but—not much; it
was so meager that it was tantalizing. All that it accomplished was to let me say, "Now I'd like to see this church
and tower, or that ruin, and you'll have to tell me all
about it. I know only that it's here!" But I came to
grief in any town where I didn't find a friendly Pole.

Fortunately, I wasn't helpless in Zamosc, for some one
at a luncheon in Warsaw heard me say I was going there
and gave me a card to a friend. I'd written ahead to announce my coming for three hours, that I'd arrive fright-
fully early, but might I call about nine, just to ask if there
was something else besides the famous market-place that
I should see. And there they were to meet me, the Senator himself and a friend who spoke English.

(If only the Warsaw lady had explained that she was
introducing me to the most important people at Zamosc—
to a host in the Polish Parliament, to a hostess who was—
well, you'll see as I tell the story. She'd acknowledge

only that she served on this board and that committee, but I had the feeling they'd started things and were supporting or winning support for more than one interesting movement in Zamosc.)

"Please, tell the porter I want to leave my bags here at the station."

"No, no, you're to stay at our house."

"I'm leaving at ten, and I don't need luggage just to see the market-place."

"But—my wife has planned everything for you for four days. Some dancers from the Warsaw opera are giving a performance, there's a special movie she wants you to see, and excursions, and—well, we'll just take the bags along and talk it over at breakfast."

Which we did, and compromised on my staying till noon the next day. With so many extra hours it was with the greatest difficulty that I saw Zamosc.

My banker was right. The market-place was worthy of all his enthusiasm, and mine added to his. It was worth the discomfort of the journey. It was, as he'd said, just about perfect. From the Senator and Mme. Senator, from the friend who spoke English, I pieced together bits of history and learned of Jan Zamoyski, the hetman who founded the town. (There were four hetmans in Poland, the most important officers of the king.) That explained his name, for *ski* is the Polish equivalent of a French *de* or a German *von,* and means "from"; Zamoyski then means "the man from Zamosc." Now this Jan Zamoyski must have been a very important person. I'd seen his full-length portrait in the gymnasium in Warsaw, named for him. He was rector of the university of Pavia, and chancellor under Stephen Batory. And Batory, they reminded me, was perhaps the greatest and the wisest king who ever ruled in Poland; when? in the sixteenth century.

I was speechless with joy over the market-place, as many times as I went into it that day and the next. An architect from Italy designed it—what to-day we'd call "city planning"—with high brick walls surrounding the whole town, with the market-place arcaded all around, and streets put in where there was space left. Half shut my eyes and I might have been in Italy, for it was perfect Renaissance architecture. I gazed and gazed at the arcades; I strolled along through them, peering into the dim little shops, exclaiming over the vaulting, measuring the walls—four feet thick, or five, with heavy buttresses; the whole place in such good repair.

Above the shops were three floors of apartments with plastered walls—blue or buff or white. So strong is the Zamoyski tradition that no one has remodeled a house, in all these years, nor introduced any other style; probably no one has ever wanted to. Not one touch of Gothic, not a hint of baroque with its curls and fussiness. The town hall may be a century later than the rest, but with its fine tower it belongs in the picture. The place is an absolute unit. And over it all the medieval spell.

Though they're called by another name, Zamosc has adopted zoning laws. For the old part of the town the rules are very strict and permit no one to build or to rebuild in a style that doesn't harmonize with the Zamoyski original.

Several houses had niches for statues, and three had lovely plaster ornamentation. In the old days, Mrs. Senator explained, every house facing the market-place was so decorated, but more than a century of Russian rule had effaced much that was distinctly Polish, especially in a small town so near the frontier.

Vaguely I wondered why the market-place was so much more attractive than others I'd seen. Suddenly I sensed that it was clean and tidy. This was in August, when wilted flowers and decaying vegetables can make themselves so prominent that a tourist notices them more than picturesque costumes.

"This isn't a market-day?" I asked.

"Yes. Do you want to see the Zamosc market?"

"But—where is it? Don't your peasants sell their vegetables and flowers and chickens here?"

"Not in Zamosc," answered Mrs. Senator. "A short distance away there's a regular market. We'll drive past later and stop if you like. No, this isn't any modern scheme to make our town a beauty spot. Jan Zamoyski—or perhaps his architect—must have planned it so. At any rate, it's always been so from the very beginning. This great space was for assembling the people, not for selling."

A few minutes' walk brought us to the big building that had once been the Zamoyski palace, then barracks of

Russian soldiers, now used by the courts; and to what was once the Zamoyski University—the one and only university in Poland founded and supported by an individual; all the others were state enterprises, and are so to-day. The Russians closed it, of course. Now it houses the normal school and a gymnasium for boys and one for girls—about four hundred and fifty pupils, but in two separate schools. In the wide court both groups have athletics, for Zamosc, like all of Poland, has taken up sports seriously and with a purpose.

We went to the parish church, Renaissance architecture also, but the high altar was changed, when rococo came into style, and as I don't happen to like rococo I didn't grow enthusiastic even when they said it was all of silver. Many Zamoyski monuments, over a period of three centuries and more. With lighted candles we clambered down into the crypt where generations of this family are buried; each body in three coffins—an outer one of wood, then one of metal, and the innermost of silver. The church has one real treasure, in a chapel all by itself; back of long blue hangings that just match the blue of the painting is a most lovely Annunciation by Carlo Dolci, with all the sweetness of his master Raphael.

I saw the ruins of the town's walls and fort. Jan Zamoyski built here as a frontier defense against the Tartars, those relentless foes of Poland on the east, and strong defenses he needed. The place was besieged by Swedes and Tartars and Cossacks, but never captured. His fortifications stood till the eighteen-sixties when, after the last insurrection, the Russians took them down and left only fragments—here an arched entrance, there a round tower, half a story high, an underground passage, part of a prison, gates, bastion—all built of brick.

For military reasons it was against the law to build within so many kilometers of the walls, and when the town outgrew its limited space people had to go far out, beyond that line; consequently Zamosc is to-day very much spread out, with a new district on either side of the open space where even now no one may build—reserved for gardens.

That was the end of the sightseeing suggested in the book, with far more than it told; so my amazement grew and grew as I found other things in that town of twenty thousand—before the war, only ten thousand. There was first the House for Mothers and Children. Now I've visited baby welfare stations in New York City and I knew all the details of getting one started in a Middle West town, but I've never seen one like Zamosc's! We open a station in a congested, foreign neighborhood, taking any house or empty store that's available, clean it up a little, dab some white paint around, install a nurse, and that's that. Zamosc has a separate building that was planned for this special purpose, and a most attractive building it is—buff-plastered on the outside, red-roofed, two and a half stories high.

There was a laboratory where three girls in white were preparing special milk for special babies; a waiting-room with benches for the mothers and older children, and parking space for the babies; an office for the head nurse and her secretary. I looked at the records and though I couldn't read the Polish, I could see they are far more complete than ours. Then the mothers' room, for this is more than a station for babies, it's welfare for mothers too. In every room there were flowers—all Poles are fond of flowers; and a health poster—most of them the head nurse had made herself—how to bathe the baby, what children need, fresh air, flies.

"Do the mothers come?" I asked. "How many?"

"From eight to thirty-seven in a morning. Yesterday I had twenty-five."

"Come and see this," said Mrs. Senator. "This" was a wooden chest with handles at the ends, fitted with a tray like a trunk, and containing everything the nurse needed when a baby was born. They opened one of the bundles, done up in a blue and white blanket, for me to see what a new baby gets in Zamosc—two flannelette night-gowns, six dipes, two dresses, two shirts, soap (very costly all over Poland) and talcum powder. From a glass case they brought out all the things that came from America; some they weren't sure about; Philadelphia was on one label, was that in America?

"Where did you learn?" I turned to the head nurse.

"I began under Mr. Hoover. The Relief Commission gave me four months' training, and later I had a course at Warsaw. Now they send me out to start new stations—this is my third. How many babies in Zamosc? I have on my books—I must just look to make sure—two hundred and thirty-one. They don't all live right in the town, they come from several districts. But each child is visited once a month—otherwise I'd never see the well ones."

"The Amerikanka is writing a book," explained Mrs. Senator.

"About Poland? You're going to put my Station for Mothers and Children into it? Then I'll write my name for you, so you'll be sure to get it right." And she did.

On we went to the Community House, a large building that was once a church, confiscated by the Russians. One part is now a motion-picture theater, one part an assembly hall, with smaller rooms for committee meetings, and a museum.

"This is only the beginning," apologized my hostess, "and everything is crowded into one room—Roman remains, found in excavating; peasant costumes, some of them now rare; quaint objects made by hand; specimens in geology. The important thing is to have a place where people can bring their gifts. The museum will grow and some day it'll have a building of its own."

"What American town of this size, if you except Lexington and Concord, has a place like this?" I wondered aloud.

We visited the boys' trade school and saw all the things they make out of wood and leather—furniture, harness, cases and bags of many kinds; not a public school, this one, but a hobby of the young priest who took us through. Now having proved its worth in teaching boys a trade that makes them self-supporting, he has a group of interested persons who help finance the school.

Then we drove out to the agricultural school for boys, like the one at Lowicz—hen houses, cow barns, stables, the dairy where they make two hundred pounds of butter daily, the vegetable gardens, the most immaculate I've ever seen, not a sign of a weed anywhere, splendid fields of tobacco which they grow for the government, and wheat-fields, already harvested and shocked. We went into the building where classes are held, and stopped in one room where a young woman was giving a lesson on pigs.

"This lady is a visitor from America," the principal introduced me to instructor and boys, with much emphasis on the America.

"Did you wonder about it?" Mrs. Senator asked me later. "There's a reason. Many of these peasant boys have never been out of the district. Warsaw and Poznan are just words to them, till one day some man comes to the school and they're told he lives in Warsaw, then it begins to mean something. So this was an opportunity not to be missed—a visitor from America!"

A boy of eighteen came up to speak to me—in English. He was born in the United States, not far from Pittsburgh, and went to Poland seven years ago. His mother has a little farm near Zamosc and when his year in the school is finished he'll take charge of it for her. Yes, he feels already what a great deal he's learned in the school. Would I, he asked, like to see a boys' dormitory?

Indeed, yes. Into another building, with wide halls, and walls of blue and white, and a sleeping-room with forty beds in two long rows, each with a gay striped cover, no two alike (these they bring from home).

I should have liked to stay longer, but we were due for a brief visit at the hospital for animals, where a veterinary, paid by the town, looks after dogs and horses and cows.

Then to the Zoo.

What! in a Polish town of twenty thousand? Why, we don't have that in America! I know we don't, and now I wonder why not?

The Zoo and the Botanical Garden are all in one, near a public school. Much of the work is done by boys and girls, who build cages in the school workshop and help get beds of rich earth ready. There were groups of plants for class study—a water garden, an Alpine garden with mountain plants, a tropical garden (in a glass case eight or ten feet long), and beds where special things were growing. There were ducks and turtles, two brown bears, two wolves, over a hundred birds, storks, peacocks, eagles from the Caucasus.

"Where is your white eagle?" I demanded. "I particularly want to see a white eagle like Lech's!"

They all stared at me. How did the Amerikanka know the story of this founder of Poland? Why, I explained, it was Lech who brought me to Poland.

"The Zoo," Mrs. Senator told me afterward, "was started about five years ago. One interested man was

[66]

responsible for it. Many of the animals have been gifts.
The director hears of a certain animal for sale and broadcasts the fact; almost always somebody offers to meet the
bill. No, there's not another zoo, so far as we know, in
any town this size in Poland. But it's a fine thing for the
boys and girls of Zamosc, and often children come from
other towns to see our plants and animals—once a trainful came from Lwów.''

Another of the modern things is the city park, started
six years ago in what was once a part of the fortress.
The trees, they apologized, are not very large yet—trees
do grow slowly! The shrubbery and flower-beds were
lovely. Tennis courts (free!) and a football ground.
A pond made from the medieval moat, with boating in
summer and skating in winter.

In a brick building that the Russians used as a military
prison, the town has opened a peasants' hotel. How astonished the Senator was when I begged to go inside! I
wanted to see the rooms. And how did they happen to
have a hotel for peasants?

''It didn't just happen,'' he answered, ''it came to meet
a desperate need. A few years ago there were hundreds
of homeless people wandering over Poland, especially in
the eastern part—they were coming back to their homes
from Russia. Gradually this has adjusted itself and today there are few such cases, but just after the war we
had so many—jobless, homeless, with literally no place
to go. Very dirty, often with vermin. So this house was
opened for them. For twenty *grosze* (that's just over

two cents) a man can sit here all night, where it's dry and warm; for forty he can lie down. Ah, here's the care-taker. Now we'll see just what accommodations they get, for different prices."

The men's room had twenty—what word would de-scribe them?—wide lounges of wood, the end slanting a little. The women's room had these with ticks filled with straw. For people who can pay one *zloty* each (eleven cents) there are up-stairs rooms with sheets and pillow-cases. And for affluent folk two rooms, with four beds each, supplied with linen and towels. Every one can have tea. They bring their own food, or buy a little. But it's not a place where they may loiter about all day; they must leave in the morning, and at half past eleven we found the rooms empty.

"Well, if your homeless refugees are no longer so nu-merous, who comes to this hotel?"

"Plenty of people," said the Senator. "Fathers and mothers who come to visit their children in school. Some one to see the doctors. Men with business that can't be finished in one day, for in Zamosc is centered all the bus-iness and the court work of five districts. The place is never empty at night, I assure you."

All this sightseeing and social service had been broken up by second breakfast at eleven—a real meal!—a tiny nap (for which I had to beg!), guests for dinner at three. About half past five we set out in the motor for a long drive to one of the most interesting things I saw in Po-land—a school for peasant girls. It's not like the boys' farm school, in a fine new building specially planned for it, but in the one place that was available—a gentleman's estate, with the girls living in the manor house and the outbuildings utilized as far as they would serve. Some day they'll have a new building, exactly fitted for their needs; and some day they'll have a two-year course instead of only one year; for the present they are carrying on.

I saw vegetable and flower gardens, a small greenhouse where the girls learn how to pot plants and care for them in winter (very important in Poland!), and the new hen house, with its model roosts and ladders, and a special breed of Polish chickens with greenish feet; the cow barns with concrete floors and drains, and the piggery where three girls in red headkerchiefs were feeding carrots to the pigs, one of them slapping a fat porker who didn't want to go into his own apartment.

In the main house the sewing class was finishing a lesson. Each girl was making a different thing. I exclaimed over the tiny stitches, like convent work, and the beauty of the designs in blouses and table-cloths. They make their own designs, the teacher said, and merely bring them to her for comment.

We looked into the recreation-room, once the salon, and then went up-stairs to see a dormitory. Twilight had come and four girls went ahead with lamps. The sleeping-rooms were plain and simple, but spotlessly clean. Each girl had a place to keep her things, but all the shoes were in lockers in another room, for in winter

they wear such heavy boots and walk so much in the
mud and the wet.

Then we had to eat something. I groaned inwardly,
for *collatya* would be ready when we reached Zamosc.
Tomatoes, stuffed with chopped egg and celery; white
bread, the very best I ate in Poland—that seemed to me
a good omen for the future, for the girls had made the
bread themselves; enormous raspberries, out of their
own garden, with plain cake and of course tea.

"Turn around," the Senator spoke in a low voice. As
I happened to be sitting at the end of the table, I hadn't
heard the double doors quietly opened. There stood the
forty girls in a half-circle, the lamplight shining on their
white or red or figured headkerchiefs, their gay striped
skirts and full white blouses. They sang for me—an
aria from a Polish opera, peasant songs, a hymn to the
Virgin.

The motor sounded its horn. The Senator rose abruptly and said we must be starting.

One of the girls made a speech—in Polish, which somebody translated into German. They wanted to thank me
for coming to visit their school, and to make sure that I
shouldn't forget them, as they shouldn't forget me, would
I be kind enough to accept this little gift?

"Bardzo dziekuje," I managed to gasp out, *"bardzo
dziekuje,"* (I thank you very much), and added in German, "I shan't forget you."

What do you think they'd chosen as my gift?

An embroidered blouse.

CHAPTER IV

DIVIDED INTO THREE PARTS

ALL Poland was divided into three parts: one the Germans ruled, the next Austria, the third and largest the czar of all the Russias. For something over a hundred and twenty years the country was thus partitioned, so it's not to be marveled at that a visitor runs up against reminders of this very frequently. Before the war travelers had much to tell of difficulties and delays when they wished to cross from one section of Poland into another. What fascinated me was the reaction of the Poles.

Warned repeatedly in Krasinski's plays and poems that they must not hate their oppressors, for hate reacts and in the end harms most the hater, the Poles do not speak bitterly of Russia and Germany and Austria. They state facts—just plain bare facts, coldly, calmly, making no comment. At first I thought this was because the Countess P. could not talk of her uncle's tragic death, that the young doctor who took many walks with me must be thinking of his grandfather that he spoke so briefly. Little by little I realized that the exiled Krasinski, one of the three outstanding names in Polish literature, had been like a school-teacher, telling the whole nation what they must not do. Whether they sense it or not, nothing they could have solemnly bound themselves to practise could be more impressive to an American than their bare facts. It's as if a czar's order had gone out, and to all classes of people. It's well-nigh universal.

In Poznan I had tea with the head-mistress of a girls' school. She had gone twice to Berlin to what we call a normal school, and spoke gratefully of the excellent training they gave. (I noticed that often. People would say, "We must give the Germans their due.") When the policy of Bismarck and Von Bülow became more and more drastic, with attempts to stamp out the Polish language and so stamp out all memory of Poland, this woman started a circulating library of Polish books— against the law. The finding of one or two books would have been sufficient to close the school, for the inspectors were always hunting for an excuse. So the girls—four hundred or more—were put on their honor not to tell of this forbidden library, and were specially cautioned not to bring the books to school save on the day they were exchanged.

"One morning, just after I'd given out the Polish books," began her story in answer to my questions, "I heard the signal. The *Herr Oberinspekteur!* All the servants in the school were Polish, of course, and had instructions to detain German visitors, taking all the time possible to admit them, delaying with their hats and coats, speaking of the weather, of this and that. I had a minute and a half, perhaps two minutes. Oh, German inspections were thorough. Not that the man looked into every single desk, every girl's bag, but he'd do a few in each room; and not a girl in the class but had a Polish book that day.

"We weren't in the present school then, but had half of a building; the other side was apartments. I had to think quickly. I ran over to the ground-floor apartment and by good fortune there was a big basket of soiled clothes. No time to explain who had come. I dragged the basket back to the classroom. Very quietly, but quickly too, for they knew how much was at stake, the girls brought up their forbidden books and buried them deep under sheets and table-cloths. Two girls carried the basket out and we had begun a lesson in the geography of Germany when the *Herr Oberinspektcur* walked in. It all happened in far less time than it takes me to tell you. This was only one of countless experiences I had, but—our circulating library was never discovered."

She had taught a whole generation of Polish girls their language. I remembered Bismarck's bitter complaint, "Yes, our colonization schemes have failed, in spite of the millions of marks we've spent. Send a German colonist there, he marries a Polish woman, and their children—why, the children aren't Germans, they're Poles! It's the women of Poland who have defeated us."

And it was the women who helped nullify the Prussian project of making the land itself German. The Colonization Commission bought up whatever land was for sale and settled Germans there. The Poles organized a bank to provide funds for buying land and managed it so well that actually more acres were purchased by Poles than by

Germans. The men did this, the women planted the idea deep in the minds of their children.

"This is Polish soil," the mothers would say over and over, very earnestly, "this is Polish soil," leaning down to touch the earth, "and you must never sell an inch of it!"

This passionate love of the soil has not died out, now that Poland is free. It is still a matter of patriotism to hold on to the land. One instance that came under my notice: my hostess at a country house received a letter from her eldest son. He had inherited a piece of land from his grandmother, but had not been able to make a success of his farming. (It's not only in the United States that farmers have been having a difficult time the last few years.) Things had gone from bad to worse, what with a poor crop one year and a big crop with very low prices another. He couldn't meet his interest charges, was utterly discouraged, and had decided to sell the farm (two thousand acres), pay his debts and start anew.

"It is Polish soil," she said again and again as she sobbed over the letter, "and my son must sell it. It is Polish soil!"

"K-o-z-l—a barred l—o-w-s-k-i," I spelled after a man as I wrote his address down, "please look, is that right?"

"Don't make your z like that," he said sharply, for I'd made it come below the line, like a g or y.

"Why not?"

"Because," he explained, "that's a German z."

He took the pen, drew a heavy line through the word, and wrote his name with a *z* like our printed one. It was, I learned, a matter of patriotism to use a Polish form for *z*.

Poznan is to-day one of the most Polish of Polish cities. The census says over ninety-six per cent. Polish, half of one per cent. Jewish, the rest German. Now this was the center of all the Prussian campaigns against the Polish language, Polish soil, the Polish spirit, so naturally I expected to find a very large number of Germans living there.

"Yes," some one explained, "before the war their figures—well, this is how they counted: a family that spoke both Polish and German was listed as German. They kept an enormous number of officials here as well as many regiments of soldiers, and though they were only temporary, they were all counted as citizens of Poznan. Yet juggle the figures as they would, they never made the city out more than half German."

"It's only on the surface," a Polish woman warned me, "that it seems a German city. The streets have that imprint, particularly in the center of the town, which was all destroyed by a fire—in the eighteen-forties or fifties, I think it was—and rebuilt in the solid, stolid German way, with architecture that might easily remind you of Berlin or Hamburg. The pretentious palace of the kaiser—you've been there? it's one of the university buildings now—with its square tower dominates every view of Poznan. Yes, you're right—that's just the way I feel about it; it cost a huge sum of money, and certain details have beauty, but—it's wholly lacking in atmosphere.''

In Danzig too, for I saw Danzig with Poles and not with Germans, I heard a great deal about the census-taking. How cross one of my Polish acquaintances was when I showed him a booklet some one on the steamer had given me—*What to See in Danzig*—and the first paragraph said that ninety-six per cent. of the Free City was German.

''But everybody knows the Poles are fifteen per cent. by one count, and eighteen by another! This is what they do, these Germans, wanting to make Danzig out a German city: I know a Russian woman who came here after the war; she can speak German; therefore she's listed as a German!

''Now, tell me, where have you been to-day? To the town hall? I suppose you went through with the German guide. Did he show you any of the Polish things? only the bust of a Polish king? Didn't he tell you the copper weather-vane is a figure of our king, Sigismund III? Did you see the Polish eagles on the fountain in front of the *Artushof?* Of course they told you only that it was made in a German town. Did you see the palace over one of the city gates, built for Sobieski, who came here for a week? Tell me, did you see the Polish eagle, carved in the *Hohes Tor?*

''And yet I must be honest and say, culturally Danzig

is a German city. What you see here is German architecture. All its background is German. But its future is bound up with Poland's. Look at the figures of its shipping—very large in medieval days when all trade was by water, when Polish grain and timber floated down the Vistula to Danzig, and purchases of kings and nobles from all over Europe came through this port; then it dropped to a fraction of those figures, while Hamburg's grew and grew. See how its trade has leaped in the last decade—Poland's imports."

"What do you think the future of this Free City will be?" I asked.

"If it is left alone, in ten years, thirty, perhaps fifty, in time it will come of its own accord to Poland, as it did in the fifteenth century when it threw off the yoke of the Teutonic Knights and voluntarily placed itself under the protection of the Polish kings. To-day it's economics more than politics that determines a question, and economically Danzig belongs with Poland and not with Berlin."

"Gdynia? By that time Poland will need two ports."

For the claim that Nicholas Copernicus was a German the Poles have nothing but scorn. Yet I noticed that in Torun, where they took me to see his birthplace, and in Warsaw, when we passed his monument by Thorwaldsen, and in Krakow, before his statue in the library courtyard, some one always spoke of that claim and brought forward the facts that disprove it.

"This is what the Germans say: 'Copernicus was born in Torun. Torun is a German city. Therefore Copernicus was a German.' There's mixing of tenses in a syllogism for you! It's true, he was born in Torun, but they don't add that his father was a Krakowian, living there as a wholesale merchant. Torun a German town? Seven years before Copernicus was born the Teutonic Knights ceded that district to Poland and it was a fief of the Polish crown. This settles the question—after the Latinized form of his name he himself wrote the word 'Polonus.' "

Here is the story I heard from a Pole, head of a department in an American firm in Warsaw. I write it just as he told it one day in the mountains, for all the literary skill in the world couldn't dress it up and make it more telling. Not that he volunteered this. It came out in answer to my question, "Have you ever been in prison?"

"Why, certainly," he replied indignantly. "What do you think I am? Don't you know the old saying"—he quoted it in Polish and then slowly translated—'Show me the Pole who has never been in prison, and I'll show you an arrant coward.' What happened to me is only what happened to scores and hundreds of others—only mine began early.

"I lived in Poznan when I was a boy. I don't need to tell you that meant German schools and the strictest of German rules. And one of these rules was that we must

not speak Polish in the school—only German. One day—
I was nine years old at the time—as we were changing
classes I asked a boy to lend me a pencil. I forgot and
asked in Polish. It wasn't during class. I wasn't speaking to a master. At the end of the day the teacher read
out the names of several boys, mine among them, telling
us to go to the principal. He gave minor punishments
to the others for slight misdemeanors, then turned to
me.

" 'Ha! so you were heard speaking Polish! Has that
policeman come? (This last to a servant.) Yes? Tell
him to come in. Here's the boy, officer, take him.'

"And I was led off to jail and locked up in a cell. Nine
years old. No chance to send word home, no chance even
to ask another boy to tell my father. Nothing to eat.
At midnight the cell door was unbolted and I was told
I could go home. It was nearly one when I reached there,
but late as it was, my father was waiting up for me—
with a strap. And such a thrashing as I got! I must
have looked pretty white and—what is it you say in America? all out—no, no, all in, for suddenly my father asked,
'Have you had anything to eat?' I shook my head.
'Well, you ought to have something; wait a minute.' He
came back presently with a bowl of steaming soup and
some rye bread. Oh, it tasted good!

" 'Now, my son,' he said when I'd finished the very
last of the soup and the last crumb of bread, 'this is a very
serious matter, going off in the morning and coming in
at one o'clock at night. Answer my questions. First,

[79]

where have you been?' I looked up at him and gave the briefest possible reply: 'In prison, father.' He stared at me. It was as if a half-miracle had taken place, for all the anger was gone from his face and in its stead was a great wonder. 'In jail,' I heard him whisper. A long wait. 'My son in jail.' And after a long pause he asked, 'What for?' Again I looked up at him. 'For speaking Polish at school.'

"Not a half-miracle then, but a whole one. The tears rolled down his cheeks. 'My son,' he said, 'my little boy—Michael, why, child, I've made a true Pole of you before I knew it—and you're only nine.' He was still crying when he'd undressed me. He took me into his bed and I fell asleep in his arms. None of my other prison experiences—in Warsaw, twice in Siberia, in Lwów— had an ending like that."

It was not only school children that the Germans thought to depolonize by harsh treatment and humiliation. I spent a day at Kornik with a Polish countess, a descendant of the Jan Zamoyski I'd learned to know at Zamosc, and of the Dzialynskis—I don't know which family is the older and more famous. The house was a medieval castle with towers and battlements and a moat (with real water!) and drawbridge; the first mention of it in the records is in the fourteen-twenties, but it wasn't new then by any means. And the museum—— But I didn't start out to tell the story of Kornik, but of my hostess and her parents.

"I was born in Paris where my father lived, not a voluntary exile, but a general, formally proscribed after the rising of 1830. His sister went to visit him; on the day she was to return there came some outbreak in Paris—barricaded streets full of revolutionary crowds and soldiers; he insisted it wasn't safe for her to travel alone, and went with her. He reported his presence at once to the German officials and asked permission to stay a few days with his mother. It was thus he met his future wife. There was a difference of many years in their ages and they were distant cousins, but—he fell in love with her.

"From France he wrote to my grandparents, formally asking for her hand. My grandfather read the letter to my mother, touched on the great honor paid her, and asked what her answer was—yes or no? 'I don't know,' sobbed my mother and began to cry. 'I don't know—I feel so sorry for him, there all alone in Paris, so far from his people, and never allowed to come back.' My grandfather sent her up to her room, with stern orders to stay there till she'd made up her mind, and to bring him a letter accepting or refusing this offer of marriage.

"My poor mother! Often she told me this story—how she sat down at her desk and tearfully wrote a refusal; as she read it over she pictured him, all alone in Paris, tore it up and wrote an acceptance; cried some more and wrote a no, sobbed and wrote a yes, till after some hours her desk was littered with tear-stained scraps and she was no surer of herself than when she began. Then with a sudden resolution she swept all the papers to one side, wrote accepting him, and carried it to her father. 'Will this do?' she asked timidly. My grandfather glanced it over and said yes, and he too wrote to the exile.

"Of course as they were cousins, it was necessary to get a dispensation from the Pope. Once that was done the real difficulties of the wedding appeared. The Prussians determined this marriage should not take place— either they objected to the uniting of two such families, or they would sanction nothing that might mean happiness for my father. The banns, as you call them in English, were announced by the priest, but after one reading he was notified by the police that the marriage was *verboten*. They tried in another place. Again the priest was told *verboten*. A third time. The same result.

"It was necessary to go to a parish where banns were not required—there were some such; but it was also necessary to find a parish where they owned property, so that they could say they belonged there legally. Fortunately both families had land here and there, and after a long search they found a place that met both conditions. Without any fuss and feathers they went one morning and the priest married them. As they left the church after the ceremony, a policeman arrived and handed the priest an official order forbidding the marriage. But— what could be done then? They were already married.

"They lived in Paris where my father bought a house, on the Ile de la Cité. My brother and I were born there. But how they longed to come back to Poland! It was here at Kornik, after my father died, that my mother started a girls' school—a plan she'd long had in mind, a school to prepare girls for life. Bismarck ordered the school to close or move, charging that it made Polish patriots out of the girls and sent them out with a patriotic message. You visited the school—at Kuznice? Now a second school has been started here at Kornik, small as yet, thirty girls, while Kuznice has a hundred and twenty, and last year turned away four hundred."

On one occasion the countess and her mother returned to Kornik to visit a sick servant, and promptly reported themselves to the Prussian police. They felt that something was about to happen and that evening the mother said, "They will come. You are young, you must live out your life and do something for Poland. I want you to leave me—yes," as she saw the daughter was about to protest, "yes, you must go. I will stay and face them. I have done nothing wrong." So the young countess slipped out by a side door and hid among the trees in the park, with one of the men-servants to watch over her. At three in the morning the Germans arrived, threw their soldiers around the castle, demanded admittance, forced the mother to rise and dress, took her off to prison. Twenty-four hours they kept her there, in the ward with criminals; she could not lie down, she could not eat what food they took her. A crowd of the villagers was waiting when she was released; no one dared say a word, but the father of one of the pupils silently handed her a little bunch of flowers.

"Here the flowers are," she added, "my mother pressed them and placed them in this box under the glass."

Now that the period of Prussian domination is ended and they have some perspective, the Poles see that all this hardship and suffering were not without a purpose.

"Our country was not perfect," men said to me more than once; "it had many faults, many weaknesses; and it was because of these faults and weaknesses that the Partitions came about. But some good resulted. The Germans taught us valuable lessons—to be punctual, orderly, thorough, thrifty, to stick at a thing day after day. That's why you'll find the best organization, the most efficient business methods in the west of Poland. Indeed, I've heard Americans say that a fortnight of business dealings would be enough so that they could pick out the Poles who'd had Prussian training. A costly school—yes, but we needed it. Now we must make these qualities tell in serving the new Poland."

The happy nation, says the proverb, has no history. This is almost true for the last half-century of Austrian Poland—happy, I mean, in comparison with the other parts of the partitioned nation. In the beginning Austria neglected the Poles, repressed and exploited them; but after 1861 there was a decided change of policy. Galicia, as the province was called, was to be an integral part of the Austrian Empire, with loyal citizens. The people had local self-government, with their own parliament at

Lwów (Lemberg), and they sent their representatives to Vienna. They could hold important government positions. Twice the premier was a Pole. As a result they were more loyal, more contented than their countrymen under Russia or Prussia.

"I'm astonished," said a Poznan resident on a visit to Krakow, "to hear Polish spoken by officials!"

On the wall of the drawing-room of a country house near Krakow I saw a great piece of blue taffeta, edged with gold, irregularly shaped. I'd seen nothing just like it and was curious at once.

"Oh," said my host, "that's the caparison for my horse—it had to be always a white horse—when I rode with the emperor (Franz Jozef). He had two Polish chamberlains and two Hungarian, riding directly behind him in state processions. We must have made a striking picture, all four of us in the old costumes. I suppose you've seen so many sashes that they're an old story? You'd like to see one more? Here are two that belonged to ancestors of mine—gold with purple flowers on one side, the same design in black and silver on the other; they could be folded either way—one side for festive days and the other for mourning."

A visitor in Krakow notices many things that Russian and Prussian officials would never have allowed to exist. This was the only university that was not closed, its record runs without a break from 1364. The Academy of Sciences, now considerably more than a century old, encouraging research, publishing, forming valuable collections, helped to make this city the intellectual capital of Poland. While I was there, an art society celebrated its seventy-fifth anniversary. Would Matejko have been allowed to paint and to exhibit *1863* and *Prussian Homage* in the domain of czar or kaiser?

In Lwów I went to the Lubomirski Museum and when I exclaimed over some of its treasures and asked more about it, the secretary replied, "These two families (Ossolinski and Lubomirski) collected everything that was Polish. That's how we have Sobieski tents from Vienna and Kosciuszko objects and the Matejko canvases, and so on. This was a little island of Polish influence in a foreign sea, after the Partitions."

"But how could they have this large collection and throw it open for Poles to see, without the government's knowing of it? They would shut it up at once, wouldn't they?"

"Ah, Count Maximilian Ossolinski was a personal friend of the Emperor. He went straight to the Emperor himself and asked permission. See, we even have this full-length portrait of the ruler of Austria. You must remember, it was different under Austria."

When the Poles wanted to raise a mound—that's a distinctly Polish custom—in honor of the three hundredth anniversary of the union of Poland and Lithuania, they knew they couldn't do it in Lublin, where the treaty was actually signed, because that was on Russian soil; so it was planned for Lwów, where the permission was easier to obtain. At the pension I met an old lady who told me

[86]

Photo by Swiatowice

Photo by A. Pawlikowski

In Polish museums I gazed at gorgeous saddles and inlaid armor, exclaimed over a nobleman's sash, woven in two colors with threads of silver, and stopped short just to look at a doorway

Wilno: here life goes on in quaint medieval courtyards

Photo by Jan Bułhak, Wilno

of carrying a load of earth, to do her bit toward raising this monument. It took several years to complete it (it's about fourteen hundred feet high) and even a hot August day could not take away the thrill with which I climbed its zigzag path clear to the top.

It was in Lwów too that I saw a statue that belonged, by right, in Warsaw—the shoemaker Kilinski, who led the citizen-soldiers in withstanding a Russian siege in 1794; as great a leader as Kosciuszko, some Poles told me. I thought of Nathan Hale when they translated the inscription: "I have one soul and I offer it as a living shield to protect my country."

Americans think of Kosciuszko as merely one of the f igners who came over to fight for liberty in our Revolution. We know the story of Washington looking up from the letter of introduction to ask, "What can you do?" and the quiet reply, "Try me and see." We know that he planned the defenses at West Point and suggested a military school there. But we know only vaguely that he went back to Poland and fought again for liberty. To the Poles all that he did here was but preparation for his great service to Poland.

For he refused to accept the Partitions and headed an insurrection. He called to arms not the nobles only, but also the peasants who had never before been given the opportunity to fight for Poland. He armed them with scythes and farm tools, for lack of muskets, and led them to victory. In Krakow I saw the house where he lived, the little chapel where he went to have his sword blessed, in the market-place the great stone where he stood to take the oath. But it was in a city many miles away from the scene of his great victory that I saw the *Panorama of Raclawice.*

An inspiring, thrilling picture, the work of three Polish painters; an enormous thing, nearly four hundred feet around and seventy high; so cleverly arranged with some tangible objects—charred logs and earth, branches, a plough—that it's hard to tell where they leave off and painted objects begin—a burning house, ravines, a wooden cross. It tells the whole story: Kosciuszko in a peasant's coat and the dress uniform he would wear at a ball, his soldiers in the square red caps that are still known as Kosciuszko caps, with flails and scythes, capturing Russian cannon with their bare hands—("Impossible! impossible!" cried the czar's general when this was reported to him); here a group of prisoners led off to one side; there Polish nobles galloping along a narrow road as reinforcements; old men, women, children kneeling at a wayside cross; Cossacks in red coats and tall fur hats, Russians in green, peasants in white smocks; smoke of battle, victory!

Still the Poles under Franz Jozef were never Austrians. Their chains did not bind so tight, but they were chains. Never did they give up their dreams and hopes. The love of the soil itself, the desire to keep it in Polish hands, was no less strong here. I heard a story of burning patriotism from the sister of the nobleman who bought Zakopane.

"The newspapers announced its sale at auction—that great valley, thousands of acres, that included the town of Zakopane, forest lands and mountains. My brother wept at the thought of its passing into the hands of Austrians—but he was no more anxious than all the Poles. He counted up all the ready money he had, all he could borrow, then came at night and begged my mother's consent to mortgaging some lands we held; and she agreed—was it not for Poland? He sent a man to the auction to bid for him, with orders to offer a penny more, no matter what sum was bid. Amid great laughter the bidding went up and up, the man always giving one penny more. When at last his opponents were worn out and Zakopane was ours, the newsboys shouted their head-lines, 'Zakopane bought for a penny!' For a long time afterward strangers used to stop my brother on the street, in Krakow, in Lwów, and congratulate him in the name of patriotism.

"For years he carried on, at his own expense, a lawsuit with the Austrian government to settle the boundary, for he claimed that Morskie Oko—the beautiful lake that's almost a perfect circle—the name means 'eye of the sea'—belonged to Poland—to Galicia, he had to say then. At the end of twenty years an international jury decided from the ancient documents that it belonged to us. People could not understand why he spent so much time and money on that suit, since no matter where the line was drawn, it was all Austrian territory; but my brother used to say, 'When we're free again, it'll be very important to have this additional land; it's very valuable indeed, and it must belong to the new Poland.' And that is literally true to-day, for my brother died recently and willed the whole estate to the nation, the income to be used for education.''

Quite a different story I heard of the czar's government, when my Polish acquaintances would speak of that tragic period. For the most part I got only touches here and there, little things that came out incidentally, perhaps the more impressive for that reason.

On one of my first days in Warsaw, the first when I was going about by myself, I went to see the Krasinski palace, once the finest private house in the capital. (To-day it is used by the courts.) What was the garden is now a public park, filled with mothers and babies, with boys and girls—especially boys. In front of the palace were two monuments of black marble, very plain, marked with a date—1823. My vivid imagination at once suggested there was a story here, they must stand for something tabooed by the Russians and so there was no inscription; doesn't that sound logical? I would make sure. So I did what was to an American the most natural thing to do—I went up to a policeman.

In half a minute, before I'd found out what language we could use, half a dozen boys had gathered around us. While he signaled his colleague at the corner, a man who could speak German, the crowd grew and grew. I made them understand my question, but neither of them knew; they must ask a student. They called up two or three and at last I learned that the two monuments had nothing whatever to do with the Russians—they were fountains and the date was when the Krasinskis gave them to the neighborhood; nothing historic, nothing thrilling. A waste of time.

"You are blocking traffic. Please step into the park," they gestured.

I glanced up. Behind my students both policemen were busy keeping people back. It was a throng such as we have at a serious street accident, or when finals are being played in baseball. And all I'd done was to ask a question. I walked eight blocks before I shook off the last of that crowd.

"Don't you understand?" my landlady explained when I told her of this adventure. "It's a grave comment on conditions in Poland. Why, you asked a policeman! A policeman!" she repeated.

"Well? Of course I hunted up a policeman. In England, in Italy and France, and in the United States as well, a stranger always turns to him. Ask a man in uniform. It's his job to set you right."

"But you don't understand. In another generation perhaps we'll do that in Poland—look on the police as our friends, appeal to them for help of all kinds. But for over a century we've been taught to regard them as enemies and spies. Why, those people all thought you were being arrested; when word went around that you were a foreigner, they were more curious and excited than ever.

Watch now as you go about—you'll almost never see a Pole speaking to a policeman."

"Then I mustn't?"

"Oh, yes, yes, it's all right. You've met only courtesy, haven't you? Only—it isn't done in Poland, that's all. It will take years and years to make our people feel that the police are their friends. That's one thing we owe to the Russians."

"This is the church," the doctor pointed out, as we passed Holy Cross on the main street of Warsaw, "where the people sang the patriotic hymn in 1861."

"Is that the same as your national anthem—the one the band played when our steamer landed at Gdynia?"

"No, that was really the national anthem, like your *Star-Spangled Banner*," and he hummed the first bars of *Jeszcze Polska* (Poland Is Not Yet Dead). "What we call the patriotic hymn is something different. Watch for a chance to hear it, for it's not often played nowadays. But in 1861, Sunday after Sunday, the congregation at this church used to stay, when mass was over, and sing it— new words fitted to an old tune, words that were a prayer, asking God to give us back Poland.

"The Russians objected and complained to the arch- bishop, but he replied he could do nothing, as the singing was after the service, when the priests had left the altar; and if the people were really breaking the law, was it not for the police and not the clergy to interfere? So inter- fere they did, putting spies into the church to chalk-mark the shoulders of the leaders, who were then arrested at the steps. Arrests did not lessen the popular enthusiasm and the singing of the hymn kept on. Exasperated, the Russians surrounded Holy Cross with their Cossack troops, who burst in at a signal, arrested many, and sent them off without trial to prison or to Siberia. Desecration, and the church was closed for many months. It was one of the steps that led to the insurrection of 1863.''

Small wonder the Russians objected to that hymn, I thought, when months later I ran across a translation of its poignant words. This is, I take it, a literal translation, but rough as it is and suggesting nothing of the poetry of the Polish, it interested me—and perhaps may interest you.

O Lord, who for so many centuries didst surround Poland with the magnificence of power and glory; who didst cover her with the shield of Thy protection when our armies overcame the enemy; at Thy altar we raise our prayer: deign to restore us, O Lord, our free country!

O Lord, who hast been touched by the woes of our injured land and hast guided the martyrs of our sacred cause; who hast granted to us, among other nations, the standard of courage, of unblemished honor; at Thy altar, etc.

Thou whose eternally-just hand crushes the empty pride of the powerful of the earth, in spite of the enemy vilely murdering and oppressing, breathe hope into every Polish breast!

May the Cross which has been insulted in the hands of Thy ministers give us constant strength under our sufferings! May it inspire us in the day of battle with faith that above us soars the spirit of the Redeemer!

[93]

In the name of His commandments we all unite as brothers. Hasten, O Lord, the moment of insurrection! Bless with liberty those who now mourn in slavery!

Give back to our Poland her ancient splendor! Look upon our fields soaked with blood! When shall peace and happiness blossom among us? God of wrath, cease to punish us! At Thy altar we raise our prayer: deign to restore us, O Lord, our free country!

Speak of 1863 and you feel Polish patriotism burning like a flame. The revolt was hopeless from the start. It took the best men—in battle, by exile and imprisonment—for two generations. Its tragedy is embodied in the drawings of Artur Grottger, one of the greatest of Polish artists, though he died at thirty. In Krakow, in Warsaw, in Lwów I saw his work, each time with a Pole to explain. A stranger might well think he was portraying the horror and cruelty of any warfare; to Poles the pictures are the story of 1863, vibrating with grief and patriotism, the experiences of the artist and of his friends.

One of my guides was a woman who'd had in her girlhood a favorite nun, Grottger's niece. Tears stood in her eyes as she showed me *Death Walking through the Forest*. I felt as if I were getting it at first-hand: the signal at the window, summoning the husband to war; the vow of the soldiers; peasant and noble; the Jews; service at church—only women; the battle-field; the wife sees the man's ghost in the doorway; the Madonna of Czestochowa appears to the exile in Siberia; the widow, in mourning for Poland.

"I see you've been looking at that portrait," said Mme. T., the first time I was in her home. "It's my mother, done by a celebrated Pole. After the last insurrection she dressed in mourning to the end of her life. She had lost her only brother—my uncle," she added as if in a parenthesis, "was for a long time a prisoner in the Citadel in Warsaw, he was beaten to death by the Russians, and a few minutes before he died he was hanged; but she's not in mourning for him, but for Poland. All the ladies did that." Her voice was calm and even as she stated the bare facts.

One morning I was walking down the Krakowskie Przedmiescie (that's the main street of Warsaw, and the name means "the street of the suburb toward Krakow") with an elderly woman who stopped in the square where a monument to Adam Mickiewicz (Meets-kay'-vits) stands. I knew vaguely who he was—the greatest poet of Poland.

"You'll find Mickiewicz statues and monuments all over our country. I remember the day this one was dedicated. We came early, but the Place was crowded. More people came, and more till it seemed as if not one more could find standing room; and still they came—thousands of Poles, and every one of them silent—men, women, boys and girls. He is more than our greatest poet, he's the poet of patriotism. Perhaps more than any one person he kept alive, in the hearts of thousands, the spirit of Poland—love of her, pride in her past and all its glories, and—most important of all—belief in her future."

[95]

"Tell me more about him, please," I urged, turning to her.

"It's a dramatic story. Born in Lithuania, not far from Wilno, in a beautiful country of lakes and forests; arrested while a student in the university of Wilno and sentenced to Siberia; for the rest of his life an exile, living most of the time in France, lecturing in Paris. When the Crimean War broke out and he saw an opportunity to make a move for Poland, he went to Constantinople to enlist a legion of Poles—and died there of cholera.

"There was some doubt about the Russians' giving a permission to erect this monument—you know, they were always opposed to anything that might fan the spirit of nationalism—but they did grant it and the committee went ahead with their plans. Henryk Sienkiewicz was to make the address, and he had prepared a splendid one—everybody was sure of that. Then, at the eleventh hour, the governor-general gave his orders to the committee: no demonstration at the unveiling, no music, no eulogy of the poet, no songs, no cheering—nothing.

"And that morning, with thousands of Poles gathered here in the Place, not a word was spoken. Sienkiewicz went up the steps, the folded sheets of his address in his hand, stopped a moment, then gave the signal and the curtains were drawn aside. Not a word. Why, it was so still I could have heard a pin drop. We looked up at our poet's face. Suddenly the silence was broken by sobs. I glanced around—tears were running down everybody's cheeks. Still without speaking, people turned and left the

Place. I think of it now when I walk past—how we dedicated a monument in the time of the czar.''

She told the story so simply, so vividly, that I felt as if I'd been present that morning. The Russian governor was not the only one who could give an order, and have it obeyed implicitly. Did the Poles realize then that a silent ceremony before the figure of a patriotic poet was many times as impressive as the ordinary dedication?

As she had said, I found Mickiewicz statues and busts in many a Polish town. One was in the oil-fields. Why, I asked in surprise, had he ever lived there? No.

"It proved, under the Russian régime, that this was a Polish town," was the oil man's answer.

One of the most interesting was in a church in Wilno. In Russian Poland the people put up in their churches monuments and tablets that we would place out-of-doors, because as a rule there was no interference in the churches themselves. They could have there what would never have been tolerated for a moment on a public street. So on the hundredth anniversary of Mickiewicz's birth they put up this monument in St. John's church in Wilno.

"And the Russians allowed it?" I asked in amazement.

"Well, the first official who should have prevented it was so stupid as to believe the poet was buried here; and once the monument was up, the second was bribable. Don't you know the old saying, current everywhere in Russian Poland, 'Absolutism can always be softened with baksheesh'? That was proved true over and over in Wilno.''

"Oh, you can't understand," exclaimed a sad-faced Polish woman I met in Warsaw, "what it was to live under Russia. You say we were better off here than in German Poland, because there they had to fight for their language, for the soil itself. There was progress in Germany. The Russians prevented all improvements. I was in Lublin last month—a town of a hundred thousand—and as I drove to the hotel my first evening the street lights were turned on. 'See!' the driver called my attention, 'see how bright the streets are! We've had electricity only a few weeks. The Russians would not allow it.' It's true that Warsaw was the one city with modern sewers—that was only because so many Russian officials and army officers lived here.

"However, all that is tangible, and tangible things are not the worst—not by any means. It is dreadful," she went on seriously, "to bring up your children in an atmosphere where every one knows you can do anything— almost anything—if you spend money in the right places. For a short time, a few years even, you could make them understand that it's temporary. But when it goes on for one generation after another, it's almost fatal, it's so demoralizing to character. It eats into character like acid."

In the center of Warsaw there is to-day a great open space, empty, covered with gravel. This was the space chosen by the Russians for their cathedral—a very large building of typical Russian architecture—towers, domes, mosaics. They wanted to give the impression that Warsaw was a Russian city; the cathedral dominated it, the domes showed up in every view. The Poles regarded it as an ever-present grievance, the church of their conqueror and oppressor planted in the heart of their capital.

It was nearly twenty-five years in the building. There were engineering difficulties in the ground underneath. There were frequent changes in the plans. There were many accidents among the workmen. Always something wrong! The Russians knew there was a saying current among the Poles that when the cathedral was finished and the first service held, the czar's rule in Warsaw would come to an end. In 1904 it was almost completed—almost, but not quite; one excuse after another for ten years longer. Then, in July of 1914, when there were no more possible excuses for delay, it was dedicated. Before a month the war began.

The Germans took the copper-gilt plates from the roof, the chandeliers, the radiator coverings. They did, to be sure, put on a substitute roof, but the work was badly done and the water dripped through and ruined the frescoes. Not a penny was spent for repairs for a whole decade. Then the people of Warsaw demolished it.

"A crying shame!" was the vigorous protest of some Americans who'd seen pictures of it and had set their hearts on seeing the cathedral itself and hearing the Russian choir. "Why couldn't the Poles have kept it as an unusually fine example of Russian architecture? Art has nothing to do with politics and oppression. By all means, it should have been kept."

"Be practical a moment," urged one of my Polish friends when I quoted those Americans, "you can't let a big cathedral take care of itself, it has to have constant care and yearly repairs. Tourists couldn't see the condition it was in. It needed a large sum spent on it immediately, with more and more to follow. Who would meet the bills? Not the Poles. Not the Soviet. And there's only a handful of Russians living in Warsaw today."

"You've been in Paris?" I asked him. "You remember the Place de la Bastille—that great empty space where a white line in the pavement shows the outline of the prison walls? I think it would be interesting—and dramatic too—if you showed here the outline of that cathedral. If there was a tangible line to look at, so that tourists could see how huge it was, they'd understand how it dominated the city."

"Why should we?" he demanded impatiently. "We want to forget it. We don't want to remember, to be reminded of it every day. No, no, we did the only thing possible—tore it down."

In the most important square of Wilno the Russians put up a monument to Michael Muraviev, the governor-general whom the Poles called "the hangman." When the last insurrection was put down with iron hand, he condemned to death more than five thousand men and sent other thousands to Siberia, after he'd confiscated their property. This was one of the most desirable neighborhoods, but the Poles moved away as soon as the monument was erected, and the houses stood empty; rents were reduced and reduced, to the dismay of the owners; but no Pole would live there.

"A group of boys found some wolves' fat," one of my Wilno guides told me the tale, "and smeared it over the Russian's monument. All the dogs of the whole city gathered here and howled—you know, they hate and fear wolves. No one could understand why, but when the howling kept up the Russians put a guard of their soldiers here, night and day. And when they left Wilno, the monument went along with them—Muraviev's as well as Catherine the Great's; it was as if they knew their monuments could endure only as long as they used force."

From that square we went to the university which has recently been reopened, a center of Polish culture for the northeast of Poland. Closing it was part of the punishment meted out by Russia for the insurrection of 1830. Later one of the buildings was used for a Russian gymnasium, where the rules must have been as strict as at Poznan.

"This," explained my guide, "was the room where the university used to confer degrees. The gymnasium used it for an assembly hall. I must tell you one thing that happened here. The whole school was called together, and a group of boys publicly reprimanded and expelled. Why? Because they spoke Polish. One of them was Jozef Pilsudski."

[101]

"Perhaps," the countess laughingly tried to explain, "that's because I come of a family of insurrectionists. My great-grandfather was one of the 1830 men and was sent off to Siberia. His cook and butler, who were husband and wife, followed him there; they had no idea where he was, they couldn't read or write, they knew only that the master was in Siberia—somewhere. It took them more than a year to find him; then they settled down and lived for years in that village, serving him just as they had done at home. Yes, the Russians allowed it. Touching, wasn't it, their wandering in Siberia and asking everywhere for their old master?

"My grandfather was a child of seven when 1863 came. He was mad to go to war. For days and days he saved his sugar and plums, and with that as his sole supply he ran away early one morning and walked—oh, many kilometers, eating his plums on the way, till finally he reached a Polish camp. He told the sentinel his story and insisted he wanted to be a soldier and fight for Poland; so he was passed along from man to man till at last he got to the general's tent. A messenger was sent to his family. The general took my grandfather on his lap and talked with him, said he was made of the right stuff, that Poland needed such boys and such men, thanked him for coming, gave him tea, and made him quite a hero in camp till somebody arrived to take him home again."

One day she and I were walking through the cemetery in Krakow and came upon the grave of the men who fell in the brief, sharp encounter there between Poles and

Bolshevists. Suddenly I had a strange feeling of the use-
lessness of the World War—of all the suffering, the hardships, the deaths. I stopped in the path and turned to
her abruptly.

"To what end? What good was the whole war? What
did it accomplish, to balance the deaths and the suffering?"

She stopped too and stared back at me, her eyes wide
with amazement.

"What came out of it all? Why," and she flung up
one arm with a strangely emphatic gesture, "why—Poland! Don't you know how many years we've been waiting, waiting, hoping, praying for some great change in
European affairs, so that there could be a Poland again?
People expected it in 1913; there were scores of rumors
and prophecies afloat that in 1913 something would happen. Month after month slipped by and nothing dis-
turbed the surface of things, and some lost heart and said
hopelessly, 'It will never come. Better give up hoping.'

"Then August of 1914 and suddenly the thing we'd all
been waiting for was upon us. Whichever side won,
there'd be a new map of Europe and that meant at least
a chance for Poland. You see, the tragedy of 1863,
the loss of the best blood of Poland, of our finest young
men, was too great a loss to be repeated; it was useless
to make a move unaided. Only in some general shake-up,
some new arrangement of the chessboard, could we find
our opportunity."

"And did you," I slowly asked, "did you see clearly,

at the beginning of the war, that Poland would emerge?"

"Some persons didn't, but most of us were sure. Of course there were a few who argued that come what might, Poland couldn't benefit; that if Germany and Austria won they'd take Russian Poland, between them; that if the Allies won, the czar'd demand the rest of Poland as his reward. But with the revolution in Russia, many Poles began to hope. When America came in we felt we had a friend at court. Woodrow Wilson taking such an important part among the peace-makers, and making Poland one of his fourteen points—you know, thirteen used to be the unlucky number; but when Wilson wrote his thirteenth point, demanding that Poland should be put back on the map, with access to the sea (Poles never mention that point without the sea phrase!), all that was changed and people began asking for thirteen because it brought good luck."

In Krakow the chairman of the restoration committee for the royal palace (which the Austrians used as barracks and left as a ruin) talked with me of its treasures. I'd read a brief paragraph about the tapestries—a hundred and fifty some, made for the wedding of Sigismund August and Catherine of Austria, twelve years to make them. That was no preparation for their amazing beauty. Speechless I gazed and gazed as he pointed out the threads of gold in the drapery of this angel, of silver in that background of verdure, and told me how a workman was given a square meter to do, in a year's time.

"There are several distinct sets—Biblical scenes with the story of Adam and Eve, of Cain and Abel, of Noah and the tower of Babel; another with the arms of Poland and Lithuania; a group of small pieces with S. A. as the main design; and a series of grotesques, with queer animals and birds and landscapes. And now they are here at last, in the rooms for which they were originally made."

Something in his voice made me look up.

"Tell me—where have they been?"

"When the capital was moved to Warsaw, the tapestries were all taken to the palace there. At the last Partition the Russians confiscated them and carried them off to Moscow—St. Petersburg—other places. It was one of the conditions of the peace treaty after the war with the Bolshevists that they should be returned."

He stopped. I could learn the rest of the story only by more questions.

"Did they all come back?"

"Not all."

"Were they in good condition? To my untrained eyes they look very clean and new. It's hard to believe they were actually made in the sixteenth century. Did the Russians then take good care of them?"

"I saw them when they were unpacked. They were unspeakably soiled and dirty. Many of them needed a great deal of mending. Come close up, I'll show you where this one was patched, that one darned. Fortunately by its very fabric tapestry makes this possible with less risk of its showing badly. The Russians cut one, because there was a door in the room in Moscow. Another they slashed into—for windows. And one large piece was returned, not as a hanging for the wall, but as upholstery on a sofa and a dozen chairs.''

The beauty-loving part of me boiled over as I heard this, and I couldn't keep my voice steady, I was so incensed at that wanton destruction of sixteenth-century beauty. My Pole made no comment whatever.

I felt much the same way at the palace in Warsaw, once the home of kings, then of Russian governor-generals, now of the President of Poland. The rooms were repeatedly stripped by the Russians. It seems to have been the proper thing for officials to carry away whatever they liked. This began with the last Partition. After each insurrection they took more. When they abandoned Warsaw in 1915, they took from this one palace ninety vanloads of furniture and treasures. Some of these things were returned—portraits, tapestries, the Canaletto paintings, a series showing Warsaw streets and buildings in the eighteenth century. But to-day only a few rooms are completely furnished.

The guide's tale runs like this: You are now in the ''marble room''; the Russians took all the marble from the walls, and the decoration over the windows; they left only the inlaid doors. This room was called so-and-so; here's a painting showing how it used to look. Here, in the study of the Russian governor, they papered the walls; only recently we discovered that underneath there are frescoes. Experts are working in what was the pages'

Photo by Polskie Tow, Krajoznaweze

Recently the Russians sent back the Canaletto paintings to the royal palace in Warsaw

"And now, at last, the Sigismund August tapestries are hung in the rooms for which they were made!"

Something in his voice made me look up to ask, "Where have they been?"

room, to find out if valuable frescoes are hidden there too.

Just once did I find that the Russians had saved a Polish treasure. In Lublin I went to a royal castle, converted into a prison.

"A great profanation!" said the Pole who was taking me, "it was sacrilege for the Russians to change the home of our kings into a jail!"

But it is still used as a prison, and there was some formality about our admittance. At last the great gates swung open and we crossed the court to a little Gothic chapel in the very corner of the enclosure.

"This is old—old, even for Poland, for it was rebuilt—not built, mind you, but rebuilt by Ladislas Jagello in 1410. After the Partitions the Russians whitewashed the walls and people gradually forgot there'd ever been a chapel here. Shortly before the war the whitewash fell off in one place and showed a bit of fresco—Jagello and the Virgin Mary. At once the Russians began a systematic destruction. You can see, here on this pillar, how they hammered at the stone and peppered the fresco with tool marks till nothing could be made out.

"Just then by good fortune arrived a learned commission from St. Petersburg and announced that this was a Russian church with Byzantine frescoes, and must be saved. The work of destruction ceased, and we never argued with those learned men. Byzantine? It's the work of Master Andrew of Wilno, court painter to Jagello. A Russian church? Look at this inscription. They've chipped away till much of it is illegible, but one word is perfectly clear: *kosciol,* the Polish word for church, where the Russians say *cerkiew.*"

The experts set to work, slowly, patiently, peeling off the whitewash. To-day more than three-fourths of the frescoes of the chapel show; with a few blank spaces, to be sure, with colors faded and softened by the centuries, but fascinating as when they were fresh from the hand of Master Andrew.

To the surprise of the onlookers, I painstakingly copied down two inscriptions on the front of the city hall of Warsaw and carried them to an American to translate.

"This one says, 'In memory of the one hundredth anniversary of the death of Tadeusz Kosciuszko, 1917.' You'll find many such tablets in Poland, they made a great point of them in 1917. And this"—she frowned in a puzzled way—"I can't get all of it and I'm afraid I'll make a mistake. You must ask a Pole."

On the train I submitted it to a man who was taking me to see Wilanow. He too frowned with the effort to make me understand all that it stood for.

" 'To the warriors of independence, liberty, justice,' " he began, " 'mistreated'—how do you say it in your English? much mistreated——"

"Sorely," I suggested.

"No, no, sorely will not do. Sorely isn't good enough. How can I tell you, madam? They beat and kick, they burn——" He leaned forward and made a circle on the back of my hand. "They burn—so——"

For a second the flame blazed up in his voice, in his eyes. I looked quickly down at my glove to see if there was a burn there, it was almost real. For a second only. Then he went on calmly.

"They no let to sleep, no food, and you say, madam, sorely mistreated. Give me a better word."

"Shamefully."

"That is better, but it's not enough yet. Haven't you any more words in your English? Well, I translate again: 'To the warriors for independence, liberty, justice, shamefully mistreated within the walls of the City Hall by the Russian government, from the grateful population of Warsaw.'"

Another day he took me for a walk past the Citadel, a fortress-prison like the Bastille in Paris, he said, where political prisoners were confined. The czar built it, after the insurrection of 1830, and tore down whole blocks of houses and gardens to make space for it. As a defense of Warsaw it was of little or no use; indeed its cannon were kept trained not toward an enemy on the west but on the city itself; at the least outbreak the Russian troops would fire down on Warsaw, warned the czar, and destroy it; and once destroyed, he was not sure that he would ever rebuild it.

"There," pointed out my Pole, "is the Traugutt cross."

"Please tell me about Traugutt," I said in my ignorance.

And standing there by the plain wooden cross, which the people of Warsaw put up in 1916, I heard the story:

1863, and Traugutt was the head of a group of five men who made up the provisional government of Poland. One by one the Russians captured them. Traugutt was very ill. The five were given a pretense of a trial and condemned to death.

"They met here on that August day in 'sixty-four. Some of them had never seen the others, so secretly was their business carried on. Traugutt was brought in a cart; when he was lifted down, soldiers had to support him the few steps to this spot—where the gibbet was. There's talk now of putting up a fine monument here."

"I like this plain wooden cross better," I said, "and the boulder with just the five names and the date. It's far more impressive than a great pile of marble, especially when you see how long the Poles had to wait to have a simple cross."

He said nothing about taking me inside the fort and it was a year later that by chance I learned that visitors could go; there are strict regulations, as the place is under the Ministry of War, with some thousands of soldiers stationed there.

"Oh, I want to go! Is it possible? Do you think you could arrange it?" I appealed to Panna B. in one of the government offices.

"Yes, I could arrange for it. But—you must go with just the right person. Otherwise you'd wander around and the guide would point out this and that, and you'd get nothing more. You must go with just the right person," she repeated.

She was staring out of the window, with a strange look on her face.

I waited.

"I will take you myself," she announced in a low voice. "You see, my mother was a prisoner there."

Thus it came about that, with just the right person, I went inside the Citadel. It's an enormous place—I could well believe a dozen city squares made its site, for there were many, many buildings, sometimes far apart: barracks for six thousand troops, officers' houses, hospital, a social room for each regiment, a garrison church, and high walls with gateways separating the whole into sections.

"The Russians kept heavy guards by all these gates," she explained, "so if a man did escape, he could never get far. This one, opposite the rooms of the court where prisoners were tried, was called 'the gate of execution'; it was built exactly like the entrance gate and sometimes the guards would play a particularly cruel trick—political prisoners were brought here from pavilion ten—you'll see that presently—and told they were to be released; the gate swung open, the men walked through, and on the other side were lined up and shot—or hung. We'll go through and see the place."

A chestnut tree to which prisoners were bound, the firing squad opposite them; it's riddled with bullets, more than a third of the trunk is completely gone. Near it the gibbet, with places for five at a time. Evidently five or six at once was not sufficient, for a few rods away the

Russians built a "waiting house" where the Poles waited their turns to die. The Russians deny, she said simply, that any one was tortured here, but our men have found bloodstains on the walls that tell a different story.

Over three thousand Poles are buried here. No stones, no tablets. Half a dozen wooden crosses. But on the first day of November (the day when all Poland remembers the dead) many Warsaw people come with flowers and wreaths and candles. On the brick wall is an inscription. I asked what it said.

"'To those who died for an ideal,'" she translated with a catch in her breath.

We walked on slowly to pavilion ten, built around three sides of a hollow square, with a high wall on the fourth side. It had room for five or six hundred prisoners, row after row of cells. In the narrow corridor, under the eyes of the guards, the Poles had each day a few minutes of walking up and down—all the exercise they got. Some of the cells have the original doors, with peculiar openings, less than an inch square on the inside, giving a view of only a tiny bit of the corridor, and four inches on the outside, so that the guards could see the whole cell.

"The place looks cleaner and fresher than I expected. How is that?"

"Oh, there's a reason. The Russians were always afraid prisoners would write on the walls and give some message, some important information to their successors. So every room was repainted or replastered for each newcomer. Consequently it's less drab and forlorn than some other prisons.''

"How large is this cell?" I asked when we stopped in one of the small rooms.

She stepped it off and estimated, "A meter ten by two meters fifty. And notice—no heat in winter. The larger cells are three or four times this large, and some of them had stoves.''

Traugutt's cell was marked by a tablet. Two others bore the names of noted patriots. Pilsudski's too she pointed out, with the dates of his stay here—about six months.

I'd just been reading (in translation) a lecture the Marshal gave, *The Psychology of the Prisoner.* He'd served many sentences and was "up" on prison life. The Citadel was evidently one of the places where he had a better time than in some, as his cell was large enough to walk about in, to move the furniture around; and moving furniture was one of his greatest pleasures. Was this where he'd taught himself English? If you ask the Marshal to-day, he replies that he does not speak English. He learned it all by himself during one of his prison terms, saying the words as if they were Polish. He knows now that his pronunciation is all wrong, but if you talk with him through an interpreter and watch his face, you can see that he gets what you are saying long before the man puts it into Polish.

To generations of Poles, he said at the end of his lecture, prison gave a certain training; it put into a man's character valuable qualities—a grim enduring courage that left complaints and lamentation to the weak, devotion to an ideal and quick response to its call, loyalty to comrades. What will this generation have instead of prison? What will mold their characters as prison terms did ours? They must live for the new Poland, not only be willing to die for her; but if they have no prison life, will they not miss something?

CHAPTER V

The Poles and America

I'VE traveled in nearly all the countries of Europe and in Canada besides, and I've watched to see how people regard Americans. I've seen clerks' and servants' faces brighten when a group of American tourists entered a hotel. I've heard prices in shops suddenly increased to travelers who didn't know how to bargain. I've heard some Americans abusive to pension servants, just because they couldn't understand the language.

"Your name makes people think you're English," I was frequently warned on my first trip abroad; "be sure to say you're an American. Why? Because in Holland (or Italy or France or Switzerland, it mattered not where we were) they like Americans better than they do the English. We're better spenders!"

Sometimes I wondered if they'd like us at all, if we weren't spending money. Stay for any length of time in a country, particularly in a private house, and you sense how quick people are to blame us, to pass judgment without knowing all the facts, seldom to give us the benefit of the doubt. But not in Poland. Put European friendliness and interest together and multiply it by four—or by forty—and you won't have a total equal to the interest and friendliness I found in Poland. It is without a duplicate on the Continent.

After a few weeks I got used to being stared at—on the street, in a railroad station and on the train, in a church or museum. Something in my dress, my opening a map, my speech, the moment I asked a question—all announced as plainly as if I'd worn a huge placard, "This woman is a foreigner!" But they couldn't make out where I came from. I remember a lady at Jaremcze (that's off in the very southeast corner of Poland) who stared till she made me uncomfortable, turned my luggage over to see if there was an address or a betraying label, and finally asked pointblank, "Madam, where do you come from?"

That question was usually followed by these: "Where are the others of your party? Are you here all alone? Then you have relatives in Poland; or friends, surely? Where is your husband? Then, madam, how many years have you?"

Once, curious to see how long we could play the game, I answered merely "No," to a woman sitting in my compartment on the train when she inquired if I came from Germany.

"From France, then?"

"No."

"Surely you're not Italian?"

"No."

"Nor Spanish?"

"No."

"Well, you'll have to tell me then, for I've guessed all the countries in Europe."

"Oh, no," I teased her, "Norway and Sweden, Hungary, Greece, Roumania, and—and—— But perhaps I don't live in Europe."

"Oh, I understand. Australia!"

I shook my head.

"South America?" she guessed wildly.

I surrendered and said quietly, "I come from the United States."

"But that can't be!" she exclaimed, looking me over sharply from head to foot, "no, that can't be. Where is your uniform?"

It took me a few seconds to realize that the only Americans she'd ever met must have been war workers, always in uniform. I explained as well as I could.

"And are these really American clothes?" she asked, leaning over to feel their texture.

"No," I confessed, half sorry, "this is a French dress and a London coat, and my gloves are Polish. But at least my shoes are American."

As had happened often on the Continent, Poles sometimes took me for an Englishwoman and commented on the fact that I didn't have an American accent.

"Why, you're the first American I've ever talked with that I could understand," the young doctor said. "You speak slowly (he didn't guess what an effort I was making!) and distinctly."

"And you don't talk through your nose," others commented frankly. (So all foreigners describe our peculiar tone placing—not meant in an uncomplimentary way.)

But the minute they knew I came from America, one and all, they were keenly interested and anxious to help me. I think there were several reasons for this. Firstly, Poland is not yet a tourist country. Oh, it will be before many years go by, when our people learn how interesting it is, that it isn't as far off as they think, that it's possible to travel without knowing Polish, and how little things cost—say, in comparison with Germany. Taxis eleven cents a mile; a four-course dinner, with the tip, fifty-five cents; a large room in a pension for six or eight *zlotys* a day. The Poles know how many millions we spend in Italy and France, and would like for a few thousand of us to put Warsaw, Krakow, Poznan on our itineraries, when we're going to Prague or Vienna or Berlin; to fill their hotels and spend generously in their shops; and without knowing just how to go about it to advertise Poland they feel that one way to help bring this to pass is to give what visitors do come the best possible impression.

Secondly, they are naturally kindly and courteous and generous. Realizing that their language is difficult for foreigners, they look after them as Frenchmen and Italians, say, never do—in pensions and hotels, in trams and trains. Never before did I have a busy pension hostess go herself to show me a church or take me for a drive and afternoon tea. In one city I had an introduction to a man in a bank who could go about with me only after five o'clock; but he would plan for the next morning and when I reached a palace or a museum, I'd find that he had telephoned and a special person would be waiting to take me through—a special person being some one I could talk with.

To give one instance out of many. This in Krakow. Wanda, translating a paragraph from a Polish book, read, "The Nativity figures in the convent of St. Andrew's church are perhaps the oldest in Europe."

"Oh," I cried, "I must see them! Figures that were really used in the old mystery plays! Let's go—to-morrow."

"They are still here, but we keep them put away," she translated the nun's answer to our eager questions. "They won't be unpacked till Christmas time."

"But this lady is from America. She won't be in Krakow in December."

"From America! Wait—I will speak to the Mother Superior."

And presently we were told to come Tuesday morning at ten.

A young nun unwrapped the figures as she took them from a deep basket, and the Mother Superior, who was over seventy and very deaf, passed them out through a grill for me to see and touch. A gift from Queen Elizabeth of Hungary, Wanda said, the sister of Casimir the Great; the earliest "cradle figures" existing in Europe; fourteenth century.

Gently I put down Joseph with a flowering staff and took up the Virgin Mary, who had no dress on. The Amerikanka must understand that her hands were new, for they were broken off. Once a new costume was being made for her, and to make her body thinner somebody sliced off part of her breasts so that she looks sadly mutilated now. Three musicians in peasant dress, carrying book and banjo and trumpet.

The Wise Men with their negro servant in a white turban—they're later, made in the sixteenth century. One had a red coat and yellow trousers, very full, a blue satin shirt with silver braid. The second in red velvet, with a long gold cape and jeweled crown. The third in crimson satin over a skirt of gold brocade, and a cape of rose and silver. All three with jeweled scepters.

Rachel, the tallest of them all, about fifteen inches, wore yellow and green, with a violet cape and pearl necklace. There were two citizens kneeling, and two Polish nobles (later). The cradle and the gilded manger weren't old at all—eighteenth century. The four-inch figure of the Christ Child was dressed in white satin, laced across with gold cord to suggest swaddling clothes.

"Tell the lady that we would not get them out, not till December, except that she comes from America," mumbled the Mother Superior. "Tell her we would not do it for Polish visitors."

"Tell her," I turned to Wanda as I pushed the tallest of the Wise Men under the grill, "that the Amerikanka thanks her—many, many times. And ask her to take this money for the convent."

Thirdly, the Poles do not forget that Kosciuszko and Pulaski fought in our Revolutionary War, one of them giving his life for our cause, and that gives them a friendly feeling for present-day Americans—following the old rule that you care for the person you've done something for. They beam all over when they point out a memorial of one of these heroes—Kosciuszko's commission, signed by John Hancock, I found in a museum in Krakow; a miniature of him in Warsaw; a Pulaski portrait—and when I would answer, "Ah, they belong half to us. They are our heroes too!"

Fourthly, they themselves have many ties in America, with four million Poles living here, many of them sending money home regularly and generously. Asked a cleaning-woman in the Ukrainian Museum in Lwów, "Madam speaks such good German. Madam puts all the endings on. But—please, madam is not a German? What? From America? Oh, oh, oh! I have a friend living in the next street—she's gone on her vacation, or I'd send for her so you could meet her——"

"Why in the world should I want to talk to her?" I thought impatiently, for I had little time and was eager to see the old vestments and the church paintings.

"Do you know, she has a brother in America, and every month he sends her a hundred—and—fifty—*zlotys* (just over sixteen dollars)! Why," and she clasped her hands, "why, it must be just heaven in America!"

The fifth tie is still stronger. This many years after the Armistice people said over and over to me, "You can't know—because you could never know all the details—what splendid work your Red Cross people did in

Poland—at the end of the war and afterward. How efficient they were—and how kindly!''

''Please tell me,'' a young woman appealed to me when our hostess happened to say that I was an American, ''do you know Miss Simpkins? (That name, and one other in this book, are unchanged.) She stayed at our home for— Ducha, was Miss Simpkins with us three days or four?— for four days. Surely you must know her. She's with the Red Cross, and she lives in a town called Ohio.''

Had I ever met Major Phillips, was asked repeatedly; did I know his book about his Red Cross experiences in Poland? And other workers were inquired for by name. It was very plain that the Poles have to-day only the happiest memories of all of them.

''We got to know them so well,'' one man said of some of the Hoover Commission, ''working side by side with them for month after month. One thing they did that we can never forget—they gave out supplies with the friendliest manner in the world; not patronizing, but rather with this air: 'Here, you're down-and-out, let us lend you a hand. You'd do the same for us if things were reversed.' Which wasn't always the European attitude.''

One lady told me that the Red Cross asked her to be responsible for giving out five hundred women's—what's the word? not uniforms; perhaps bundles will do— dresses and petticoats, shoes, gloves, winter coats, and various accessories. They asked her to promise one thing—that the garments wouldn't be sold. She stared at the man and repeated, ''Sold?''

"He'd had a bitter experience in one town, he told me. In a hospital of convalescents he'd given out a supply of sweaters—this was in the dead of winter—only to find, two days later, that every Jewish second-hand shop was offering them for sale. On investigation he found the soldiers were dismissed from the hospital without a cent of money; and as they left Jews stood at the gate and offered a few *zlotys* in cash—in cash, mind you!—for their sweaters. I couldn't find it in my heart to blame our poor soldiers, yet I understood how the Red Cross felt too. So I made every woman promise she'd keep her things and never sell them. I could have given out twice five hundred and not have had enough then."

"What I remember best about the Americans," commented Mrs. D., "was the amazing efficiency with which they did everything. I wrote up to Warsaw to present the needs of two hundred children, mostly orphans, who were being looked after by a little group of ladies in our town. They sent a man to talk with me, and shortly afterward the boxes of supplies came. Such complete outfits! Nothing forgotten. Shoes, underwear, dresses, coats, blouses, a supply of insecticide—they seemed to think all Polish children were in the sad plight of the refugees from Russia—and, how we laughed over this! a gallon of castor oil!"

And whenever they talked about the relief work, my throat would fill up and I'd ask myself, "Oh, did we do enough? Couldn't we have done more?" But when I asked Poles if we'd sent enough, they answered, often with tears in their eyes, "You're the most generous people in the world!"

Things like this occurred, over and over again. I was invited to Mme. M.'s for *collatya*, and her youngest son, a boy of fifteen, came into the room. Four or five at the end of the war, I figured.

"May I introduce my son, Stanislas? We owe his life to Mr. Hoover."

It was in Lublin that I demurred, for the first and only time in Poland, over one piece of sightseeing. A doctor was taking me about and he gave some direction to the chauffeur and announced, "Now, we'll visit my hospital. Yes, yes," as he saw the doubtful look on my face, "you must come. I particularly wish it. And Sobieski built the chapel," he added as a final bait. After we'd seen the chapel he summoned the head Sister (who might have served as a model for a painter's ideal nun, so spiritual was the look on her face) and we went into one of the wards to see not the patients, but the beds.

"Mr. Hoover gave them to us—in 1920—this whole room full (about thirty). I want you to see what good care we've taken of them—not one damaged. Please tell us what these letters mean—U.S.M.S.; we know the first two."

"Medical Service," I suggested.

"And more than the beds," added the Sister, the doctor translating to me. "She says I'm to tell you these are American blankets too. Here's the same mark— U.S.M.S. All these years we've used them, day in and day out, winter and summer, and we still have the very number Mr. Hoover gave us. Will you tell him so when you see him?''

I blinked back the tears and promised. And I didn't wait till I was going to Washington, but sent a note to Mrs. Hoover who was as touched as I'd been when she learned what care they were taking of beds and blankets in that little hospital in Lublin.

And lastly, Polish gratitude to Wilson is very sincere and very deep. I heard many references to him and to the important part he played at Paris, to his fourteen points, one of them concerning the new Poland, with access to the sea.

In January I went to a church service on the anniversary of the outbreak of the insurrection of 'sixty-three. In marched a little group of veterans in their blue uniforms (they didn't have uniforms in 'sixty-three, they're new since 1920). Outside the church when mass was over, I went up to the flag-bearer and asked if I might see their flag; was it really an old one? He gestured that the embroidery was new. A woman standing by offered to interpret—in what language?

''In German, if you please.''

''But—you're not a German, surely not?''

''No, an American.''

''Amerikanka, Amerikanka,'' the word was whispered about and passed on through the crowd, while I reverently touched the flag of white and red, with its lovely embroidery of the white eagle. Up came the leader of the veterans and made a long speech, while the crowd grew and grew. The woman translated—alas! I felt that she was giving only the gist of it:

"Madam, we greet you, and through you all Americans. We can never, never forget how much we owe to your country, to your Woodrow Wilson for his aid in making the new Poland. We owe America much, and we send this message through you, madam."

With a deep bow he turned back my glove and kissed my hand. The blue-coated old men marched slowly away, and I walked down the street with my head up as if the Stars and Stripes were floating over me.

In Poznan one of the city parks has been renamed Wilson Park. On the thirtieth of May each year Lwów holds a solemn ceremony at the grave of the three aviators, the only Americans who lie in Polish soil. On Warsaw's main street there's an intersection with a little triangular park, planted with trees and gay with flowers. The Poles have named it the Hoover Garden, and the children have taken it over as their special possession. I walked through on the fourth of July. Flags were flying everywhere—the Stars and Stripes floating out side by side with the white and red of the Polish flags.

I stared at them.

What was wrong?

Then I saw the mistake. Those flags must have been made in Poland and they had only half enough stars. Evidently some one had asked, "How many stars?" "Forty-eight." So they put twenty-four on one side,

How Poland honors the three American aviators who fell at Lwów. The winged marble figure is always banked with flowers

Photo by Polskie Tow, Krajoznawcze

Every section of Poland has its own picturesque peasant costume

and twenty-four on the other. But even without the full quota those star-spangled banners in the Hoover Garden made a lump come in my throat.

Indeed the Poles are so friendly, so eager to help visitors, so anxious to have tourists know their country, that I advise your going right off and not waiting a few years before you see Poland. In a decade or so tourists will be an old story; and while I can't think that the people will be any less courteous, there'll be less need for them to offer their services. To tell the truth, I can not help dreading the day when every Tom, Dick and Harry goes to Poland, quarrels with the taxi men, rows over bills, complains at the baths and the meal hours, and generally makes himself so obnoxious that everybody's glad when he moves on to Czechoslovakia and Hungary. I pray that the time may never come, as it has come in other lands, when tourists do such unmannerly things and cause such trouble that they get into the head-lines of the world's newspapers and bring discredit on the Stars and Stripes. For to-day there could not be a more friendly feeling toward citizens of another land than that of the Poles for us.

It interested and pleased me very much to notice what happy memories my Polish acquaintances have of their visits in America. A banker, in New York for a year to study methods, an engineer, an instructor in a nurses' training school, several social workers, the head of the national parks of Poland, who spent some weeks at

Yellowstone and Yosemite, a beet-sugar manufacturer, a playground teacher, a few travelers for pleasure, even the journalist who took his wife to New York at the end of the war when prices were highest and the housing shortage at its worst—one and all, they spoke of our country with enthusiasm, with admiration.

"My husband and I hope to have one wish come true," said a woman who had lived here for a brief time, "we want to spend a couple of years in Washington."

"Your houses are so convenient. Your people are so efficient," a man summed it up. "I remember now, seven years afterward, the celerity with which clerks in your shops served me."

And I recall the young countess, one of the most beautiful women in Warsaw, who'd had a glimpse of America and wanted to go back. What time of year would be best?

"Not in the summer," I warned her. "Everybody who possibly can goes away from New York and Washington, and I think you said you wanted to stay there particularly. You couldn't stand the hot weather, especially when you're not used to it."

"But surely you'd not tell me to go in the winter. How in the world could I stand January and February in New York? How would I keep warm?"

When I laughed at that question, she only stared at me. I was wondering how I'd keep warm in Poland. I hasten to add that I was thoroughly comfortable all winter long, for I followed the archbishop's advice and chose a small room with a big stove. Of course I paid extra for more coal, to the constant wonderment of the maid who frequently exclaimed, "The Amerikanka buys extra fire and then—opens her window!"

"I confess, we were anxious when my nephew went to the United States," said a dowager-duchess type of lady whom I met at a tea, "but do you know? we all thought his manners distinctly improved on his return. He said to me once, 'I'm afraid I was careless at home, but in America I was on my tiptoes all the time, to get up quickly enough when ladies came into the room.' Yes, your countrymen are most polite, but not in our way."

Of all the Poles I met who'd been in the United States, none was more enthusiastic than General Haller. In February I spent a week in Zakopane to look on at the winter sports and have a change in that wonderful mountain air. The gong rang for dinner one day. When I entered the room I felt something electric—zip! so sharp it seemed almost as if I could put out my hand and touch it. At the far end of the dining-room were Pani N. and her niece, with a stranger—a man under average height, ruddy-faced, middle-aged, dressed in gray sports clothes. A very Polish face, keen, alive; dark brown eyes, tiny mustache and pointed beard, high forehead, hair very black with just a hint of gray. Madame glanced up and motioned me to join them.

"May I introduce our guest, General Haller?"

"Oh!" I gasped out, and then as we shook hands, "do you speak English, General—or must I think it out in French or German?"

"I have not forgotten English, I hope. Didn't I have to make speeches in America?"

"I have a letter of introduction to you, but I had no idea I was to find you in the Tátra Mountains, so I left it in Warsaw."

"You must bring it to me," he said severely, but with his eyes twinkling, "it must be presented in person at my home in Poznan. Then we'll be sure to have a visit from you."

Sitting across from him at meals, I was all the time conscious of the electric personality of the man. No wonder his soldiers adored him if he exercised the same influence over them that he did in the pension. The commander who went through the ranks of the Allies to pick out the Poles and then welded and fused them together to make a Polish army, who used it in France and on the eastern frontier against the Bolshevists and for the defense of Warsaw—could this be he, this alert keen man whose hair was far less gray than mine? Yet I noticed how lame he was; crossing the room to the little table for coffee he did not try to walk without his stick, and then he had a decided limp.

I asked him to describe for me the ceremony on the northern coast, when he rode into the sea and threw in the ring to wed Poland and the Baltic.

"Two rings," he corrected me, "platinum rings they were, given by the merchants of Danzig. Did you know they suggested the idea? That was a real marriage, for the word *Polska* is feminine and *Balticus* is masculine.

It was a rainy February day, yet hundreds of people came, thousands, massed on the hillsides above the bay. Cavalry on one side, the artillery on the other, in the center an altar for the mass—my chaplain and a field bishop. Representatives of all the Allies were present—Italian and French and English—and one American too."

"But, General, you haven't asked who gave me the letter to you. Judge M., your host in Philadelphia."

"Yes, yes," he answered quickly, "his daughter took me to Independence Hall where I saw the bell of liberty, and sat in Washington's chair to write my name in their book. I'll never forget Philadelphia—but then, no one could forget America. That was a marvelous trip. All the way to the Pacific coast I went. You know, I had over twenty thousand Americans—nice boys," he added with a happy smile, "nice boys—and good soldiers too!"

"You come from the New World," said a scholarly Pole with whom I had many talks. "You can't know what a glamour and romance it has for us. What's so wonderful about your country is—not your prosperity— a job for everybody and a high standard of living—but the fact that you have no problems in America."

I stared at him, speechless. No problems?

"Now in Poland," he went on, "well, this is true all over Europe, but here especially, there are so many problems and such difficult ones—almost unsolvable. Our whole economic life's like an apple-cart upset, as you say in English; the question of land for the peasants; mi-

norities and their rights; relations with our neighbors—
Lithuania, Germany, Russia. In America you don't have
neighbors or minorities. Perhaps as a result you don't
have to keep up an army—yours is actually smaller than
ours, I understand—and so taxes are far, far less and
maybe that's why you're so prosperous!''

"But you're wrong. We do have neighbors, only—
we're good friends with them; at least, we are with Canada, and relations with Mexico are getting better right
along. And we do have our own problems—the negroes
are one, both north and south; and the immigrants are
another—why, our four million Poles might be called a
problem, with their own churches and schools and their
exclusive social life. Of all our foreigners they're the
most difficult to get acquainted with. You're wrong if
you think it's heaven in America.''

What questions they asked me about our country, and
how many! Where did I live? In New York City part of
the year, and in Illinois. The latter word meant nothing
to them, but "five hours from Chicago" they understood
at once; and naturally, for Chicago has the largest Polish group in the whole United States. How far was it to
Illinois? Distance told so little, and I would answer,
"Twenty-eight hours.''

"Twenty-eight hours! Impossible! Why, in less time
than that I can go from Krakow to Wilno, and that's
slanting clear across Poland.''

And when I spoke of the overland trip to California,
they shook their heads as if it were a fairy tale.

Does' New York really have tall buildings like the pictures? How tall? Are they safe? What about fire? Why do we build them? How often do our working people have meat—more than once a fortnight?

Is it true that we don't have enough house servants? How much does a cook get a month? Would I put that into *zlotys*? Why don't we change the quota and let Polish peasant girls in; in a couple of years they would make good servants. Who lives in the villages in America, if it isn't the peasants who own the near-by fields? If there are no peasants, who does the work on the farms? Are people good friends if they go to different churches? And why did we have so many sects?

Our queer system of educating girls and boys together—did it have any advantages? Did we think it good for the boys? or for the girls? What—for both? Could it be true that boys were named Lindbergh? Why do so many Americans go to Europe?

Children in Poland always asked me about the Indians. Did any live in New York? or in Illinois? Did I know any? I rejoiced at my friendship with Os-ke-non-ton, the Mohawk singer, and at one country house had a spellbound audience as I told his story and described the deerskin costume he'd made himself, from chief's head-dress to moccasins and tom-tom. But Adam and Nusia and Marya looked askance when I added, "His concert is almost as unique with us as it would be with Poles."

"There's one thing I've heard about America and I want to ask you if it's true," a portrait painter's wife appealed to me. "Do people use dollars as we do *zlotys?*"

"Living conditions are so different that it's almost impossible to make a comparison. But most decidedly it's not true that the average American hands out a dollar where a Pole gives a *zloty*. For example, how much do you pay the porter at the railroad station if he carries two bags from the train to a taxi? One *zloty?* Well, I'd give more than one *zloty*, but not as much as one dollar. How much did those shoes cost? Fifty-six *zlotys?* Well, I'd never pay fifty-six dollars for a pair of shoes. How much is butter? Tell me, how do I put kilos into pounds? Why, butter in New York costs very little more than in Krakow." (Butter is very good in Poland, but high in proportion to other things. You must order it extra in a hotel or restaurant, and a small portion costs more than two rolls.)

But we came to grief when we tried to compare rents, for rent in Poland doesn't include heat (you buy your own wood and coal, and your servant makes the fires in every room; you must allow so many minutes for each tile stove, and time for bringing up the coal from the basement) or hot water (you heat your own, by gas or in the reservoir of the kitchen stove); you paint and paper and make every kind of inside repairs yourself, even to rebuilding a tile stove that you couldn't take along when you move.

"Well, one more question, please. Why does an average family get along with one servant, where we have three or four?"

COMPARISONS

"You must remember," I answered, "that our one servant is paid far more than she would be here in Poland. She doesn't go to market, and nearly everything that comes into the kitchen is ready to use—where your cook spends three-quarters of an hour getting the roast ready, and makes the chops herself. Ice is delivered, or we have electric or gas refrigeration. If the laundry isn't all sent out, there's an electric machine to do it in an hour's time. Why, our one servant does far more than she could here, for she has all manner of things to make her work easy. Isn't she worth more than five dollars a month?"

More than once Poles asked me about taxes in America. I suppose it's a remnant of 1776 and our no-taxation-without-representation principle that makes us resent petty taxes in addition to the large ones? In Poland one is reminded of them daily. There's a tax on your hotel room, on theater and concert tickets, sometimes on railroad tickets. I remember one woman who got out pencil and paper and wrote down the figures as we talked and compared—or tried to compare.

"Now," she began briskly, "let's take an individual—say, a small farmer who has a thousand dollars a year. How much income tax does he pay in your country?"

"None. The tax starts now at fifteen hundred; and then he gets certain deductions—so much for each child, for interest paid, for contributions to charities and colleges, and so on."

The exemptions she could scarcely believe. We discussed local taxes and I could scarcely believe how many there are in Poland.

"No, there isn't a capital tax now," she explained, "that was levied only twice when the new government was just starting. But we pay a land tax, quite separate from income from the land, and a manufacturing tax—if the estate makes beet-sugar, for example, or spirits (from potatoes). Then there's a luxury tax—for a motor, a carriage and carriage horses, riding horses, a gun, and so on. Village taxes. District taxes. National taxes."

"I wonder you have a *zloty* left," I commented.

"Oh," she cried, "you don't know how well off you are in America!"

"We have now in Poland," said the owner of a very large estate, "a persistent campaign for peasant lands. One result of that is the sliding scale of land taxes. Do you have anything like that in your country? Yes, I can give you an illustration: here are two adjoining fields, the same size—say, twelve acres each. One belongs to a peasant and it's all the land he has; the tax is fifteen *zlotys*. The other is part of a great estate and the tax is a hundred and twenty *zlotys*—eight times as much. Tax the large owners till they sell is being done in other places than England."

One morning I went into a bank in Krakow—not the largest bank in that town of two hundred thousand— and saw at the teller's window a pile of paper money with an American five-dollar bill on the top. Was it various kinds of foreign money? I asked.

"No, that's all American bills. We keep a supply on hand."

"How much?"

"Never less than fifty thousand dollars, and often twice that much. Why? Because many contracts nowadays stipulate that payment must be made in dollars. People lost so much in the deflation periods that they're afraid; it isn't enough to say this must be paid in *zlotys* at such and such a rate of exchange, they insist on dollars."

"But your *zloty* is stabilized. I've been here nearly a year now and it hasn't varied more than a tiny fraction of one per cent. Pounds sterling changes from day to day in New York more than that."

"Yes," he agreed, "but the bank has to be ready at any time to pay out large sums in American money. It's a sad state of affairs for Poland, for all of Europe," he added with a serious look on his face, "that exchange in every country is now reckoned in dollars. Financial leadership for you means losses for us. And yet," he went on quickly so that I should not misunderstand, "no one could be more grateful to America than the Polish bankers. Your government has been most friendly and let us sell our bonds; your bankers too, who made a market for them. We can never forget that."

What else did they ask? The lady comes from America; does she know my brother in Albany? Do you know my cousin in Argentina (this from a little girl of seven)? If it is true that prohibition doesn't prohibit, why do we have laws that aren't enforced? But not one person asked, as I was so often asked in England, "Why do you send us such bad motion pictures?" They like our pictures and would invite me to go to the Kino as if it were a great treat.

"You must come to-day. It's an American film!"

And they were amazed at my enthusiastic endorsement of the two Polish pictures I saw—one based on a novel by Zeromski, the story of the son of a soldier of 'sixty-three; and *Halka,* with music from the Moniuszko opera and settings from the romantic mountains called the Pieniny. There was not one scene in either where puritanic I could object, though there were several where I said to myself, "Here an American director would have overstepped the line, jazzed it up, and made it common and vulgar. The Poles have better taste than we."

While I was in Krakow, the main in the city water pipes burst; and though men worked overtime, repairing was a matter not of hours but of days. No water for the whole population. Everybody had to carry it from the nearest well. Long lines formed, with buckets, pitchers, washtubs, babies' baths, coffee-pots, any sort of receptacle. What surprised me was that nine-tenths of the carriers were women, on days so cold that spilled water froze.

"They are servants," explained my landlady, "or else the wives of working men." As if that made it all right for women to be carrying buckets of water, sometimes three or four blocks.

"But in America," I protested, "a working man wouldn't let his wife carry water like that. If he had to go early to the factory? Why, he'd get up fifteen minutes earlier and make at least one trip for water, and go again at night."

"Don't you know," asked my landlady a bit sharply, "that in America all women are spoiled?"

CHAPTER VI

Lowicz for Color

"Please, lady," my little Warsaw maid began in Polish when I came in one Saturday afternoon, then went on in German, "to-morrow morning, half past eight (showing me on my watch), station, Professor R., Lowicz, you understand, lady?"

"The train goes at half of nine, Rosa?"

"No, no, lady. Train—eight and fifty minutes, but it is Sunday, and many, many persons. The professor will find you at half of nine. *Dobsche, dobsche?*"

"Good, good," I repeated in Polish, twice for emphasis. "Shall I wait at the gate, Rosa?"

"On the train, lady. He will find you. Your break-fast—twenty minutes before eight? *Dobsche, dobsche.* And hot water fifteen minutes before that? No, the lady does not need a taxi; it will be a fine day and the tram takes you right to the station. *Dobsche,*" and Rosa, greatly impressed because I had a professor to take me to Lowicz, completed all my arrangements as if she were Mrs. Cook herself.

Lucky that she started me off so early, for the station was crowded when I arrived at a quarter after eight. I stood in line at a ticket window till eight-twenty-seven, and twelve minutes, moving up inch by inch, seems a very long time to an impatient American.

"One—third-class—to Lowicz," in my best Polish, which brought a reply I couldn't understand—so many *zlotys* and so many *grosze*. The man hunted for a scrap of paper and wrote it down, but demurred when I handed him twenty *zlotys* (two dollars and twenty cents for a ticket costing about seventy cents).

"Has madam no change?"

I searched. Not enough. The man shut and locked his window and went off. All the Poles in the line back of me grew impatient, afraid they'd miss their trains; and I didn't blame them—one woman holding up so many travelers. They began to talk, scoldingly I fancied, so I turned and announced in German, loud enough for the first ones to hear me, "Amerikanka—it is necessary that I ask." Not another word out of them.

I got a slip of a ticket and my change and found the gate. Two trains to Lowicz—eight-fifty and nine. I gestured to the guard, I want the eight-fifty train, but he wouldn't let me pass. He explained volubly in Polish, then called on a passer-by to put it into German: my ticket was for a local train—at nine o'clock; the other was an express; it would cost more; did the lady really want to pay extra just to go on that train? Then I must go back and buy an express slip.

"Stand in line again?" I cried aghast. "I'll miss my train!"

"No, no," he comforted me, "go right to the window and say, '*Schnell Zug, bitte,*'" which I did, quieting the first man in the line by announcing again, "Amerikanka—a mistake—express train."

I raced back and ran along by the train till I found a seat in a third-class compartment, all the time saying to myself, "Make a note of this: special tickets for express trains. Tourists need heaps more small change than in England or Italy." In two minutes appeared my professor, dismayed at finding I'd bought my ticket (how did he expect me to get through the gate?), but refusing my prompt offer to pay for the one he'd purchased. Frantically he ran about till he found somebody to take it off his hands.

It was a ride of an hour and a half across the flat, uninteresting country that makes up the vicinity of Warsaw. There ought to be a sign put up to tell foreigners that's the most monotonous, uninteresting section in the whole of Poland, and they mustn't judge the country from this one sample. But the time flew by, for we talked hard.

Did I remember, began the professor, that Lowicz was the background of Reymont's *Peasants?* I'd forgotten, probably I'd known when I was reading the book. The Reymonts had lived not far away. We had to go on a Sunday. No regulation sightseeing to do in Lowicz. The thing visitors go for is to see the peasant costumes, and of course they don't wear them during the week—a few put them on for market-days; but on Sunday they all dress up for church. Such color as we'd see at Lowicz!

"You'll find stripes in other districts of Poland," he went on, "but not up and down stripes like these; they're peculiar to Lowicz. You know how they began? Well, there are two stories. One is that the peasant women

Photo by Henryk Poddebski

Stripes belong to Lowicz, but not slender lines

Photo by Polskie Tow, Krajoznawcze

A typical peasant home with thatched roof and outside crucifix and the people in Sunday-best

A peasant in the north of Poland in every-day dress; his kindly blue eyes
look out frankly from a face bronzed by wind and sun

wove just what they saw when they looked out of their windows—long, narrow fields that at a distance look like stripes on the landscape.

"You can always tell the old costumes because the wide stripes are of red. That was what everybody had until one day a Jew discovered (for the Jews were—and are to-day—the shopkeepers of Lowicz) that orange dye was a little cheaper than red; so he spread abroad the word that red was out of style, orange was the newest fashion. And all the peasant women of Lowicz followed his dictation—just as New York follows Paris—and to-day they all make orange the foundation of their patterns."

"But the second story," I reminded him.

"Oh, yes! The other story is that one of the archbishops of Gniezno had been in Rome as chamberlain to the Pope. It was just at the time that Michelangelo designed the costume for the papal guards at the Vatican. You've been to Rome? You remember the tall guards with halberds, in gorgeous striped clothes? Well, the archbishop wanted a similar dress for his peasants and thus the Lowicz stripes came into being. Take your choice."

"About how much does a costume cost?"

"Four to five hundred *zlotys* (that's forty-four dollars to fifty-five), provided you could find one to buy. They're all home-made; the cloth's hand-woven—pure wool, and it wears—well, there's almost no wear out to it. The wives and daughters weave it for their own garments and their men folks', they don't make it to sell. Now you can buy cheap, ready-made clothes for far less—say, fifty *zlotys* for a dress; and every year more and more girls are wearing them. I'm afraid," he shook his head sadly, "it's only a question of time till real peasant costumes will be a thing of the past, seen only in museums."

He asked some one to change seats so that I could be by the window for the last ten minutes. I gazed and gazed. Across the fields came peasants, single file, along the narrow paths that separate the fields (there aren't any fences in Poland); here two together, there five or six; old women, young women, girls in their teens, maids of six or seven, in striped skirts and striped capes and white blouses and gay, spotless headkerchiefs. Such colors! Orange, green, dark blue, pink, black, red. Primary colors as vivid as those in a child's paint-box.

Very wide stripes—two inches or more—of orange or red, then narrow stripes, four, five, six, eight of them, all different, and this design repeated time after time. Never two skirts alike. But all of them yards and yards around, gathered in at the belt. Sometimes an apron of the same, and the cape; sometimes of a different striping. Out-of-doors, against the green of the fields or against the snow, they suit perfectly.

"There comes another!" I cried, "and two more. There's a whole family—five, no—seven. Why, even the men are in Lowicz stripes; how the trousers show up against the long white coats! One picture after another!"

"Slender lines are not popular in Lowicz," commented

the professor with a chuckle. "The skirts stand way out, for every woman wears six or eight white—what's the word? Thank you—six or eight petticoats, each with many ruffles."

Most of them were carrying their shoes—high, laced shoes, black, with pointed toes, always worn with white stockings.

"Oh, what a shame! Look—two young women with flesh-colored silk hose and light slippers with a strap!"

"Lowicz flappers. Those shoes don't fit with the striped skirts, do they? But even Lowicz thinks it must be in style. Too bad, isn't it?"

I was still looking at costumes as we walked from the station to an exhibition in the boys' gymnasium (that doesn't mean athletics, but the equivalent of our high school). I was surprised at the size of the building and asked how big Lowicz was.

"About fifteen thousand."

"And how many boys come to this school?"

The professor asked to make sure.

"More than one thousand. Not all are Lowicz boys. Some come from far away—many kilometers, on bicycles. The gymnasium's grown enormously in the last few years."

"Please," said a voice at my elbow, in French, "are you the American?"

I turned to a lady in mourning and said wondering, "Yes, madame." How did she know of my coming? I never found out.

"The American who's come to write a book, *Why Not Go to Poland?*"

"Yes."

"I am Mme. Reymont," she said simply. "Would you like to see the exhibit with me?"

I gasped, explained to the professor and went with her. What better fortune than to meet, in Lowicz itself, the widow of the author of *The Peasants?* She was so glad I'd come that day, for I'd see Lowicz at its best, and more peasants than usual—oh, many more, for they were all coming to the exhibition. It was, she answered my questions, a regional exhibition showing all the new movements of the district. Though I couldn't read the Polish, I could readily understand the charts that told of better farming, public health, education and so on. Here a little girl with a book, then a larger girl, and a big girl, with figures of book sales; how much wheat to the hectare without fertilizing, and with; how much rye; how many new schools, how many patients in the new hospitals—all illustrated with pictures, colored squares and oblongs, graphs; splendidly done!

Still more interesting were the peasant rooms, completely furnished. Mme. Reymont called my attention to this or that, as typically Polish or typically Lowicz: a door with very old carving; the rafters covered with paper cuttings—the peasant women make them in the wintertime, with just a sheet of colored paper and shears, and designs they think out themselves—every-day things, flowers and chickens are the commonest, a few with peasant figures, and one was a nobleman's coach with three horses. They must have an innate sense of beauty, or they'd never do such work. The crudest shows a vague reaching out for beauty.

"That's a part of every peasant girl's dowry," she went on, "a feather-bed, very thick, with very fat pillows, and deep lace on the pillow-cases—hand-made, of course. And see how the ends are laced back and forth with tape of two colors, because the pillow's always too fat for the case.

"Many of the skirts are double," she explained when we came to the old costumes, "and so are very heavy, yet the peasants wear the same ones, winter and summer. They last almost for ever—I know women with dresses twenty, thirty, forty years old. They don't get a new one every year, or every decade even, for they're expensive; with apron and cape it takes nine meters for a costume— that means a long time spent at the loom."

There was a showing of linen too, hand-woven and embroidered—cuffs, strips for collars, napkins for afternoon tea, no more than five inches square. Those would be easy to pack, I thought; were they for sale? But it was Sunday. I appealed to Mme. Reymont who began, "The lady is from America," when the woman in charge interrupted, "Oh, then we'll be glad to sell her some, even if it is Sunday," and helped me choose a dozen with old Lowicz patterns.

We moved on to the Frederic Chopin room—did I know he was born in this district? There were letters to and from him, many photographs, his Bible, manuscript sheets of his waltzes, of a polonaise, a bust, the cast of his hand, printed music on which he'd written dedications, programs of concerts in Paris, pictures of his grave at Père Lachaise—a remarkable collection. (Part of it was loaned by the Chopin Society in Warsaw.) I recalled it vividly when later I visited his birthplace, when I heard a concert by Rubenstein, next to Paderewski the greatest player of Chopin's music.

"And here," said Mme. Reymont as we neared a case that had always a big crowd around it, "are the Stephen Waleski things."

"Waleski?"

I searched my memory. The name meant absolutely nothing to me and I said so frankly. If I'd read this in a book, I'm not sure I'd have remembered; but a lesson in Polish history with such a teacher made the facts stick in my mind.

He was the son of Napoleon and Marya Waleska, the reigning beauty of her day and the leader of Warsaw society when the Frenchman lived here for six weeks—it was in the winter of 1806-7. The son bore the mother's name, but spent most of his life in France.

"Was he a man of great importance?" I asked.

"Well, Napoleon III made him Minister of the Interior."

"Did he ever do anything for Poland?" I persisted.

"I think not—nothing definite," was the vague answer.

I looked at letters, photographs, his sash of red, miniatures of him and of his mother (a real beauty!). People crowded up and pushed us along. They were not interested for Stephen Waleski himself, but because he was the son of Napoleon. That was the first time I met it, but I found it over and over and over, in every part of Poland—an overwhelming admiration, almost adoration of Napoleon, such as to-day you notice only here and there in France itself.

I slept under his picture in many a hotel and private house. I saw David's portraits of him in the Potocki country house near Warsaw, and in a reception room at the American Ambassador's. I saw cases of Napoleonana in Count Krasinski's library—articles for which French visitors have offered huge sums, in vain. Person after person told me proudly of ancestors who had fought under the Little Corsican. They showed me banners which the Polish legions carried in France. In Poznan they pointed out the grave of a general who died in Spain, leading a charge that won for Napoleon a great victory.

The more I saw and heard of this inordinate admiration and devotion, the more surprised I was. Now I've never made any study of Napoleon and his relations with the Poles, but my impression was (and my professor said it was correct) that he made them vague promises and did—little or nothing. The Duchy of Warsaw he created wasn't even allowed to use the old Polish flag, and it lasted only a few years, till the Congress of Vienna made a new map of Europe; indeed hadn't I read somewhere that even while he promised vaguely and enlisted thousands and thousands of Poles, using their legions in Egypt, in Spain, sending them to the West Indies to die of fever, he was assuring the czar that the partitioned country should not be patched together? But if he'd won at Waterloo, the Poles argue. Well, if he had, would he then voluntarily have decreased the size of his empire to put Poland back on the map?

"Did Mme. Reymont show you everything?" asked the professor.

"I think so—the peasant rooms, the charts and graphs, the Chopin and Waleski things."

"And not the Reymont case? I might have known she wouldn't, that's just like her."

"Like a Pole," I commented to myself as we made our way back through the crowd to a room I'd passed by. It was—if not the treasure of the exhibition, one of the special features, and only a chance question had told me it was there; why, I wouldn't have missed it! Photographs and snap-shots of Ladislas Reymont, alone, with his wife, with friends, in Warsaw, in Paris, at his country house which reminded me of Mount Vernon, a big, white house set close to the ground, with tall pillars; his books, *The Peasants* in Polish, Russian, English, French, even Japanese; manuscript pages in clear firm handwriting, with almost no corrections; medals; a framed parchment announcing the Nobel prize; just think of seeing these things at Lowicz.

"Oh," I exclaimed when I saw the limited edition of *The Peasants* with full-page colored illustrations, "that's needed far more in the English translation! Every time I've been in the country here, I've had the feeling of looking up from a page and seeing a living illustration of some scene in Reymont's story—a girl with a wooden yoke, carrying water, an old woman spinning, why, just the people going across the fields to church, as we saw them this morning—things Americans can't visualize. What our copies need isn't the usual illustrations an artist would make, but drawings of every-day things, not formal and posed, snap-shots rather. Wayside crosses and fenceless fields and Lowicz stripes are all strange to the U. S. A.''

"Why don't you talk to Mme. Reymont about it?" asked my professor.

Just then in came a Lowicz man who had read *The Peasants* and modeled the important characters as he pictured them. He was bringing his busts to the exhibition, some in plaster, some still in wet clay. I studied his face as I watched him carry in Boryna and Yagna and Antek. He might have walked out of the book himself.

In the village church after luncheon I had my second lesson that day in Polish history. Did I know about the Primate? In utter ignorance I shook my head. The Archbishop of Gniezno was head of the church in Poland and was besides the Primate; the word would tell me the story: on the death of a king, before the election of another, sometimes a matter of weeks, he was at the head of the government, the first man in Poland, hence Primate. When the capital was moved from Krakow to Warsaw, it was too far away to have the Primate in Gniezno (it's in the west of Poland, near Poznan), so the king gave him the Duchy of Lowicz. The peasants here were much better treated than the folk who belonged to the average over-lord, and were immensely proud of the fact that they be-longed to the Archbishop; and they are to-day a superior group. All this was to explain why in the Lowicz church are the tombs of perhaps a dozen archbishops, some flat against the wall, with the figure at a slant, so that I had the uncomfortable feeling the poor man was falling out of bed—a pose I was to see often in Poland.

Then we went to the commercial high school to see the Lowicz museum. It's a collection made by one man, long the music-teacher of the town, who had an idea but no money. It goes to show what one man with an idea can do. There was a case of papers with seals and signatures of Polish kings; fans, snuff-boxes, costumes of an earlier day; old religious pictures; primitive stones for grinding grain; a heavy iron door labeled 1571; a lady's black lace scarf, the national mourning after 1863; and—not to make the list too long—half a dozen yellow arm-bands marked "Kriegsgefangen," worn by Polish soldiers in 1914-18.

"Are you tired?" questioned the professor. "Can you walk out to the agricultural school? It's two kilometers or so. You'd rather walk? Good!"

I was glad we did, for then I saw the new park—not very large, but well planned, and so tidy it would put an American park to shame. My guide hadn't been to Lowicz recently and was amazed to see the progress the town had made, since it was no longer under the Russians—new schools, the electric light plant, the park, better roads, with no less than six signs for motorists at the crossroads. That's true all over Poland—progress everywhere now that they are free.

The farm school made me open my eyes. It was four years old, an attractive group of buildings, white or buff plastered, with red tile roofs; the main house with class-rooms, library, dining-room, and dormitories; a shed for machinery; cow barns and stables; the assembly hall. Poland has been divided into two hundred and forty districts, each of which is to have a school like this for boys and one for girls; and half of them have already been built and are going concerns. The eighty boys live there for a year, paying a very low tuition and doing all the work on sixty acres. They were seventeen years old, eighteen, up to twenty-two. I found two boys who spoke German, and was listening to their story of how they got more wheat from a ten-acre field when the professor interrupted with, "Time to go. Dancing, yes, old peasant dances on the lawn, and then a play."

In front of the school a great circle had formed—many peasants, labeled as such by their costumes, with a sprinkling of city people. First came a little cart, trimmed with flowers and branches of trees, with dolls dressed like a wedding-party; the man turned a crank and they went round and round. Five men sang, accompanied by a violin, triangle, drum and two home-made wooden instruments that made a clapping sound; and five girls with bright red headkerchiefs ran in and out of the group, throwing water (a symbol of rain).

My professor looked at his watch—half past six—and said how sorry he was, but he must go back to Warsaw on an early train, but I should by all means stay for the play. I'd find Mr. Blank or Miss Soandso, whom I'd met that morning, and they'd look after me.

"Did you tell them I was to go back with them?" I asked with a vague feeling that I might not be able to get along alone.

"No, but you'll see one or both of them. You'll have no trouble. The train's at nine-thirty."

"I won't think of what may happen," I resolved as we shook hands and he started off; "I'll just enjoy everything to the utmost and then see about getting home."

While we'd been talking, the spectators had gone into the assembly hall. I found every seat taken, every window-sill crowded, many persons standing. And suddenly I felt tired. Could I stand up all through a play? Could I follow what was happening without some one to explain? I glanced around. Yes, there in the aisle stood Mr. Blank.

"Hello!" I accosted him gaily, "I'm so glad I've found you. Professor R. had to go back to Warsaw, and he says, will you take me with you on the late train?"

From the expression on his face I might have thought that what he most longed to do was to pilot a strange American back to Warsaw. Indeed, he would be delighted, and where was I sitting for the play? What, no seat at all? Come down this way. About seven or eight rows back, the choicest place in the room, he spoke to a man who rose and bowed as he offered me his seat. I protested, but to no avail. This was best for me, for in the next seat was the French teacher from the Lowicz gymnasium, she would interpret as the play went along.

Group singing, with the Lowicz music-teacher directing; the finest part singing I've ever heard, for girls and boys of twelve to sixteen; splendid shading, gradually getting louder, dying away to pianissimo. Just the least explanation was sufficient: a religious song; a dialogue between two girls in love with the same man; a harvest song which they acted out—sowing, the wheat growing taller and taller, the men coming to cut it.

Then came the play, *A Lowicz Wedding*. Part of it I could have followed alone, but without comments I'd have missed the Lowicz touches, certain customs that are fast dying out and will soon be only local traditions, others that are typically Polish, that I'd find anywhere. There was no change of scene—a room in a peasant's house.

The mother, weeping because her daughter of sixteen is not married, complains to her husband. Enters the marriage agent and the three discuss the matter; he returns with the young man's parents, then the young man himself. They all eat and drink. The groom's parents hold out for a dowry of nine thousand *zlotys*. After much bargaining the girl's father agrees to pay eight. (That's a very large dowry, even for a well-to-do peasant.)

"And," the agent reminds them, "you must give besides something to the priest, for he will do nothing without money." (Laughter—the only time the audience laughed.)

They all drink (from one glass), each one singing before he drinks. They go to sleep—on benches, chairs, wherever they can. Curtain.

I used the intermission to make notes on their costumes: the men in high black boots, trousers of orange with stripes of green, blue, red; coats, short-waisted with very full skirts and big buttons; overcoats of a white, homespun material, very long, skirt full and gathered in the back; flowers on their hats. The women in the costumes I'd been seeing all day.

The bride's mother wakens them; they wash (only one towel!); the mother weeping all the time. (That made the audience smile; several persons turned to me with, "Notice, madam, how much the mother of the bride cries. That is Lowicz!") Four bridesmaids and four men lead in the happy couple. Her Lowicz head-dress, over a foot high, was made of paper roses, blue, white, pink, and ornaments of silver paper, with at least a dozen streamers of colored ribbon, each a yard long.

The weeping increases—both mothers, even the two fathers. The girl's godfather makes a speech, blessing them as they all start off to the church—all but the parents of the bride, who must stay home to get things ready for the feast.

The next scene shows the return of the wedding-party.

A dance, with the orchestra sitting on the stage—two violins, accordion, cornet and drum. The men all kept their hats on, perhaps because they were specially decorated?—some with silver ornaments, some with beads, some with a narrow band of home-made trimming. They danced, with much stamping of feet and clapping of hands; once the men held their handkerchiefs by the corners, high overhead, and the girls passed under them in a sort of ladies' chain. The wedding-supper and more dancing.

"In a rich peasant's family the wedding celebration often goes on for a whole week."

"Yes, it was so in Reymont's book, I remember."

Then the girls bring in a wooden box and take out a new head-dress for the bride. She protests, they insist, she objects, they urge her, a third time she protests, then yields (three is the traditional number at Lowicz); the godmother lifts down the bridal head-dress with its mass of paper roses, and in its stead places on her head a cap of white net with a narrow band of tiny pink and blue flowers.

"You are no longer a maiden," sing the girls. "You're now an old, staid, married woman and must wear the married woman's cap!"

Then a man announces in a speech that he has a girl for sale, the price is a hundred *zlotys*. In come two young farmers, say they might buy, but insist on seeing her. The bride is pointed out to them. They find many flaws and object to this and to that. Finally the bridegroom

[157]

pushes them to one side impatiently, saying he'll pay a hundred *zlotys* for her, and the two men are hustled out.

The music strikes up and with the bride's mother still weeping and all the young folks dancing, the curtains come together and the play is over.

I had that most enjoyable feeling—not as if I'd been seeing a performance in a theater, but as if I'd seen a bit of Lowicz life.

It was nine o'clock. Why, the play had lasted more than an hour and a half. Suddenly I realized how tired I was. Could I possibly be pleasant on the train and talk to people?

"Please come, Miss Humphrey," said Mr. Blank, "you're to go in the governor's car."

I supposed they were driving to the railroad station, but no, they were motoring back to Warsaw. I groaned to myself. When I was so weary, when my head was full of Mme. Reymont and the wedding and the school and Lowicz stripes, how could I be polite and chat with strangers all the way to the city?

"I am sorry, madam," apologized the governor's wife, "but—I am quite fatigued. We left early this morning and have been meeting people all day long. You will pardon me if we do not talk on the way back?"

I assured her, and meant it from the bottom of my heart, that that was just what I'd like. It was like a page out of *The Peasants*—the last of the sunset; here and there a group of peasants, barefoot, carrying their shoes; level country, with long lines of trees at the roadside; white houses; twilight, quiet, peaceful.

It was half past ten when they dropped me. Tired out, a bit hungry too. I couldn't go to a restaurant at that hour all by myself. I'd just forget that I'd had no supper.

"Panna Amerikanka?" called Rosa as I tiptoed past the kitchen. "Your supper—in a moment. Yes, yes, madam left word you would be hungry."

Lowicz—color—a red-letter day.

CHAPTER VII

Thirty-Six Kilometers from Nowhere

"If you're going to be in Wilno," wrote a friend of my sister just before I sailed, "do please inquire for Gabrielle C. who was my good friend years ago, oh! many years ago, in a Prague convent. I've not heard from her since the end of the war, but she lives—or did live—near Wilno—rather near, I take it. The address is

Mme. Boleslas de K.

Szemetowszczyzna

Excuse, I had to make two tries at the name of the estate."

No wonder, thought I as I painstakingly copied it into my note-book, for I never learned to pronounce it without stumbling, without two tries or more.

Wilno, one of the treasure cities in Poland, was certainly on my itinerary. Overnight by the fast train from Warsaw, way off in the northeast corner. The first evening I made inquiries in the hotel, with the one waiter who spoke a little German to translate for me: Was this family well known? Was Madame still living? Did I have the address right? How far was it from Wilno? Could I telephone, and would some one talk for me?

A famous family, very old; every one knew the name. Yes, Madame was still alive, and her husband. Please, why did the American lady ask? When I explained that I had an introduction from an old school friend of Madame's and was anxious to meet her, waiter and clerk suddenly got excited and announced eagerly, "Just the right time! The son of Madame is to-day a guest in this hotel." I looked up quickly to see if my fairy god-mother's wand was over my head. Would they give him a message?

"He is in the restaurant now. We will send for him."

In two minutes up came the handsome young man I'd passed on the stairs that morning. He was so interested, so cordial, so utterly astonished. His mother was in the country, and wouldn't be in Wilno for some weeks, as there were many guests. I must come to them. He was leaving the next day. Would I write a note to his mother? And they would wire me what day and train.

When the telegram came it was in Polish. No one in the office could translate for me. The clerk went around asking guest after guest if he knew English, French, German. At last a woman volunteered and read, in hesi-tant French (nearly as hesitant as mine!):

Come Monday train to Lyntupy will send to meet you welcome.

"But, please, doesn't it say which train?"
They talked back and forth. At last she turned to me.
"There is only one train. You leave at eleven-forty and arrive soon after three. How far is it? Over a hundred kilometers."
So Monday found me buying a railroad ticket to Lyntupy and hunting a place in the local train. A journey

I shall never forget. The country was flat, with many
fields of wheat and rye, with stretches of forest, but no
villages, almost no people. Once for more than an hour
I saw not one person. The very landscape seemed de-
serted, desolate.

But it was sociable enough in my compartment, though
I had only one companion—a woman physician, bound for
a town past Lyntupy, where she went twice a week to see
patients. She asked me countless questions (in French)
and in the hospitable Polish way offered me half her
lunch, which she produced from a sort of Boston bag, one
little newspaper package after another—rolls, meat,
pickles, cake. (Don't think all doctors in Poland are so
unhygienic; their standards of hygiene are European,
not American. Moreover paper of every kind is costly
in Poland. All the time I was there I saw waxed paper
only twice, in American households.)

"No, no, thank you," I replied. "Last week I arrived
at three in the afternoon, to find they'd ordered dinner for
me, and I had to eat it when I'd lunched in a railroad
station at half past eleven and knew I'd have tea at five.
So this time I planned better and had a late breakfast.
I thank you ever so much, but I can not take your lunch."

When she ate and ate till every little newspaper package had vanished, I wondered what she would have done
if I'd said yes.

I hopped off the train at Lyntupy—a station of one
room, and one little house. One other passenger got off,
a peasant woman who climbed into a cart, was kissed many

times by her husband and two kiddies, and off they drove. I was left alone. The train pulled out, with my woman doctor waving good-by. I felt rather scared and asked myself aghast, "Oh, why did I come?"

(There is really a village of Lyntupy, I learned later, a village of about four hundred, three kilometers from the station. All over the Russian part of Poland the stations are far from the people they're meant to serve. Villages and towns were there first; railroads were built according to the lay of the land. Why dip down into a valley, or spend money on difficult grading, or go out of the way to reach a town? Let the people come to the train, not the train to the people.)

Presently a peasant came around the corner of the station, looked all about, approached me and said something in Polish.

"I don't speak Polish."

"Amerikanka?" He fumbled in his pockets and brought out a letter.

"Mme. de K.?"

"Yes, yes, yes."

He took my bag, wrapped it up in a blanket, and strapped it on at the back of a carriage. Is carriage or cart the right word? It was made of yellow wood, no top, two seats upholstered in green velvet—faded velvet. One gray horse and one bay.

"They don't match!" I exclaimed aloud. "Oh, why did I come?"

At my last private house I heard daily talk about their

horses. My hostess would say, "Shall we go in the car or with the grays?" And before I could answer, "Of course you'd rather drive, the horses are so perfectly matched."

"They don't match!" I repeated and opened the letter. It was in French, to bid me welcome as the friend of Clara Brent, and to explain, lest I be worried, that the coachman spoke only Polish, and we must stop to rest the horses on the way; it was a long drive—thirty-six kilometers. My heart sank. Thirty-six kilometers. I multiplied by five and divided by eight to put it into miles—twenty-two and a half. Oh, why did I refuse to share that lunch? But there was nothing to do but go on, as I couldn't stay in Lyntupy and there was no train back to Wilno, whose hotel began to seem very fine indeed.

Out from under the seat the man brought a long, very heavy, blue cape that came down to my feet, and awkwardly put it around me. He watered the horses, carrying buckets of water a long distance, economically packed away in the carriage what hay they hadn't eaten, boosted me in, and off we started. The first half of the way the road was sandy and the horses walked; now and then there were little hills where they raced down and poked up.

It began to rain. The coachman produced an umbrella for me, a robe, and a water-proof apron; buttoned his brown jacket over his smock, turned up his hood; and on we went in utter silence. I counted the signs to see how many kilometers we'd done. At eleven we met a peasant girl, coming out from the forest with a basket of red berries. Then on and on. Not a word spoken. Not one house, not a person. It rained, stopped a bit, then rained again; once quite a downpour. We had one long wait to rest the horses.

We drove through a manor with a very fine big house, a mill by a stream, many farm buildings, and a row of cottages, unpainted, thatch-roofed. Three times we came to villages—twenty houses, forty, fifty, drab and monotonous, with a few barefoot peasants in drab clothes. It grew darker. The sun set in a dull bank of gray clouds. We splashed along through puddles, once over a corduroy road that was the roughest stretch of all. We went between two long rows of trees. And then suddenly, there were lights ahead!

The horses galloped. We swung around a great circle of lawn and shrubbery and pulled up in a wide porte-cochère with four enormous pillars of gleaming white. The glass doors were thrown open. Servants ran out, a barefoot girl in a white headkerchief. Somebody said in German, "I am the daughter," and reached up to shake hands and help me out, for I was stiff from the cold and from sitting still so long. Madame was waiting at the top of the steps, tall and very straight, with a crown of perfectly white hair, and the saddest look in her eyes.

"You are Clara Brent's friend—and Lillie's too?" she asked, kissing me on both cheeks, many times over. "When did you see them last? We are so glad you have come to us. We've hoped and hoped to have Clara and Lillie come to Poland. It is so good of you to visit us."

Every one was introduced—ten persons to get straight—Pan de K., a niece who spoke English, the son I'd met at the hotel and another son, home for the long vacation from a Belgian university, an army captain, two sons-in-law, and a guest from Poznan, there to learn Polish as an offset to his German education. At the time I could only bow, give my hand to be kissed, and try to catch their names; for instead of saying "I'm glad to meet you," or its Polish equivalent, Poles on being introduced repeat their surnames—they realize their names are hard.

Madame took me off to my room which was on the ground floor; we reached it by walking through room after room. I found this arrangement in many country houses. With a few quick changes they could transform a bedroom into a drawing-room, or vice versa. In the old days the nobles moved about continually—for hunting, for war, for pleasure, or for business; they took with them rugs and wall hangings, some small pieces of portable furniture, and made themselves at home anywhere.

My room, as nearly as I could tell from stepping it off, was twenty feet by fourteen, not counting the alcove, separated by four white columns, large enough for the bed and a prie-dieu under an elaborate crucifix. The bedstead was beautifully carved, with two thick mattresses and a down quilt covered with purple taffeta. The walls were gray, darker at the bottom; the parquet floors were highly polished. There was the inevitable white tile stove—a huge one. But—the dressing-table had gray cardboard where the mirror should have been.

WINDOW SCREENS ARE UNCOMMON

The double windows were screened—this was one of two Polish houses where I saw screens. Weeks later when I told about this adventure, a woman said in a puzzled tone, "But, madam, you've seen screens at my house, there's one in my bedroom. And where did you sleep at my cousin's? Wasn't there an embroidered screen in your room?" I had a hard time making her understand what window screens were, and discovered that they are well, not quite an unknown quantity in Poland, but not common in homes that had all the comforts and many luxuries.

All these details I noted the next day. That first evening Madame was so eager to talk that she stayed while I freshened up. She had hunted up the photographs of the two Americans she'd known in that convent—Lillie in a tiny fur cape and a dress with big sleeves, Clara in gorgeous evening clothes, short-waisted, with a belt ending in a big bow in the front, puffed sleeves, elbow length, long gloves, her hair elaborately done. "Vintage of '95" they were invisibly labeled. Thus they'd looked when Madame and her husband visited them in Switzerland on their wedding trip.

"How did you happen to go to school in Prague?" I asked.

"I lived near Poznan when I was a little girl, and went to a convent there. It was one of the schools Bismarck suddenly ordered to close or to move out of Germany— part of his campaign to stamp out everything Polish. Nuns and girls went into exile together in Prague. My six daughters all went to that same convent—six daughters," she added very proudly, "and all of them married."

It was nearly half past eight when supper was announced and you may guess how rejoiced I felt when Madame said, "You are to have dinner, you must be hungry after the long drive." For *collatya* is rather like Sunday-night suppers in America, generally one hot dish, with tea, and all sorts of little dishes—pickles, cheese, honey, jam, cakes. It's ample nourishment when you've had a big meal at two and tea at five; but I'd had nothing for nearly twelve hours, and did full justice to what they were having plus soup, roast veal, and ice-cream (made with cream, duplicated only once in my travels in Poland).

Shall I try to describe the house as I saw it the next morning by daylight? A long, low, central part with a balcony looking down on the porte-cochère, whose pillars were two floors high. It was plastered in white on the outside, relieved by many vines, and the trees, now taller than the house, made an unusual background. The steep roof (Polish roofs are very steep because of the snow) had its long straight line broken by a drop—very typical of Polish architecture of that period, but now rarely seen.

On either side of the entrance hall were the living-rooms—four or five in all. In one the walls were done in crimson velvet. (What had happened that some of the panels had great slashes?) The dining-room was about forty by thirty feet—I paced it off when no one was around. There was only one stove; in winter, Madame said, they stoke it constantly—yes, with wood; how could they use coal? Its paneled walls held fifteen paintings, some large ones—an Italian Madonna, a portrait of Savonarola, a Polish girl visiting her father in prison and finding him blinded by the Russians, a scene in Venice, and others. There was a small canvas by Matejko; Pan de K. said he'd tell me the story, but we never got back to it, so I missed one lesson in Polish history and don't know why the young prince and his mother were in prison, who this visitor was, why the monk by the door motioned to them to say nothing.

At right angles to the house, but entirely separated, were two annexes—like three sides of a square with open corners, the center a lovely stretch of lawn. They were only one story, of unpainted wood, weathered a silvery gray, with flowers in front and vines climbing up to the roof. One side was for guests—I don't know how many rooms there were—Theresa and her husband, just back from a month in Paris, her little daughter and the nurse, the sons-in-law, other grandchildren and their nurses, all had rooms there, and some were not being used.

The opposite side was quarters for the servants and the kitchen. (I used to wonder in Poland how food came to the table so hot—sometimes it didn't! But often Poles would wait till hot food cooled, especially soup and tea. How could I drink my tea so hot? they asked over and over.) Madame was now using a smaller kitchen, but took me in to see the old one. (Why was there a sign in German, "No admittance except on business"? I was to learn later on.) I exclaimed over the white tile stove on which the meals used to be cooked. How large was it? She measured it carefully with her head on one side. Five meters by eight. Hotel size, I commented to myself. And that wasn't all—a separate oven for baking bread; a separate reservoir for heating water; a separate stove, a little one, when the cook wanted only one or two pans; when I say separate, I mean, each one had its own fire. Next door were two rooms for the cook and her family, and huge storerooms for supplies. The place was like an estate in the South before the Civil War, sufficient unto itself for many things—food, clothing (in large part), schooling, amusements, religion.

To my eyes the farm buildings were far from the house and more scattered than with us. They were all of brick— the son told me the brick was made right on the estate— and each bore a date: the newest was 1907. Their doorways were arched—a Polish carpenter couldn't make them absolutely plain, such a sense of beauty is part of every one of them. One building was evidently not being used— the spirits factory, Pan de K. explained. Before the war they made spirits (methylated alcohol) from a certain kind of potato which they raised in great quantity; in fact, this was one of the largest income-producing things on the estate. Now the making of spirits is a government monopoly and the amount is strictly limited.

Tuesday, Wednesday, Thursday I stayed at Szemetowszczyzna, and then back on the night train to Wilno. So full the days were that I found it hard to get in a little rest, and later I had to take a morning off and stay in the hotel to catch up in my note-book. We walked about the grounds nearest the house—through the gardens and a stretch of forest land—and watched an American reaper cutting the last field of wheat. We drove in a hayrack to a lake where we ate apples and cookies on the sand while Andrzej showed me in the distance the frontier and Lithuania beyond (that made me feel very far east and very far north!) and told the tale of how the Germans mined the lake, and when the Russians started to cross it on the ice, set off the mine and a whole regiment was drowned.

We spent a morning gathering mushrooms and had them for supper, in one of the delicious Polish concoctions. Be sure you order mushrooms often in Poland! And once we walked to the De K. Switzerland, a high bluff above the river; a walk of several miles, but we were never off the estate save when we passed a village whose peasants owned their land, given them by Theresa's grandfather at the time the czar freed them. That was my chance to ask her all the questions I'd been saving up, for I sensed that the real adventure at Szemetowszczyzna was not my getting there, nor the things we did, but seeing the estate itself and learning its story. To-day railroads, motors, the telephone and radio have changed many of the country homes in Poland till they're no more isolated than those on Long Island; but this house was typical of many a generation or two ago—the kind you read about.

"How many acres is it? Have we really never been off

your land in all these walks and drives?" I asked incredulously.

"The picnic at the lake was off our estate, a kilometer or so. In 1914 we had something over eighteen thousand acres, but since the war my father's sold some, three of my sisters have had their portions given them in land, and now it's not nearly so large—seven or eight thousand. But in medieval days, when it first appears in the records, they didn't count by hectares but by villages, and Szemetowszczyzna had fifty-two.

"You saw the long avenue of trees, the night you came? My great-grandfather planted them, over a mile, two rows deep. The ponds in front of the house are artificial, dug years ago by the serfs, and always kept stocked with fish. They're very deep in the center. My brothers caught a hundred and sixty pounds one day, and sold them all to a Jew pedler."

"What could even a Jew do with fresh fish, this far from a market?"

"Carp are shipped in tanks, all over the country; they're fresh when you buy them in the city. They're a great delicacy in Poland and always bring a high price."

The house itself, she told me, is more than three hundred years old, and is under the protection of the National Commission. If they wanted to, they couldn't alter it or sell it, without permission. How many rooms? Not counting the guest house or the servants' quarters, fifteen; they never used the up-stairs rooms, but the Germans did. I knew they'd lived in the house during the war?

"One of my sisters," Theresa went on, "married an officer in the Polish army. She met him while we were in Poznan, at the end of the war. He'd lived in that section and had, of course, served in the German army. When they came here for a first visit, as they entered the house he exclaimed, 'Why, I've been here before! I remember this room. I remember that Canteen.' And in the military cemetery—you passed two of them on the drive to the lake, near the old trenches and the holes where the dugouts were—he found names of men he knew. Strange, wasn't it?"

I was ready to hang my head in shame for thinking that the horses didn't match, for noticing the faded velvet of the carriage, the mirror missing. Oh, I'd come close to the war more than once—at the monument of the three American aviators; at the tomb of the Unknown Soldier in Warsaw, where I stood looking on one day when two women in mourning knelt down and tearfully laid their flowers by the words that told of this nameless Pole; at the rows and rows of short graves where lie buried the heroic children of Lwów who saved the town from the Ukrainians by holding out for more than three weeks until help could come. But never did the war come home to me so grippingly as at this far-away country house.

For the Germans had come into this district, come in October of 1915 and stayed till just before the Armistice. The house became for three years headquarters; the dining-room was an officers' club; the brick carriage house and smithy were used as a Canteen. (I'd noticed

Soldatenheim in big black letters.) Trains ran direct from Germany, marked *Berlin to Szemet*; the Prussians couldn't pronounce it either! Madame and her six daughters, the two younger boys, and the three governesses were promptly sent away, in a long procession of farm carts. The father and the eldest son stayed on for a few months, living in two rooms at the end of the house.

They'd seen the war coming closer and closer as the Russians retreated and the Germans advanced their lines. Looking ahead, they made up their minds that the Prussians would occupy Wilno and places beyond it. For weeks their living-rooms were in disorder as they packed things away, took down the most valuable of the paintings, supervised the peasants who hid some articles in their cottages and sheds, building in false partitions to store boxes behind, burying chests in their gardens.

In 1915 Madame had had everything ready for the winter. She took me down to see the vegetable rooms in the cellar, because they had vaulted ceilings; I was interested not only in architecture, but in seeing a peasant shoveling in a wagon-load of sand, to pack beets and carrots in. All supplies, especially food and wood, were on a hotel scale. Well, the Germans helped themselves to everything. Often officers would say to Pan de K. as they poured out his wine and ate his potatoes and carrots and took a second serving of Madame's preserves, "*Ach*, we didn't live so well in Berlin!"

Many of the German officers, he said, were pleasant acquaintances. One general he mentioned by name and described as "a very fine man." For what they took they gave him slips, I. O. U.'s from the German army; if they'd won the war, they'd have paid in full.

"In my desk there's a pile of those slips, nearly six inches high. If the Dawes Plan works out and reparations are actually made, if Poland gets some, and if our government gives it to individuals with such claims as ours, why, some day there may be money enough to put the estate into good order again. Payment for the timber alone would do it, for they cut on four thousand acres; what they took, they themselves told me, was worth more than three million gold marks."

He spoke not bitterly, but hopelessly, just stating plain facts. I reminded myself that it was now twelve years since the Armistice. If—if——

He showed me the kodak pictures of the rooms as they looked on the day of his return. Windows broken, a few pieces of furniture upside down, everything in disorder. And photographs of these same rooms as they had been before—a dramatic comparison.

"So much old silver!" I exclaimed.

"Yes. The glass case in the dining-room was filled with silver. Some of it was made for my great-grandmother; see, here's her coat of arms on this piece."

"What about this bowl? Isn't it porcelain and silver?" I pointed to it in the picture. "It's strikingly handsome—a real museum piece."

"Yes, a museum piece. I came into the room one day and found a German using it for—what do you think? to feed his dog from. We never knew whether they broke it or took it with them.''

''And the paintings?'' I glanced at the copy of a Veronese, a large canvas with several ruthless gashes.

''We thought the war was over and brought the paintings back. The Bolshevists did this. Only one's been mended—the small portrait of my uncle; you see, there by the eyes. We must have an expert come from Warsaw and do the large canvases here. But there were so many other things more important than paintings, before we could live here at all.''

From one person and another I pieced together bits of what had happened. It wasn't only timber and food that the Germans took. Their automobile, all the farm machinery—three tractors and five reapers and other things in proportion; the copper pans and kettles from the kitchen (Madame pointed sadly to three long shelves with empty hooks where they used to hang); and more than two hundred horses and oxen and cattle. It took courage to make a fresh start—Polish courage!

Pan de K. and Konstanty, the eldest son, bought horses and cattle, put things in order, and began life again. Then came the Bolshevist invasion, with Szemetowszczyzna right in their line of march. They led off all the stock and destroyed what they couldn't take with them, leaving a desolation behind them like Sherman on his march to the sea. They ruined the water system—the house used to have running water everywhere; after I saw a peasant girl bringing two pails of water with a wooden yoke, I didn't use an extra drop. They broke up the electric light plant the Germans had built, threw stones at the church windows, thrust their bayonets through the paintings in the dining-room, smashed all the mirrors.

The De K.s scoured the country, bought horses and started a second time. The Lithuanian troops came for a brief three or four weeks, long enough to undo all that had been accomplished. Again they purchased horses and put their men to work in the fields. And once more the Bolshevists marched across the estate, taking, destroying. What to do then? Not that their funds were gone, but literally there were no more horses, no more cattle, in all that section of Poland.

"That's why we can never be grateful enough," went on Pan de K. "If it hadn't been for the Anglo-Americans —you know? Certainly, I haven't made a mistake in the name. I'll never forget—the Anglo-American Committee. Wait, I'll show you," for my face must have looked perplexed. He brought me an envelope marked "The Anglo-American Committee of the Society of Friends."

"Oh, yes, yes, indeed, the Quakers! Of course I know something of their war relief work." Then I had to explain, as best I could in German, who the Quakers were and how they got the two names, and why they came to America; and heard in return a fascinating story, perhaps not reported in detail in their records, of what they'd done in that far-away corner of Poland. Four of them made this house their headquarters, giving out supplies and loaning horses for a month's work in the fields.

[177]

"They gave us six horses, on condition that we plow and plant for some widows near us. It was a godsend, I don't know how we'd ever have made another start without those Anglo-Americans."

(I hope they know how grateful this family is, a decade after their visit.)

They spoke of Konstanty frequently, the father and mother always with unsteady voices, with their eyes full of tears. They showed me many pictures of him—snapshots with his sisters, on his pony, playing on the lawn, in the motor, in uniform; a handsome boy indeed. Griefstricken as they were, it seemed a relief to talk to some one. He was very young, but served all through the war; he was so glad to volunteer. Almost at the end of the struggle with the Bolshevists, he was shot—somewhere in the forest, a few kilometers away from their house. They knew only that he had fallen.

"When spring came," a sister told me the next part of the story, "the peasants buried both Poles and Russians as soon as the frost was out of the ground—buried them just where they lay, marking the places with wooden crosses. For weeks, for months after we returned, my sisters and I searched for Konstanty's body, looking at countless ones, but never finding his. It was too hard on my mother, hoping, hoping, always disappointed. People would send us word that more bodies were found, and two of us would go.

"In February, nearly two years after his death, an officer saw a pack of wolves, starved by the winter, tear-ing at a shallow opening in the ground. He summoned help, drove the wolves away, dug down, and found the body of a Polish officer. He turned back the coat. There was an identification even my mother could not question— K. de K. embroidered on the shirt. She's done it herself, on all Konstanty's shirts. So the body was brought back to Szemetowszczyzna and reburied in the crypt of the church.

"We've set aside one part of the gardens and called it 'Konstanty's garden.' There isn't very much money now, but every year my mother spends a little on it. She's built a low brick wall around it and planted his favorite trees and flowers. She plans to make it the beauty spot of the whole estate. I'll take you to see it."

One morning we went over to the church, about ten minutes' walk, and suddenly I was carried back through centuries of time. I've seen churches and chapels in Italy, in France or England, given by one family or even by one individual, in medieval days. Here was a twentieth-century church, built by one man.

"A chapel just for your family?"

"Why, no, for every one," Pan de K. replied in surprise.

"For the estate people, then?" I persisted.

"Why, no, it's a very big parish. Our priest (never my priest, I noticed) has over three thousand people to care for. He lives in that brick house—almost in a park, isn't it? You see, there was no church nearer than fifteen kilometers; we could drive, but in winter the roads are bad and it's very cold; and the peasants had to go on foot. Why not have a church here where it was needed?

"That was a terrible time to live through," he went on as we passed the priest's home with its attractive garden and the organist's house, both of which he had built. 'Under the rule of Russia we had to have a permission for everything. I knew they'd never give a permission for a Polish church—you know, after the Partitions, every Roman Catholic church was a center of Polish influence— so I just went ahead and built it. And had to pay much money at St. Petersburg."

"What a hard time you had! Your family had the money—why didn't you go to America?"

"What?" he stared at me in amazement. "Why, we never once thought of going to America! At that time no Pole could buy land here; if a man had to sell, he must sell to a Russian. You thought that was true only in German Poland? Oh, Bismarck wasn't the only one who tried to crush out all memory of Poland by forcing us to give up what we held dearest—Polish soil. No, no, we had to stay on to keep the land for our children and grandchildren."

That passionate attachment to the soil! Perhaps we'll have it in America too, when we've lived more than three centuries in one house and filled it with traditions and memories. And in Poland this love for the land is closely bound up with a burning patriotism.

We went up a long flight of stone steps, very wide, to the church, cream-plastered outside and in. It has a separate bell tower, open at the sides, where they had put three bronze bells, one a gift from Pan de K.'s mother. The Germans took all three, to be melted up and made into cannon. A Polish committee found two of them in Leipzig, identified them from the inscriptions in Polish and the names of the givers, and sent them back.

"My mother's came shortly before she died. She was so happy to hear her bell again. Hark, that's it that's ringing now."

"How many people come to church here?" I asked.

"Not many on week-days, just now everybody's so busy in the fields. Over a thousand every Sunday. It's far too small. I'm sorry now we didn't build it bigger."

"I call the church," Madame turned to me with her gentle smile, "my husband's tenth child. He loves everything in it—the windows with the Polish saints—yes, they were made by a firm in Warsaw—and the chancel frescoes, by an artist we had come from Munich. The hanging bronze lamp is a copy of one in Rome, and the pulpit——"

"I know," I interrupted eagerly, "it's like the one in St. Casimir's chapel in the Wilno cathedral. See, here's the Polish eagle, and the chalice, a symbol of Christianity. The Russians cut off the eagle's head; they showed me where it was put on again."

"Why," Pan de K. cried, "you remember what you've seen, don't you?"

I didn't tell them that the details of that chapel had been impressed on my mind by a Wilno professor who'd explained at great length that the old carved pulpit was one proof that it was the Poles who brought Christianity into Lithuania, for here the two symbols were united.

We went down into the crypt where he pointed out the graves of his parents, a sister and brother, and then Konstanty's. They've put a marble tablet on the wall with his name and part of a verse from John's Gospel:

"The best have I chosen unto myself."

Standing by it was the cross they'd brought from that roadside grave—a plain, wooden cross, unpainted, with letters of red:

"Here lies an unknown Polish officer,
regiment unknown,
the year 1920."

"It was the greatest comfort, the greatest comfort," the mother said over and over, "to have found the body of my son."

CHAPTER VIII

OLD AND NEW

AMERICA is a land where everything is new. We call Mount Vernon old. The most ancient places we seek out in New England date from the seventeenth century. And one result of this is that the really old things in Europe appeal to us because of their age; for we do need to be reminded occasionally that history didn't begin in 1776, nor yet in 1492.

Is this true in Poland? I was afraid that there'd be nothing to see, after centuries of warfare and destruction; that I'd feel like the school-girl who complained to her chaperon in Paris, "I'm tired of looking at just sites, I want to see a few sights!" Well, Poland offers both. Side by side with interesting, fascinating old things are new ones, very new indeed, surprising in a country that so recently came back to the map, a prophecy of the Poland that is to be. It's this combination of new and old that makes a trip over the country doubly interesting.

In Poznan a university student took me to the Town Hall and talked enthusiastically of its beauty.

"It's the finest example of Renaissance architecture north of the Alps—this is, not counting churches or chapels. Poznan knows it has a rare treasure. See,

[183]

they've put up a tablet to mark the house where the architect lived. Now, come around to this side, I want to show you something."

High up he pointed out three heads that made the ending of one of the pinnacles.

"You see them? Lech and Czech and Rus. You know the story of the three brothers who came up from the southeast of Europe—what's now Jugoslavia—when the people got too crowded there, to make new homes in the north? Czech stopped off first. Rus went farthest. Lech started the first town in Poland—Gniezno. Years later the three brothers met here at Poznan and to their surprise recognized one another. The word tells it, for Poznan means 'the place of recognition.' When was this? Sixth century perhaps, or the fifth."

Scattered over Poland, some in the province of Silesia, some in the east, some in the mountains on the southern border, are old wooden churches, the like of which I've seen nowhere else. I've seen older ones, to be sure, but made of stone. These date from the twelve hundreds, or the fourteen hundreds; the newest one I found, in the oil-fields, was built in the fifteen-sixties, every bit of it made of wood, with wooden pegs instead of nails. The interiors are frescoed, nearly every inch of surface—walls, ceiling, rafters, pillars—the colors faded and softened. There are religious pictures—favorite saints—George and the dragon are popular all through Poland; there are designs of leaves and flowers, sometimes geometrical patterns; the space never over crowded. I thought the outside of the wooden churches still more interesting. They have very steep roofs, on account of the snow; and a sort of lean-to along the sides, likewise steep-roofed, to keep the snow away from the church wall. Most of them are unpainted, weathered a lovely gray or brown.

"You must go at five this afternoon to the Franciscan church," said my Krakow landlady. "Go early and sit in the choir so that you can see. The Society of the Happy Death will march in procession around the church and through the cloisters, after their special service."

It was, she explained, a society formed in medieval times—she wasn't sure of the date, probably in the fifteenth century, if not earlier—whose members prayed for a happy death. That didn't necessarily mean they wanted to die in their beds and not on the field of battle; they wished just what the name said—happy deaths. And all these years, once a week through Lent they have this service.

There were not a great many members of the Happy Death present the Friday I saw them—about twenty-five. They wore black robes, some with skulls and bones painted on them in white—gruesome reminders of the ever presence of death. They carried lighted candles or torches. Some had skulls and bones set on poles. Some had old embroidered banners. Four of them bore a platform with a figure of Christ seated, elbow on knee and chin in hand, dressed in red silk—an ancient, ancient figure, they told me; there are only two or three like it in Europe. No one knows why, but they're always dressed in red.

"Hark, the Heynal!" cried the American who had motored me to Krakow. "Oh, I'm glad to be with you and watch your face the first time you hear it. Look up, high up in the left tower of St. Mary's church; you see the trumpeter opening the little window? Listen!"

Above the clang of a street-car and the sounds of the market-place I could hear the melody of that medieval hymn in honor of the Virgin.

"North, east, south and west, four times he plays it, every hour, day and night. You notice, each time he stops short, and always at the same place in the music—about three-fourths of the way through. 'The broken note,' the Poles call it. I suppose you know the story, from Eric Kelly's *Trumpeter of Krakow*? Oh, you'd like to hear it over again, right here in the very place?

"Well, in the year 1241 the Tartars came to Krakow and the whole population fled for refuge to the Wawel— that's a hill by the Vistula, which the kings had fortified; its walls enclosed space enough for a church and a royal castle and prison, and for all the townspeople too. Every one fled then save the trumpeter of St. Mary's; he stayed at his post, for he'd taken an oath—and to-day the trumpeters all swear the same oath—to blow the Heynal in honor of Our Lady, every hour, day and night, no matter what the cost.

"Look up at Jadwiga's tower room in the palace.
We call it the Hen's Foot. Do you understand?
The lady of the cock."

Sometimes churches were fortresses in ancient
Poland

Photo by *Swiatowice*

A circular fortress, Krakow, the style borrowed from the Arabs after the crusades

"He lifted his silver trumpet and the first notes sounded: do—mi—sol—do. Some of the Tartars feasting in the market-place looked up. One of them fitted an arrow to his bow, took aim, *whiz!* sped that sharp arrow and struck the man in the throat. The music stopped abruptly. The man fell back dead. And ever since the trumpeters stop on that particular note, in memory of that earlier trumpeter who was faithful to his oath. That's a typical Krakow story—you'll hear quantities of them while you're here; but none, I think, is so Krakowian as this tale of the broken note."

There is not to-day a Polish city with walls and towers and gates intact. Torun has kept a part of its old defenses, and Krakow has its main gateway with three of the guild towers. Each guild built and manned and defended a tower, a custom that was followed in many towns. You get the true medieval feel when you gaze at the lace-makers' tower and the joiners'. Near them is the Florian gate, once the chief entrance to the city, opening on to the road that led to Warsaw. It bears on one side a sculptured eagle, and on the other a relief of St. Florian, putting out the fire with his pot of milk. Once a year the firemen of Krakow used to hold a service out-of-doors, in front of this gate, named for their patron saint.

When the crusaders returned from the Holy Land they introduced into Europe a circular fort, a style borrowed from the Arabs. At one time they were fairly common; to-day there are only three in existence—only two, if you exclude one in Germany which has been thoroughly modernized. There's one at Carcassonne and one at Krakow. This Polish one, called the Rondel or the Barbican, is in perfect condition, unchanged by the passing of centuries, save that it now stands quite by itself, no longer joined on to the city walls by the Florian gate. I went inside, up the narrow stairways, along the passages where the defenders stood. Here were loopholes for cannon; the smaller ones in the upper part were for pouring down hot pitch or boiling water on the besiegers. There stood the men at arms, ready to fire through the slits of openings. Sentinels kept watch from the seven little turrets.

Another thing that is rare now in Europe is the fortified church. One in Krakow—St. Andrew's—still has a stretch of wall, perhaps fifteen feet high, with slits for shooting through. In one of the Tartar attacks—the time the trumpeter was killed—St. Andrew's was the only building outside the Wawel that was not captured, despoiled, burned.

At Czestochowa I saw not a fortified church, but a fortified monastery, with walls completely surrounding the group of buildings—church, chapels, library, dormitory. Even though the Russians took down the walls to half their former height, they're still high, with four gates. An easy site to defend, as the Swedes found when they besieged it with ten thousand men and gave up the task after five weeks.

Gniezno gave me the feeling of digging down to the

very roots of Polish history. I remembered asking the prince in the Consulate for the date, an approximate date for Lech and the white eagle.

"I can't tell you," he said apologetically. "Before the nine-sixties our history is legendary."

"And what happened then?"

"A Polish king married a princess from Bohemia and she brought Christianity into the land. That date's the first definite one that ties Poland up to events in the rest of Europe."

At Gniezno I saw the grave of this Bohemian princess, Dabrowka, in the place of honor in front of the high altar; and a fragment of her chapel, built into the wall of a later church. Near by is a statue of Boleslas the Brave, put up on the nine hundredth anniversary of his death. Think what a long time we have to go to reach the nine hundredth anniversary of anything, even of Columbus! That makes you realize how old Poland is.

Thanks to wars and fires, there are many ruins. In five scattered cities I saw ruins of castles built by Casimir the Great; he ought to be called Casimir the Builder, I thought, for he had a long reign with comparatively little fighting, and he built constantly—palaces, churches, hospitals, a university. He found Poland with cities of wood, and left it with cities of brick. In and near Wilno I went to ruined castles dating back to the days before the union of Poland and Lithuania (and that was in the latter half of the fourteenth century).

One of the most interesting ruins was the castle of Tenczynek (Ten-cheé-nek is enough like the Polish pronunciation so that I could ask my way), an hour from Krakow. During the Swedish wars it was burned. I had to imagine the moat which the Russians ordered filled in, and the high walls which they ordered taken down; but even so, the place was full of atmosphere. I saw where the seven gates were, which the enemy must pass before they arrived at the center of things—and at Tenczynek they never did penetrate that far. I saw part of the Gothic chapel—an arch here, a window there; and the great courtyard where tournaments were held. I climbed ladders to a station in the watch-tower, where I could see for miles over the countryside. I explored the two round towers that are still called "the towers of Grunwald," because a lord of Tenczynek built them with the labor of German prisoners who were assigned to him after the great victory won by the Poles at Grunwald—and that was 1410!

"Pray, don't ask me when this happened," begged one of my Polish friends as we started down the steps to the dragon's cave at the Wawel, "for nobody knows. Duke Krakus is a legend and nothing more. Go slowly, and I'll tell you the story when we get to the bottom."

It was a long way down—a hundred and thirty-five steps, down and down in a spiral staircase, the first part lighted by tiny windows in the wall of the bastion, then by electric lights. At last we found ourselves in a limestone cavern, one chamber opening into another through low-ceilinged passages.

"This," began my Pole, "was the dragon's lair. A fierce and bloodthirsty dragon he was, and an enormous appetite he must have had, for he destroyed growing crops in the fields, took a sheep or a pig occasionally, and then demanded human beings. The poor folk of this neighborhood were terrified, afraid to venture out of their houses, afraid to stay at home. Word of this reached Krakus who came thither, followed the dragon to this lair, fought with him and at last won the victory. Here, near the site of his great exploit, he built a town and the people named it Krakow in his honor.

"What? You don't really believe my tale, even after I've brought you all the way down into the very cave of the beast? Then climb all those steps and I'll show you—and that (with a snap of his fingers)—that for your skepticism!"

And show me he did. On the wall by the cathedral entrance hung several enormous bones which once belonged to Krakus' dragon. Probably, he conceded when I insisted on knowing what they really were, probably the bones of some extinct animals, found in excavating. But that very fact, added to the cave, made me feel once more how ancient Poland is; even the electric lights didn't make it modern.

"A message for you," reported my landlady one day in December. "Miss K. is coming to take you somewhere to-morrow, at twenty minutes of six, and you must be very warmly dressed."

A cloth dress, my heavy coat, which I'd had interlined with a Polish wadding that gave me a stuffed look but a toasty feeling; my sweater too, urged Miss K. We walked up the street to the church of the Dominicans (did I say this was in Krakow?) and waited in the great empty nave. What had we come for? As if in answer to my wondering, she began a story:

"A great many years ago there was a young Pole who went to Rome. His name was Jacek (Ya-sek), and he was young, rich, pleasure-loving. In Rome he went to hear Dominic preach—this was before he was St. Dominic; he was very popular and great crowds flocked to hear him, and as he preached he was lifted up in the air, so holy was he. And Jacek marveled. There was a commotion in the audience; men appeared carrying a body; a young noble had been thrown from his horse and killed. They begged Dominic to come into the chapel and say a prayer for his soul. Jacek followed and saw the monk stretch out his hand above the young Roman, who came to life. This and other miracles he saw, he heard the monk's sermons, till at last he went to him and pleaded, 'Will you come into my country—to Poland? We need your teaching and your preaching. Will you come? Krakow will welcome you.'

" 'I can not now.'

" 'Then you will send some one? We must have the Dominicans in Poland.'

" 'I have no one to send, for it must be some one who speaks the language.'

" 'Will you,' begged Jacek, 'let me stay with you and learn the rules and precepts of your order? Then I will go back to my own country and introduce the Dominicans there.'

"Dominic agreed and for a year Jacek sat at his feet for instruction, and then returned to Krakow—that was about 1220 or 1221. The bishop gave the Dominicans this church. Jacek was himself made a saint later, and the monks enlarged his cell and made it a chapel. Look, look."

We were standing under one of the Gothic arches. The nave was shadowy and dim, with one electric light burning. I saw the flickering gleam of candles. I heard far off the sound of chanting. Down the steps from Jacek's cell came the Dominicans, two by two, in their black and white robes, the first two carrying tall candles. There were more than forty, those at the end novices, she said. And they were singing a medieval hymn (in Latin) in honor of the Virgin—a twilight custom that Jacek started, that has gone on without interruption all these years— seven hundred and more. Before the war, she told me, each monk carried a candle, but it's too expensive now.

This spirit of the past I felt most strongly in Krakow when I climbed the hill that is called Wawel. The palace of the kings is interesting for its architecture, for its famous inhabitants, for the tragedy of its spoliation by the Austrians who used it for barracks and built a hideous military hospital and still more barracks in its gardens, and for the restoration that is now going on. A gigantic task that required amazing courage—Polish courage! Marble floors and stairs were gone, here no windows, there water had seeped through the roof and ruined ancient frescoes. More than a hundred rooms to be furnished. If the work is progressing slowly because of lack of funds, it's being splendidly done.

"Here?" I asked in surprise when Wanda guided me to one side of the courtyard, opposite the entrance we usually used, "why, I thought this part was the kitchens."

"So it was, but during the restoration they discovered something here. Down the stairs, please, then left."

It was a little circular church, built in the ninth century, and named for two saints—Felix and Audactus. All around it and above it were the brick walls of the service wing of the palace. Evidently it was completely forgotten. There are many theories put forward by the experts—that it was a chapel, a baptistery, a room for private devotion, a place for storing wine in the days of the Sigismunds.

"Choose what story you like best," offered Wanda, "it's not only the oldest church in all Poland, but the oldest building."

As it stands to-day, the cathedral on the Wawel is nearly all fourteenth-century work, but it's the fifth on this site—the fifth church of which there are definite records. Just walking along the outside was a fascinating thing to do, particularly when I went with a Polish architect.

"See," he would say, "this part of the nave is merely a stretch of the old wall that surrounded the hill. You'll notice it on the inside, where the masonry is different. This square tower is Romanesque, with round windows; the architect apparently thought it well built and kept this much of an earlier church; yes, and afterward they changed one of the windows to Gothic! The nave is regulation Gothic, but look at that gable—doesn't it suggest the Vistula Gothic you saw in the north—at Torun, for example—built of red brick, with long, up-and-down lines, with very tall and very narrow windows? And then last of all, the Sigismunds—I and II and III—added these Renaissance chapels. One of them, according to art critics and experts, is the finest example of Renaissance work outside of Italy. I think it's the gem of the whole cathedral."

Five churches on that site, one after the other; and the last one in early Gothic style, utilizing a Romanesque tower. Why, in England I'd looked at early Gothic and thought it ancient!

And churches aren't the only old things in Krakow. Thanks to a zealous friend, I received a card for the opening of the Jagellonian University. I'd been to the library courtyard, truly one of the treasures of the city, with crystal vaulting and Gothic arches which were built after the great fire of 1492. I knew the university was named for the first of the Jagellonian dynasty, that Queen Jadwiga sold her jewels to help poor students and asked in her will that her husband endow it—which he did, giving it lands and houses. But they didn't found it. That honor belongs to Casimir the Great, and the year was—1364! Why, next to Prague it's the oldest university in central Europe. It has a right to be called medieval, hasn't it? And the opening ceremony was as medieval as the date.

Lectures began about the first of October—no special date; the young and enthusiastic professors start right away; the formal opening was postponed—for a holiday, for a state funeral (Malchewski, the painter), till I began to wonder if it would open at all. The great hall was crowded—officials of the city, invited guests, professors' wives and daughters, and students, students, students. Headed by the university servants, dressed in green robes and velvet tams, carrying maces with the emblems of the different faculties, the procession of professors and deans and rectors entered.

"The deans are the ones with the long gold chains," volunteered my English-speaking neighbor. "The velvet on the togas varies for each faculty—what you call a school in an American university. Red's for medicine, and green for agriculture; violet for the divinity school—in the beginning the one and only school; black for law, and blue for philosophy—that includes history and sciences. The rector? It's hard to compare the system here with yours in America. The rector is elected by electors chosen by the different faculties, and serves for one year. And that year he does the administrative work and continues his lectures besides. The wives dread the extra work and the strain, yet are glad for their husbands to have the honor; and ever after they're called Pani Rektorowa—you sometimes meet three or four Rektorowas at one tea.''

The university choir sang, unaccompanied, a Latin hymn. The pro-rector (last year's official) read his report. From bits that my neighbor translated, I gleaned tidings of the new things going on in this medieval institution—more than a fourth of the students are now women; a normal course in physical training is offered; an aviation club and an automobile-repair club have been formed by students; a mention of the Rockefeller Foundation school for training nurses, now part of the medical faculty.

''Look—the rector!'' whispered my neighbor.

The report was finished and the speaker turned directly to his successor who rose. He wore a red robe with cape of ermine, red gloves, a square red cap.

''You have been chosen by your colleagues,'' I give the gist of the Latin speech, ''yours is not an easy task.'' A reference to his father who was persecuted by the Russians in Warsaw. Then he took up from the square of brocade on the table the scepter, and handed it to the new rector. ''I give you this as the symbol of your power. And this,'' a heavy gold chain with a pendant, ''the symbol of your dignity. And the ring, the symbol of your loyalty to the university.''

The whole ceremony was identical with the one followed in medieval times, perhaps the very one used in 1364. And the rector made a brief reply, seated himself, took off his red cap, and read his first lecture—on evolution, from Mendel's views down to Morgan and the results of the latest research.

I could go on and on and on, telling of the old things in Poland, but I must hurry along to the new ones. The changes that have been brought about, the progress achieved in one short decade, are astounding. Take the railroads, for instance, they're everywhere a yardstick for measuring business prosperity. In the old days—before 1914, I mean—Poznan had excellent service to Berlin, Krakow and Lwów to Vienna, Warsaw some sort of service to Moscow and St. Petersburg; between Polish towns there was nothing. Indeed, for military reasons, there was literally a break at the frontier, a distance of a kilometer or so where passengers and freight crossed as best they could from one station to the other; the connecting link czar and emperor both forbade. Building lines between their important cities was a big task, and it's not yet finished.

"You'll have to go back to Warsaw and start again," I was told more than once. "You can't go from Lwów to Wilno. You'd spend far more time waiting for local trains."

Nor was this all of the railroad's problem. We heard so much of devastation and destruction in France and Belgium, comparatively little of the war's results in Poland. Two-thirds of the country was laid waste, now by one side, now by the other; neither Russia nor Germany spared the land. Just to get trains running again meant the rebuilding of more than two thousand bridges, of hundreds of stations. Not that I think service in Poland is ideal; the wonder is that it's as good as it is. Compartments are clean, officials are courteous, trains are very seldom late, and accidents are exceedingly rare.

At first the Poles bought locomotives from the Baldwin Company. Now they're building their own—engines and cars of all kinds. The compartments seat three, six or eight persons generally. They are very comfortable and attractive—red upholstery if I went first-class, brown and tan if I went second. That was the only difference I could see, except that the first-class was not so crowded.

"I hope you'll be comfortable all night," worried a man who had gone with me to the station when I couldn't get a sleeper. "You'll have the whole compartment to yourself. Lie down and get a good sleep."

Alas for his optimism! Just before the train started in came three travelers. Two places to lie down. I pictured myself napping, leaning back in my corner, arriving worn-out and cross.

"With your permission, madam," one man bowed to me and spoke in halting English, "we will make a sleeping-car."

Presto, change! Up went the back of the seats to make upper berths. The electric light was shaded. All four of us had a place to lie down, full length. Overcoats and wraps did duty for blankets. They eyed my steamer rug as if they thought me a wealthy lady.

"Madam, shall we leave the window open—two inches? The railroad knows we can't afford sleepers, but this is a good substitute. Good night, madam."

Considering that Poland is a country without stone, the roads for motoring are excellent—in spots. They are not good near Warsaw and Krakow. Very good near Lwów and Torun, all through the west. With more automobiles good roads will follow, as they have with us.

The motor-bus Poland has adopted with enthusiasm. It runs to what used to be isolated villages. It runs where no trains go at all. In one city of a hundred thousand I counted thirty-two different lines, and probably that wasn't all of them, as it was between hours. Not that I recommend the motor-bus for tourists. It's always crowded, men are smoking, in the winter there's not a crack open for fresh air. But for the peasants it represents progress in capital letters.

Gdynia, the new port on the Baltic, is a modern miracle. Men described it for me as they knew it in 1920, even as late as 1924—a long stretch of beach with a handful of fishermen's shacks and one crazy little wharf, and sandy or marshy country running back to the hills. I rubbed my eyes and saw a town of thirty thousand people—a boom town, we should say, out West, yet with this difference— Gdynia is planned as a whole, with streets laid out for many years to come; and no one may build without due reference to this city plan.

There are several hotels (mine was excellent), a yacht club, boulevards with long lines of trees, a remarkably attractive railroad station with buff plastered walls and red tile roof, three schools, and apartment-houses five and six stories high. The place was humming with activity—more building going on than I saw elsewhere in Poland. The port is not yet finished; seeing it in process of construction was fascinating—great caissons being lowered into the water, with the dredger just ahead; docks and warehouses being built; additions going up to factories; giant cranes outlined against the sky; the electric car dump unloading coal directly into the hold of a steamer; ships of eight countries waiting to coal. It's a town of the future tense—every one says "will be," not "is." In the whole world it has no duplicate—a port planned where there was no city, no commerce of any kind. A splendid example of the vitality and the energy of the new Poland, rejoicing that she has now a strip of seacoast.

It's greatly to the credit of the Poles that with everything to get started, they put so much emphasis on education. I saw new schoolhouses in every part of the country, particularly numerous in Russian Poland where there were almost no schools. There was a great demand for teachers and normal schools were started. This year, for the first time, the principal of one normal school told me, the graduates number no more than the positions waiting for them; the supply has caught up with the demand in a decade.

The University of Wilno has been reopened (the Russians closed it in 1831 as punishment for the insurrection) and the one in Warsaw too. Poznan's university and Lwów's are new, and still another is planned for. All of them have an amazing number of students, far more than can be comfortably taken care of in the present lecture-rooms and laboratories. The Jagellonian University in Krakow has four students to one before the war, so that space is taxed to the utmost and some classes must be limited.

In a Warsaw suburb where working men live, I went unannounced to see a public school. A thousand children go from eight to one, and another thousand from one till six; this two-session schedule is of course only temporary. At the end of the hall are two rooms where the morning children may study quietly in the afternoon, and vice versa. At the entrance are the coat-rooms, where each child has a hook with a bag for his street shoes. In the building they all wear felt slippers which are, explained a Pole, cleaner, quieter, more hygienic for the feet of growing boys and girls.

There were flowers growing in every window. All the classrooms had lighting from the left, and movable blackboards that could be placed higher or lower. A workshop for the boys; a kitchen and dining-room where the older girls prepare and serve breakfast to the youngsters who don't get it at home—at a cost of a cent and a half; a natural history room with an aquarium, stuffed birds, plants pressed or growing; an assembly hall that could be used for meetings, for motion pictures, for athletics; shower baths in the basement; the dentist's room—two thousand patients are enough to keep him busy (no time lost from lessons to go for these appointments); near by the rooms of the doctor, the nurse, and the woman psychologist who makes a special study of the abnormal youngsters who don't fit in with their groups—all these things the Pole took for granted, saying this school was not a shining exception, that as rapidly as people with the right training are available they'll have them everywhere.

As great strides have been made in health matters. Every town and village has its Kasa Chorych (House of Health, literally translated) where people may have without any charge whatever medical advice and care. Next to Denmark, Poland has gone farther than any country in Europe in this work and in insurance. Every worker must have a fortnight's vacation, and brain workers a full month—written in the constitution.

In one town I went to see a model laboratory for pasteurizing milk; it's expensive, as prices go in Poland, but when the demand for safe milk is greater the charge will be less. The important thing is that a beginning has been made.

Playgrounds for children are another innovation that will spread from Warsaw and Poznan to other towns, given a little time and more funds. The one in Warsaw has this advantage over any in America—it has ample space, space for many activities (slides, seesaws, basketball and net ball, circle games), for sand piles, for a children's restaurant with low tables and chairs, for a shelter (open on one side) for rainy weather, and for the offices. Every child is weighed and measured when he first comes, and at stated intervals thereafter; badly under-weight youngsters are ordered to have sun baths and fewer games. The parents, except those who are very poor indeed, pay two *zlotys* a month for each child. It's more than a playground, it's a child welfare station.

This is all a part of the new interest that has come in Poland, as in other European countries, since the war, a vital interest in physical well-being, in sports and games. I attended the finals of a field meet between Poles and Czechs. Once I saw a game of volley ball in a convent.

"The girls insist on having athletics," said the nun, apologetically.

And in Torun my hostess explained that this year, for the first time, membership in the tennis club was open to everybody, because the town had given a sum for fixing the courts.

"I've played tennis since I was ten or twelve," she went on, "we had a court at each country house. But for most of the young people sports are new, and they've gone in for them enthusiastically, with all the ardor of children for a new toy, plus a feeling of patriotism. The general in command of the army in this district made a speech at the opening of the tennis season, pointing out that the good qualities developed by athletics are the very ones that will make them valuable to Poland in case of another war—what aviators, nurses, engineers, private soldiers could learn from tennis. Did they want to be ready to serve Poland? Then they must work hard at sports.

"And notice," she suggested during the tournament, "how serious these young folks are; they're discussing tennis, the different players, yesterday's scores. I never see any flirting here. No nonsense. They don't come to the club because it gives them an excuse for meeting. They're absorbed in tennis."

Of course I was invited to the nurses' training school in Krakow, built by the Rockefeller Foundation. I asked what the words over the door meant.

"School for training maternity nurses, Medical Faculty of the Jagellonian University."

"But doesn't it say Rockefeller Foundation anywhere?"

"No. There used to be a bronze tablet by the entrance, but one of the Rockefeller staff came to Krakow and said it must be taken down, that the Foundation doesn't want its name put up anywhere."

New as this school is, it's overcrowded. And if its graduates could be multiplied by five or six, they couldn't fill all the positions that await them. This too is only a beginning.

In a mountain village of four hundred souls lives a patriotic, progressive woman who has built there a Community House, for which America gave her many of the ideas. It's built on a slope with an extra floor underneath on one side—a very large room for all sorts of gatherings—motion pictures, dances, talks, dramatics. Two rooms for the library—one for children, one for adults (with classes in reading and writing). A dispensary and a two-room hospital where the visiting nurse can look after youngsters needing special care for a short time. A laundry—later on they hope to have a washing machine and a mangle; for the present it's a great boon to give the peasant women a place to wash and to get the washing out of their crowded homes. A bakery to sell good bread at just over cost—that's far more important than with us, for bread makes an enormous percentage of peasant diet, day after day, and much of it is not well made or well baked. And last, but not least in importance, two rooms provide a store where all sorts of things are sold—whatever the people ask for. This is to teach the peasants of that village and that neighborhood that they don't have to buy from the Jews.

Nor are all the new things in Poland practical and revenue-producing. In Warsaw they've begun a large building for their National Museum. The Chopin monument is only three years old—an impressive figure of the young composer listening to the melody of the wind in the trees, with a mirroring pool and a background of trees that will, in a decade or so, give it a splendid setting; it's better placed than most statues in America. The Kosciuszko statue on the Wawel is new since the war. Even in Lodz, which I saw when the textile depression was at its very worst and the mills were running two days a week, they were putting up a statue. With all their crying needs,

Photo by Polskie Tow, Krajoznawcze

The quaint façades of the medieval houses in the market-place of Warsaw have been restored and painted in gay colors

Photo by Polskie Tow, Krajoznawcze

The Unknown Soldier of Poland lies within this arcade in the heart of Warsaw

Photo by Swiatowice

Photo by St. Mucha

Sigismund Stary had one extravagance—architecture—and sent to Florence for the experts who spent more than sixty years in building the palace on the Wawel

(See page 306)

their innumerable demands, Poles say that art and museums and universities are necessary, that they can not live by bread alone.

A unique combination—a country with centuries of background, with a history that goes back to legendary times; a new country also, with many of the needs of a land recently developed. One striking thing is the lack of capital. In the beginning Poland had an empty treasury, for none of the three governments kept any funds in these districts. What stories I heard of the efforts of the people, poor as they were, to contribute to help their nation get started! The school-teacher in Lwów who made speeches on the street and collected a wagon load of silver—spoons and forks, brooches, ornaments of every kind. Ladies gave up their jewelry and for a long while would wear only breast pins made of iron; "black jewelry," it was called and patriots wore it.

There is still a lack of capital all through Poland. Over and over and over people I met casually would start in to tell me what they could do if only they had some capital for a few years—a fisherman on the beach at Gdynia, a dressmaker, a Warsaw publisher, the keeper of a small shop. I used to wonder if they thought every American was rolling in wealth, especially writers, and all I had to do was to dash off a check and say, "Here, take so many thousand *zlotys* and go ahead with your plans."

Callers came one afternoon to a house where I was staying and I was introduced to a Mr. X. I knew only that he had a large estate within motoring distance. The minute he learned I was an American, he began telling me not of the land near by, but of sixteen thousand acres he had in the east of Poland, not far from the frontier. He was farming about two thousand acres, the rest was marshy ground; once drained, it would yield abundantly. Two years would do the work and the first two crops would pay the bill. What he needed then was a loan for four years—a thing not to be had in Poland.

"How much do you get on a bond?" he demanded. "Five, six per cent.; seven for some of the foreign bonds? Why in the world don't Americans investigate opportunities in Poland? Many a Pole would think he was fortunate if he could get a loan at ten or twelve per cent., and offer plenty of collateral too."

"Well, we had a housing shortage just after the war," I began in my ignorance one day when we were discussing living quarters, "and everywhere new apartments were put up. One of the things that's surprised me in every town in Poland is to see how little building's going on. You all agree there aren't homes enough, people live crowded into fewer rooms than they'd like to have; yet almost nothing is being done. Why?"

"Lack of capital," was the decided answer. "If you have to pay an exorbitant rate for whatever sum you borrow for your building, you must charge more rent—and no one would pay it. Here's an illustration: recently the owner of the apartment-house where I live brought an architect in to see if the walls were strong enough to warrant putting on another story—it's three floors now.

The man said yes, the plan was practical, the four new apartments could be rented easily, there was such a demand. But the best terms the owner could get from the bank—and he offered the land and the present building as security—were twelve per cent. for three months; which meant, repay the loan before the new tenants moved in. The plan fell through."

The rules of the banks are very strict. Many enterprises that an American banker would regard as A1 find it impossible to secure funds. There are almost no long-time loans being made.

Such stories made me greatly interested in what new housing I saw. The city of Warsaw helps finance one- or two-family houses on the outskirts of town, each with a garden. Very attractive homes they are. The national government lends its aid to a group of people to build a cooperative apartment-house. They must get together a fifth of the cost of land and building, and the government loans four-fifths for a period of years, charging seven per cent. instead of ten. This is a popular way for the employees of Poland to solve their housing problem—men working in a bank, in the post-office, in the railroad have erected such apartment-houses in several cities.

One cooperative building where I was frequently a guest interested me because it was a woman's achievement. I heard this story from an Englishman in Danzig, who asked me to interpret for him at the hotel and ended by giving me an introduction to his Polish friends. Like nearly all the women of her generation, Mme. A. had been brought up to do nothing—I mean, nothing that would give her an income. She lived on a great estate in the Ukraine. He described the house from photographs he'd seen, the library in one wing with the three Rembrandts. The Bolshevists came in the night and burned it, pouring oil over rugs and furniture to destroy things more quickly. With the three children—then ten, eight, five years old—she managed to get away; a ghastly journey into Poland.

"But that's not the interesting part of the story," he went on. "She found herself with barely enough funds to last a few months, if the four of them lived most frugally. Without any special business training she put all her capital into cigarette papers and doubled it; then doubled it again in another venture. Her family and various friends wanted homes, so she herself designed an apartment-house—oh, she had an architect's help on the technical part—and put it up, with a government loan of a hundred thousand—that means dollars, not *zlotys;* and she's now ahead of schedule in paying off the loan. She's built two other apartment-houses since and is planning more. A new type has developed in Poland, since the land is free, with business ability and executive gifts they themselves never dreamed of."

True of both men and women. I was greatly impressed with the high caliber of government officials. The old families have what English people have, and what is conspicuous by its absence in America—a tradition of pub-

lic service. Men have given up living on their estates to
serve in the various ministries, in the Sejm (Parliament),
in diplomatic posts. For many appointments a university degree is required. Salaries can't be very high.
It is patriotism that's responsible for the new Polish
official.

It takes courage—Polish courage! to undertake new
works with so many difficulties to be overcome, so many
delays. In the Tátra Mountains I went to see a summer
resort in the making—a "restricted development" real-
estate men would call it here. Count F. had spent a year
making a roadway (Poles are splendid engineers and
roadmakers) and another year in putting up the first of
the buildings—the electric-light plant, restaurant and
apartment-house. He was making his own brick, from
clay on his own land, baking them in kilns stoked with
wood. Progress seemed to me so slow, especially when I
compared this with such an undertaking in America, that
I could only exclaim, "Polish courage!"

On the way down the mountain—so close are old and
new in Poland—we stopped at the ruins of a castle,
perched on a rock high above the river. We clambered
up the steep path and wandered through the roofless
chambers and looked at the fragments of pillars that
date, the archæologists say, from the eighth or ninth
century.

"Nobody knows who built it," the countess explained,
"perhaps the Greeks who came this way to the Baltic
Sea for amber. The girl queen, Jadwiga, who was

brought up in Hungary, you know, slept here her first night in Poland. I'll show you presently a tablet we put up in 1910, for the five-hundredth anniversary of the victory at Grunwald, with Ladislas Jagello's name. And there are some stones in the castle wall, with strange antediluvian creatures embedded in them.

"How does it come to be in ruins? No, not the Swedes, not the Tartars. At the last Partition the day was set for the starosta (the king's representative) to hand the keys over to the Austrians and let them take possession of the castle. The night before there was a terrific thunder-storm and the place was set on fire—was it by the lightning? was it by the starosta's own hand? for he felt that he could not surrender it to the enemy of Poland. At any rate, the whole castle was destroyed and never rebuilt."

One thing I noticed particularly, and was greatly touched by, was the courage with which many persons have adjusted themselves to new work and a new scale of living, for which they had had little preparation. Here's an illustration. As we drove out from Wilno to spend the day in the country, a friend of Pani L. told me her story. They were very rich and had three great estates in the Ukraine; on one they had seven hundred head of cattle, and everything else in proportion. There was a fourth property which they thought little of and always called "the little farm near Wilno." In comparison with the Ukraine holdings the land was poor and unproductive; but they did farm it, with a resident manager.

At one blow the three estates were confiscated and they turned to "the little farm near Wilno" as a haven of refuge, glad to have some place to live. In these ten years they have accomplished wonders there. The house has electric lights and running water. The gardens are lovely.

I walked over the fields which reminded me of very stony fields in the stoniest part of New England. They've begun a campaign, to last some years longer, getting rid of the stones in so many acres each year. Slow work—here, the men were blasting, there, piling the larger stones up, so that when the snow comes they can be taken by sledges to the site of new farm buildings. In another place they were making tile for roofs.

"There's only one way to endure it," Pani L. said simply. "Not to think of the past. We must look only ahead. We must make a success of the farm for the sake of our grandchildren."

Polish courage, I call that.

To live in the present and the future is perforce the motto of many Poles who owned estates in the Ukraine and lived there in the summers, spending their winters in Warsaw or Krakow. When the Russian revolution came the land was taken from them. Very seldom would they talk about it, they want to forget; but once I found one of them in a reminiscent mood and with a few questions to keep her talking, I heard the whole story. The two sisters belonged to a noble family and had been at one time very rich. As they would say in Boston, they were gentlewomen in reduced circumstances.

"Ours was not a huge estate," began Miss Marya, "only twenty-four hundred acres. Why, I know one family here in Krakow who lost a hundred and seventy thousand. But that section of the Ukraine was called 'the Egypt of Russia,' the land was so fertile, the crops so large, so unfailing. You hear people say the peasants were so badly off—not our peasants, not in the Ukraine. We paid a dollar a day, for a short working day too. Why, the children helping in the sugar-beet fields in the spring got fifty cents a day. They didn't want any revolution. They knew they were well off. Often I've heard them say that.

"In May of 1914 we went there for the summer, as usual. The war began. With our Austrian passports we could not return. We had to stay on. Then the Russian revolution came. We were ordered to move out of our house—you see a part of it in the background of my sister's portrait, a long, low, white house with pillars. We moved into the gardener's cottage—my mother, my sister and I. More than once I was ready to give it all up and leave, to try to get back into Poland and safety, but my mother steadfastly refused: that was her home, she would not go away.

"Five years we stayed on—five years of the Bolshevists. No one who hasn't lived through it can have any idea of what that means. For two whole years we had no meat—none to be had, no matter how much we were willing to pay. And always the feeling that we were being spied on. No, no, not our peasants; they were loyal to the very last. Seven hundred and fourteen times our cottage was searched—sometimes they came just looking, sometimes with definite orders to seize a certain thing: firearms, gold, silver, anything made of copper. I remember once they said orders had come to confiscate watches, and they took twelve that belonged to my sister.''

(Not a word of her individual losses. But I'd noticed that she had no watch. At Christmas time the three Americans in the house put our pennies together and bought a wrist-watch. ''For twelve years I've been without one,'' she said simply.)

''Why did we leave in the end, and how? One of the peasants, spokesman for them all, came to my mother and begged her to go. They had endured all they could and longed to go back to Poland; they knew the journey meant hardships, but nothing mattered if they could only get out of Russia. 'Very well, you are free to go,' answered my mother. But they didn't feel they were free, they could not go and leave their mistress; they begged her to go too, and at last she yielded.

''Such a trip as that was!'' She stopped, her voice tired out, her face drawn as if even the memory of those days hurt her. ''We had first-class tickets, but Bolshevist soldiers crowded into our compartment and ordered us out. We found standing room in a third-class car. Somebody gave up a seat for my mother. Ordinarily it was a ride of two hours; this time it lasted fourteen. The next days are vague in my mind—we rested and slept if we could by day and traveled by night; our mother in a peasant's cart; always going west—toward Poland. At last we came to a river. My sister and mother crossed on a raft, poled along by some peasants. I forded it at midnight, shoulder deep. Once across I set off to find a Polish sentinel to arrest us and so get to headquarters. The frontier was closely guarded and presently I found one and brought him back to the group. We had to stay a few days till the health officers were satisfied as to our condition, and then went on to Krakow.''

For weeks they'd been saying to themselves, ''Everything will be all right when we get to Krakow.'' But it wasn't. Thieves had broken into their apartment and taken all their silver and their linen. They had nothing! With a most splendid spirit they went to work—and neither of the sisters was young. One taught school, the other gave special talks in schools. They lived in one room and took paying guests into their home. Somehow they carried on. Polish courage! I take off my hat to the new women of Poland.

Because it is a new country, because for so long they had no votes, no voice in the government, the Poles are enormously interested in politics. Nine times out of ten the men sitting in a café, drinking tea out of glasses and talking with such animation, such absorbed interest for an hour or more, are talking politics. A group of peasants loitering in front of the village store, people on the train, guests at tea or dinner are discussing politics—local affairs, trade, improvements, the government monopolies.

It's a common occurrence to see a crowd outside the Sejm building in Warsaw, impatient to get first-hand news of a vote or a debate. Ten years has not been long enough to take away from this new interest in their lives. Party politics are often at white heat, for there are—I don't know how many parties; only eight that are very important in the Sejm, one of the members told me. They disagree violently in local matters, and only a coalition cabinet such as Pilsudski formed could get the necessary measures passed.

On one thing they are an absolute unit—any question of foreign policy. If there's talk of changing the frontier, of having to give up a foot of Polish soil, immediately every one is united. There are no parties, there is only Poland.

"War may come," people say, "war may come with one or another of our neighbors—with Lithuania, with Germany, with Russia. But one thing is absolutely sure— it will not be Poland who begins it. We are all for peace. We want nothing so much as peace. Our country must have time to get on her feet. But—give up the Corridor? Never! Every man and woman and child would fight. It would be another Grunwald!"

The Marshal, as they speak of Pilsudski, is of course the outstanding figure in Poland. A very magnetic personality, people are violently for him or violently against him; I talked with only one man who was neutral. But he is not a dictator, not a czar, Poles are quick to tell a stranger; he is one of the fourteen ministers who make

[217]

up the cabinet and has more than once refused the presidency. Always modest and aloof, seldom seen in public, he is already a legend. The country is full of stories about him.

"Where are we now?" he turned to his aide when they were driving across Warsaw on the way home from some great function.

"This square has been renamed, sir. It is now Plac Jozefa Pilsudskiego."

"H—m." Then after a little, "And what street is this?"

"Marshal Street, sir."

"Well—all right," he conceded grudgingly. The motor swung into an open space and he asked again where they were.

"This is the Square of the Savior."

"No, no! This is too much!"

CHAPTER IX

"The Eye of the Master Fattens the Horse"

"Numerowy, numerowy!" I called from the compartment window as the train pulled into Kalisz. Outwardly I was calm as I followed my porter toward the gate, but inwardly excited over this week-end with unknown hosts. How would I recognize them?

A tall man caught sight of me and waved his hand. He was very slight (for a Pole); ruddy face—out-of-doors, I said to myself; standing very straight indeed; dressed in riding clothes, chamois gloves—I liked Mr. T. at once. He put me into the front seat of the motor and drove himself. The chauffeur in gray uniform with blue collar and cuffs sat in the back with the luggage. Off we went, over the finest roads I saw in Poland.

"I must ask you to excuse me," he said when we stopped in front of the bank and a young man joined us. "May I introduce my son, Andrzej? You have just half an hour to see the town. The Rubens—a bit of the park— the ruins. Mind, we mustn't be late for dinner. Good-by."

Andrew, a very handsome young Pole, starting his university life in a fortnight, speaking the best English I heard in Poland, grinned at the warning, shook hands with me and suggested that we go on foot. First to the church of St. Nicholas to see a *Descent from the Cross* by Rubens; so the experts decided recently when it was cleaned and its beauties showed up; like Antwerp's on a smaller scale. A rare treasure to find in a town of fifty thousand.

"But it's not a new town," Andrew stated proudly. "You'll find it mentioned by Ptolemy—Calisia, he calls it and tells of the amber merchants' coming here. It's only now that it's so small. In 1914 it had over a hundred thousand people. What happened? The frontier was near here—I mean, the line between Germany and Russia—and on the second day of the war the German army invaded Russian territory. Kalisz was the first town and for three days they bombarded it—no warning given, not even an hour for non-combatants to leave. Over fifteen thousand people killed, the rest homeless, Kalisz a pile of bricks. The ruins you see to-day, in places where nothing's been done. Why? An object lesson to the Poles; a gesture by which the Prussians announced, 'Thus will we do everywhere, if as we advance the Poles behind us so much as lift a finger. There must be no danger of a Polish revolt in our rear.' "

At the end of the war the people—what was left of Kalisz's population—crept back, lived as best they could in tents and dugouts and shacks, putting a roof over a few rooms of ruined houses. For lack of capital rebuilding has gone on slowly. There was none at all till 1925 and I saw only a few blocks completed. But each year there's more, all done according to a plan; some day Kalisz will be a very attractive spot.

"I have an idea!" I exclaimed. "Don't restore it all. Keep some of your ruins—part of a house wall, one story high; a chimney; spaces where windows were. In all my travels over Poland I've seen such tangible results of the war in only one other place—a village in a corner of Austrian Poland, rather inaccessible. Now Kalisz is right on the tourist's way from Warsaw to Poznan and offers a convenient stop-over. A few years from now it'll be on the itinerary of all the Americans, just because it has something to show; and forty or fifty years from now it'll be a goal for the Poles too.''

The half-hour was up. Off in the motor to their house, twelve kilometers from town. The country was very flat, almost all the land in big estates—I'd learned that large fields meant that, and small fields, long and very narrow, meant peasant owners. We turned in at a low gateway, drove round a circle to a long white house, two-storied in the center, with a porch with four great columns, and a lower wing at either side. A man in dark blue coat with silver buttons came out for the bags. Mme. T. greeted us at the door.

Bit by bit I learned about the estate and the family. It's over seven thousand acres and belongs to Madame. She has six large scrap-books of estate papers and letters. She spent one winter recently sorting and arranging them and pasting them in. The oldest is a fifteenth-century parchment, but there are family records from 1271. She is the ninth owner in direct descent, and every time the inheritance has been through a daughter—a thing they themselves said was remarkable; and she has one child, a little daughter (she's a second wife).

As for Mr. T.'s family, he laughed and said I should have asked about his first, as it doesn't seem ancient after hers, they go back only to the first half of the fifteenth century. For all these years, one generation after another, they've been landowners with a passionate love of the soil. Andrew, however, isn't interested in farming, but is going to the school of commerce at the university and means to go into business. They've lived in this part of Poland only a short while; before the war in the north, on an estate that's now just over the frontier, about two miles, and confiscated by the Lithuanian government. It was confiscated once before—by the Russians after 1863, but as a special favor from the czar they were allowed to buy it back. Mr. T.'s father spent the rest of his life doing this, working very hard to get the money together; and now he hopes that some day, somehow, relations will be straightened out between Poland and Lithuania and that he'll be able to buy back the land for his children.

What was the house like? A large entrance hall, furnished in Polish maple, used almost like a living-room. Here were the portraits of Madame's ancestors: a general under Napoleon and his wife, his father with a long beard, a priest, one in nobleman's dress, who looked like Sobieski; one lady, very beautiful, might have been an English portrait of the eighteenth century.

Madame had made some changes in the house a few years ago, and the workmen found, hidden in an up-stairs wall, three swords. Her grandfather concealed them there in 1863, to save them from the Prussians. He did the work himself at night, building them into the wall, and told no one, not even his wife. One was the sword of the Napoleonic general, the others of two ancestors; he wanted to preserve them for his descendants.

Back of the hall was a formal drawing-room, with French windows opening on to a second porch; the dining-room in one wing; the kitchen in a separate building, some distance away. Once more I wondered how food ever got to the table hot. A special boy carried it over, Madame said, and there were special covers for all the dishes. One wing is for guests and five minutes' walk is a new guest house. Twenty rooms—they can have fifteen visitors— only eight servants.

The park isn't large, perhaps twelve acres. I saw several in Poland that were much larger, but none so attractive. Walks and drives; trees—a great mass of them to shut out the orchard and the kitchen garden; flower-beds, aglow with dahlias at that season (early September); a small pond, artificial, stocked with fish to supply the table on Fridays; the tennis court; and little gardens that fitted into the scheme—the rose garden, the rockery, the Dutch garden.

After dinner we went for a drive behind a team of beautiful horses. Royal Hungarian breed, Madame said, pleased that I asked. Poles are, and always have been, great lovers of horses. We drove for three hours, just on their own grounds, and I was surprised to see what the word "estate" can cover. Nearly ten per cent. is in forest; part of this they have replanted, but it's not yet giv-

[223]

ing any income. But, Mr. T. explained, Poland needs more forest land, it's patriotic for a large estate to do its bit in adding to the total.

We drove by fields of rye, which they plant three or four years in one place, but with heavy fertilizing; and of peas, which men were cutting with scythes and women were turning over for drying, and loading on to the carts.

"What do you do with peas—on such a big scale?" I asked.

"It's threshed and part used for fodder. The peas are ground into a fine meal and fed to the pigs—they get fat on it very quickly."

In the next field they were putting in more tile—three-inch drains. Harvest was almost over. They were finishing up the odds and ends.

"But what about these sugar-beets? They look fully ripe, to my American eyes. Am I wrong?"

"That goes to seed. A Dutch firm has bought all our crop—or rather, all the seed we can supply them with—beets and clover and so on, for a term of years. That's why you see a row of potatoes planted around the beets, to protect them by taking all the flies and bugs."

Then I knew definitely what I'd guessed before—here they farmed extremely well. Fields whose product was sold ahead of time to a Dutch company were the last word. The more I saw at Kalisz, the more sure I felt this was the best farming I was to see in Poland.

"What are these names, put up in the forest paths?"

"For hunting parties," explained Andrew. "The forester assigns places to all the guests, and the placards make it easy for visitors to find their way. We always have one big hunt every autumn, a few guests now and then during the winter, and usually a small party in the spring. Game laws in Poland are very strict, but there's scarcely a month that isn't open season for something. Have you seen the pamphlet in English, *Poland, the Hunter's Paradise?* It answers all a foreigner's questions before he can ask them—when he can shoot this and that, where, what to bring, what he can buy here.''

I tried not to be a pest with questions, but so many things were new to me, so many were different from ours that I couldn't keep still. They've worked out not one rotation of crops, but three; for part of the land is wet, part is sandy, part is—ordinary, Mr. T. described it. To me nothing on the whole estate was ordinary.

''See here!'' he turned to me, ''how in the world do you know about all this? You talk as if you were a farmer yourself.''

''We are farmers. Weather and rotations, and the advantage of growing corn and then selling pigs and cattle instead of selling corn—why, I've heard that kind of talk since I was a little girl. I ought to know far more than I do—but I'm not the sister who does the farm business now. Tell me, do you keep crop maps? Would you let me see them?''

One thing was very different from a farm in the Middle West. They have a hundred and fifty employees—all-the-year-round workers. The extras, from April to October, are paid four hundred *zlotys* apiece, plus so much flour, sugar, lard, and so much wheat, barley, oats. The permanent hands live in red brick or white plastered houses, the most attractive I saw on any estate in Poland. They have a club—a very large room where they gather for games, dances, talks.

Just before my visit there was a celebration for the end of the wheat harvest. All the work people came in a body to the house, bringing a present to the master and one to the mistress. Hers was round, about eighteen inches high, made of nuts, each tied on to the framework with a piece of straw or of gold paper. It had four bells, two red and two blue. Mr. T.'s was a pyramid, each side made of a different kind of grain, with paper flowers of red and white. They are carefully kept for a year, till new harvest gifts are given. An old, old Polish custom.

The peasants sang—old songs describing the harvest. This was followed by a dance in the clubroom, with an elaborate supper. This celebration is always on Saturday night, so they can rest up on Sunday; for a Polish dance goes on for hours and hours—all night long.

"I was tired," Mr. T. said ruefully, "I had to dance with every girl."

"I was tired too," added Madame, "though I didn't dance every dance. When the evening was half over, I just sat and looked on."

He starts out on horseback before six o'clock each morning, and has given directions and overlooked the work in the fields for two or three hours when he comes in for breakfast. "Hungry as a wolf," he described himself, and quoted the old Polish proverb, "*Panskie oko konia triczy*" (The eye of the master fattens the horse), when I asked why he went in person.

The details of the work are looked after by five foremen. I saw two groups of fifteen workers—men and women together. Once when we stopped at the edge of a field, the foreman came running over, kissed Madame's hand, and reached for mine (which I held out graciously!). To my surprise, when the man went to the front seat, Mr. T. moved his arm quickly so that the kiss fell on his sleeve near the elbow, while he leaned forward and made the gesture of doing the same thing to the foreman.

"Even now," he explained to me later, "even now they can't forget the old Russian ways. I want them to feel they are men, not serfs. I don't let them kiss my hand. I salute them as they salute me. They're free now, they are Poles!"

After tea and a stroll with Andrew in the garden, I was invited into the office to see the crop maps—showing what grew in each field, with the yield, year after year. I thought our system better in one respect—ours is a slip-sheet book, and certain maps can be taken out and laid side by side for comparison.

"Ah, that would never do for a Pole," he replied seriously when I ventured to suggest it; "you know, we're not orderly as Anglo-Saxons are. If I had a slip-sheet book, before many weeks some pages would be missing. It's a continual fight for a Pole to be exact, to keep records, to finish what he starts enthusiastically. A crop book where the pages came out? That would never do.''

I asked about the oblong, near the center of the map, that was colored differently. It belongs, he told me, to the peasants, not to his wife. Her grandfather gave that land to his serfs when the czar freed them. They own from ten acres up.

''There, now!'' he cried ruefully, as a gong sounded, ''see what I've done—kept you talking here till *collatya* is ready. Not a minute for either of us to dress—and I'm still in my riding clothes, just as I started out at six this morning. Come along, it can't be helped now.''

At supper some one suggested that Madame get in touch with the M.'s, that I'd enjoy meeting them and they me. Presently she came back from the telephone and reported, ''Yes, they'll be over to-morrow.''

''You're going to Goluchow (Go-loó-hof, it's pronounced), with Andrew to show you about,'' announced Mr. T. the next morning at breakfast.

I acquiesced, wondering who or what Goluchow was.

''Get a warm coat,'' the son cautioned me, ''you're not going to walk, you know.''

''Pray tell me about Go—go something,'' I floundered over the name.

His face showed his astonishment, though he was too courteous to put it into words. How could any one be in Poland and not know all about this famous house where the Czartoryski family had established their museum?

''Oh, why didn't you say Czartoryski? I do know

The country house where I had Sunday supper, surrounded by gorgeous tapestries and generations of family portraits

A circular driveway led to this low, white, almost colonial house, the center of a Polish estate of seven thousand acres and five hundred peasants about them—The Family, the Poles used to call them. But I didn't know they were collectors and founders of a museum—I thought they were patriots."

"In Poland these often went together," he said quietly.

Goluchow didn't give me the feeling that Prince Czartoryski went out with a net and swooped up anything that was ancient or expensive, and so made this collection. Three minutes and I knew it was the result of years, in fact of several generations of discriminating purchases, into which they put love and special interest as well as great sums of money. Every object merits a superlative. Each is a "museum piece."

The treasures are now so many that the whole house, a sixteenth-century Renaissance palace, is given over to the museum, and the family live in a modern château near by. I've seen only two places in the world that can be compared with Goluchow—Mrs. Gardner's in Boston, and Chantilly near Paris; places where you're as interested in the house itself as in the collection it holds.

The Czartoryskis were catholic in their tastes. I saw treasures from Egypt, from China and Japan, Greek and Etruscan vases, paintings, tapestries, furniture, porcelains, carvings, noblemen's sashes woven with threads of gold and silver, room after room; an old stone baptistery, sculptured doorways, chimney pieces. Oh, the wealth of a great Polish family! and what a sense of *noblesse oblige* goes with it! And this, if you please, was only a part of the Czartoryski collection, the rest I would see in Krakow.

This thrilling excursion made me half forget Pan M.

and his wife. I vaguely noticed they didn't come to dinner, but nobody mentioned them. Then I was told to put on my things, we were going away for tea. It was after seven when we returned, and Mr. T. casually said, "Ah, this evening we'll have time to freshen up."

I used part of that half-hour to write a letter to my sisters, describing the house where we'd been—tall mirrors from a royal palace, with crowns above and Polish eagles made into the glass; porcelains, that were a gift from Catherine II; most splendid of all, on the south side of the house, away from the highroad, gardens such as I'd seen only once.

"Why, it's like Wilanow!" I cried aloud as I looked up, up, up, sixty feet or more to the top of the long *allées* of trees, trained to make a flat wall of living green. (Now Wilanow is a palace not far from Warsaw, built in the sixteen-eighties by Sobieski, with the labor of his Turkish prisoners from Vienna.)

"It's far older than Wilanow," said the lady with a smile, and sent her nephew to walk with me there, so that I'd get the "feel" of the garden.

I put on a simple frock for *collatya* and started to the drawing-room. At the door something, I don't know what unless it was a warning whisper from my fairy godmother, but something stopped me. I went back, changed slippers and stockings, and chose another dress—French this time. Thanks be I'd done so. For in the drawing-room were Mr. T. and Andrew and two others, all in dinner coats. One was a painter I'd met in Lwów, where he was finishing his murals in the cathedral. The other they called by a long title from his position in the Sejm (that corresponded to our Speaker of the House); and his wife, who came in just then with Madame, had that title too with a feminine ending. Two extra maids helping the butler, extra courses at supper. And no one had told me!

"I'm glad," Mrs. M. said while we chatted in the drawing-room till the men joined us, "that some one in New York advised you not to spend all your time in the cities, or you'd not see the real Poland. That is particularly true in the west. If you'd like to see another house, won't you come to us to-morrow?"

"Oh, I would like to! I don't know what plans have been made already, but I would like to!"

"Then that's settled. I'll speak to Mrs. T."

That was all—nothing more definite than that. How was I to know what they planned when they talked in Polish? Sometimes I wondered if it wasn't convenient to be able to talk and have your guest catch not a word of it all; but sometimes it wasn't so convenient for the guest!

Are we going to the M.'s now, I wondered when the Royal Hungarians drew up at the door while we loitered in the sunshine after a late Sunday breakfast; but no, Mr. and Mrs. T. were driving to church. In the afternoon I thought we'd perhaps go over for tea, but a lady drove up in a coach and four—to be exact, in what we used to call a station-wagon, with four big black horses and a footman and coachman. Andrew took me for a walk at sunset and when we got back to the house I was told, with a faint note of disapproval, "You haven't much time—we start in twelve minutes."

"Start—start where?" I gasped.

"Why, to Pan M.'s. For *collatya*."

"Pray tell me," I appealed to Andrew, "how shall I dress? Is it a formal dinner?"

"Something with sleeves. Do hurry!"

I dashed down the hall to my room and scurried into a three-piece frock of georgette, hoping vaguely that I'd chosen aright, put on my heavy coat, and over that a Polish coat (made very, very loose and full everywhere, because it's warmer so), and off we went, driving like mad.

How I longed to see that estate by daylight, but alas! it was quite dark when we arrived. Through a large park with many very old trees; the house set a long way back from the road; great pillars at the entrance; two butlers, gray-haired (in service there for thirty-six years!); several reception-rooms—I lost count—a billiard room, the library, lined with books clear to the ceiling, two rooms with paintings—so many they touched each other, to say nothing of the pictures in the other rooms; and a cook who's been there sixty-three years! Platters and plates had the M. coat of arms in the center; the silver was almost top-heavy because of the raised crest on the handles.

This is what we had for supper—at least, all I can remember; hors-d'œuvres of tomato and onion, with rye bread; bouillon (very hot!); filet mignon on a circle of toast; partridge; lettuce; ice-cream (made with cream) in a lion mold, with very sweet cake; and five kinds of wine.

"Drink some, my dear young lady, drink some," urged Pan M. when he saw me shake my head, "it's older than you are."

And indeed the cobwebs on the bottles could only have grown so thick if they'd started before I did. Then, in the salon, coffee and liqueurs. Just before we left, a fruit punch with little cakes, served in the library. And hot tea brought at the very last, to warm us up for the windy drive back. That was Sunday *collatya* in a Polish house, miles off in the country, planned the night before.

I may have left out a course or two, for how could I pay attention to food when opposite my seat at table was an enormous tapestry, a Gobelin as large and as fine as I'd seen in the royal palace, and no less than fifteen portraits, all ancestors of Pan M., I learned, when after dinner I begged him to introduce me to these fascinating people. They went back nine generations, but the records of the family date from 1310.

The old butler came to bring his master the key to the silver chest, and I asked if I could go along to see it. The key was at least eight inches long, the chest about three feet by two, with a medieval lock. It is a tradition in the household that the master must always lock up the silver after dinner—but I noticed he didn't count things.

When we left I tried to thank Pan M. and Madame, for I had greatly enjoyed being their guest. But they shook their heads and he said, as he kissed my hand with a courtly bow, "On the contrary, we thank you for coming!"

CHAPTER X

I Go on a Pilgrimage

The chauffeur tucked in the robes, stowed away the hamper and thermos bottles, and off we drove that beautiful September morning. I felt somehow that it was going to be a red-letter day.

"Did you bring your letter to the bishop?" Mrs. Sage turned to ask. "Well, my suggestion is that we go right to the monastery and hear mass, and then find the bishop and ask for a special guide. Though I've been before, I don't feel competent to take you around.

"I've just counted it up, and this is my sixth trip to Czestochowa. (That's not so hard to pronounce as it looks: Chen-sto-ho'-va. Try it.) The last time Mrs. Peyton was with us, and we decided on the way over that we'd each pray for one special thing. We were a mixed party—Miss Wallace here is a Catholic, I'm a Protestant; and Mrs. Peyton was half-way between, brought up in the Catholic church, she married a Baptist and changed to his religion. I thought over all my desires and concentrated on one; but when we got there, on the floor of the chapel lay a cripple, a boy of say eighteen; and I became so interested in him, in the intense look in his face as he gazed at the picture that, do you know? I entirely forgot what it was I was going to ask for. I prayed that his prayer might be answered. When we compared notes as we drove home, not one of us had prayed for herself, but for that Polish boy. I've decided that no one— Catholic or Protestant or in-between—could go to Czestochowa and pray selfishly. Something in the atmosphere would stop you."

"Do people go only once," I asked, "like the Turks going to Mecca?"

"No, Poles go time after time. It's a popular thing to make a vow—if my sick child recovers, if the rye turns out to be a fine crop, if this business succeeds, I'll make a pilgrimage to Czestochowa. It's been so for centuries. I know people," continued Miss Interpreter when she saw how interested I was, "who've been half a dozen times, a dozen, twenty; and others who've been only once. Like Helena S., who doesn't want to go a second time, for it could never be so wonderful again. She fainted during the mass and wakened to find the pain in her head and back gone, after it had troubled her for a long time and the doctor could do nothing for it. That was four years ago, and she's never had a touch of it since."

"And I," added Miss Wallace, "asked a man recently how many times he'd been; not since the war, but he had a marvelous experience then—not dramatic and exciting, but marvelous to him. This was 1920. Six years of the war he'd been through, and was almost worn out. It seemed as if he could not go on. Then he got a leave— three days, and spent most of it on the train; but he had a few hours in Czestochowa and somehow the picture gave him courage to go on. To him that was a miracle, he was so near the breaking point.''

Czestochowa itself, they told me, is a factory town of eighty thousand; not attractive. We saw nothing of it, but went at once to ''Jasna Gora'' (mountain of light). From far away we saw the church tower, the highest in all Poland, then the monastery buildings, like a city set on a hill, surrounded by walls and moat; one of the few fortified churches left in Europe; a splendid site for the days when men built with defense in mind. We left the car near the first high gateway.

There was a long line of booths and little shops, with peasants selling rosaries, pamphlets, post-cards, statuettes of saints, and every possible sort of reproduction of the picture that makes Czestochowa famous; cheap copies that are almost chromos, others in sepia, on silver medallions, some with a silver ''dress,'' large and small. But not a book could I buy in English or French or German. Behind the booths are the barracks. Pilgrims have a place to sleep free and bring their own food with them, for a stay of two or three days; when they leave they give whatever sum they can afford.

In the wide concrete space at the entrance was a design made of a darker stone—a palm tree, two lions, a raven; what did it mean? We strolled through the gate and found three more gateways, part of the medieval defenses, and then an outdoor chapel, roofed over at the end where the altar is. Here the priests give communion to the pilgrims—hundreds, thousands at one time.

I confess I was disappointed when we entered the church—Gothic and baroque mixed, very high windows with clear glass, the altar rather showy, with much gold and a green Polish marble, stucco decoration, modern frescoes, a few candles burning at the side altars, a handful of people coming and going. The place was so big, so light, so empty, with not one bit of atmosphere.

But without stopping in the nave, Miss Interpreter walked up into the choir, opened a door, and led the way across a passage and into the chapel. One service was just ending. I looked about, taking mental notes. Not a very large room say thirty by forty feet; Gothic architecture; vaulting; on one side two tall narrow windows that needed washing; walls of a dull red, brocaded material, hung with votive gifts. The west wall was a sort of grill with crutches and braces tied on here and there— left behind when miracles took place?

My eyes turned back to the altar—ebony and silver, with tall, oh! very tall silver candlesticks. The room was dim and mysterious. No glare of electric lights, just little flickering flames in half a dozen red glass cups. A monk lighted the candles. Another service began. The screen over the picture was raised. I gasped.

The Madonna of Czestochowa! The Virgin with the Child in her arms. I could see nothing but their faces and hands. All the rest of the picture, every inch, was covered with gold and silver; an overdress following the lines of the painted garments, in some places standing out in high relief. I'd seen in Italian churches pictures with real necklaces and crowns, in Torun and Warsaw religious paintings with certain details covered with silver or gold; but here the whole picture was overlaid, even the golden halos. The light of the candles flickered over these costly "dresses" and the crowns, rich with many precious stones.

The picture has a very deep frame, giving the effect of a shadow box. I seemed to be looking way into it. About thirty inches wide, I decided, and more than a yard high—say forty-two inches. I gazed with critical, Protestant eyes. Not a Byzantine picture—far less Byzantine than the famous Madonna at Wilno; rather, early Italian; a face sweet, calm, patient, but—beautiful? I debated that. In the dim light the two cuts across the cheek scarcely showed. I should have missed them entirely if I hadn't been told just where to look.

The service went on, with three priests at the altar. The choir sang—the best church singing I heard in Poland. They told me later that the monks are very proud of the music at Czestochowa, that the choir has twenty-four men, not volunteers, but paid a fixed salary, so that they give all their time to this. Excellent singing it was, with violins and cellos accompanying the organ.

I studied the votive gifts hanging on the wall near me. They were placed in groups—a panel of silver ones, another of gold, a third with objects made of ebony. One was a large silver plaque, dated 1752, the gift of some Polish town, showing in raised figures a procession with the picture; what great blessing did it typify?

I looked about me at the people: five Zakopane peasants in their white woolen trousers embroidered in dark blue and red, and white capes; two soldiers; a woman in expensive mourning with a lorgnette; a policeman; a peasant girl with a Madonna-like face (due to her white headkerchief?); a woman with bandages around her head; a man lying on the floor, motionless, his arms out so that his body made a cross (was he asking for some special boon? what?); a barefoot peasant girl with a basket; a woman with a tiny baby in her shawl, kneeling; all of them intent on the service, but none of them emotional. A few—some men, some women—went on their knees around a passage that led behind the altar.

What was the mysterious force that seemed to be released in the minds of those people? What was this mystic power of the spirit? What did they believe as they gazed at the Madonna of Czestochowa?

Suddenly something gripped me. I felt my throat tighten. The choir chanted a beautiful response, then the voices ceased. The organ tones swelled out triumphantly and echoed back from the vaulting; silver trumpets blown; drums rolling; the church militant—a fortified church, I reminded myself; the Virgin of Czestochowa defending the chapel. I was swept off my feet, I, the descendant of generations of protesting Protestants, of men who'd made great sacrifices to worship in a particular way. Greatly stirred, I watched, scarcely breathing. Slowly, very slowly the gold and silver screen was lowered over the picture.

What it must have meant to a Catholic and a Pole!

In a daze I followed Miss Interpreter and we drove to the bishop's house. I thought him most delightful—so interested in my coming, so gentle, so kindly. What could he do to help me? Was there something special?

"Would it be possible," I ventured, "for us to have a guide—just for our group? I ask so many questions, and we want to go very slowly. I particularly want to see the treasury." (That because the young Englishman who'd been there in 1912 had piqued my curiosity.)

"Yes, I think that can be arranged. I will telephone the prior. What do you speak? I'm not sure there is a monk who knows English."

"Oh, we'd rather have a Pole, please. We've brought an interpreter. Don't you think I'd get more if the monk just talks along in his own tongue? People always skimp if they have to translate."

"In that case you must have Brother Wojciech (Voy' check). I'll ask the prior particularly. Two o'clock? He'll be ready to take you, and you shan't be hurried."

We ate our lunch under the trees by the roadside, as Mrs. Sage had tried the hotel—once. It was quiet and restful; we all felt like listening hard and looking hard when we returned to the monastery and Brother Wojciech was introduced as our guide. A tall man with a fine scholarly face, graying hair, in a robe of white woolen cloth. It was darned in several places—Mrs. Sage liked that. Until a few years ago he'd been a teacher in a boys' gymnasium. He seemed to know, without being told, just the things we wanted. We saw other monks finishing with a group of visitors in a quarter of an hour. Some places in Poland I didn't mind going through with the herd, rushed along by a guide who told the identical story he'd been telling for years. But not at Czestochowa!

"Will you please," Miss Interpreter put my first question, "tell us about the monks here?"

"Yes. We belong to the Pauline order—no connection with the Biblical Paul, but with Paul of the Desert, as he was called, because he lived alone in the desert for forty years, in prayer and meditation. Every day a raven brought him water and half a loaf of bread. Once St. Anthony went to visit him and then, for neither of them took any thought for food or raiment, the raven brought a whole loaf. One hundred years old he was at the time of his death, alone there in the desert; and two lions dug his grave."

In the nave of the church he pointed out a fresco showing the meeting of Paul and Anthony, and sculptured above a palm tree, a raven and two lions. That explained the design at the entrance gate.

"Some persons say this is the oldest order in the church, for Paul lived in the third century; and some say it's the strictest—the discipline is very severe; lay brothers come to us, but generally they don't stay long, for they can't endure living under such strict rules—not speaking at table, for example. Well, whether it's the oldest or the strictest, it's undoubtedly the smallest order to-day; we are only forty, in three different places in Poland. There are fifteen monks here, with eight novices now.''

''Aren't you afraid the Order will die out altogether?''

''We've started a school at the monastery in Krakow, and a group of young men are being trained there who will enter the order later.''

He took us up into the organ loft, where we could look down on the chapel of the Virgin, with worshipers coming and going, kneeling on the chapel steps. And this is the story he told us, with the little explanations put in for my benefit by Miss Interpreter:

''There's a legend that St. Luke painted this portrait of Mary, that he painted it on wood, on a table made by Jesus, the carpenter's son; well, there are about fifty pictures in Europe, count them all, said to have been painted by Luke; you can accept that as legend or truth, as you like. If you want more legends, there's one that the picture was taken by St. Helena to Constantinople, and when a princess of that city married a Ruthenian prince it came into this section of the world as a part of her dowry and it stayed at Belz.

''The Tartars laid siege to Belz and the starosta (the king's representative), Ladislas Opolski, went into the chapel and prayed before this picture. To save it from falling into the hands of the Tartars, he decided to take it to Opole where he had a castle (I'll show you Opole on the map—it's a town in Silesia—not Polish now, as it's over the frontier on the German side) and his way led through Czestochowa.

"Here the horses drawing the cart stopped and refused to go on. Ladislas Opolski prayed and a voice told him to leave the picture at Jasna Gora (that's the name of this hill.) He put the portrait of the Madonna in a little wooden church here, and went on his way to his castle. And that's the first definite date in the story—1382.

"There were many Paulines in Hungary at that period, and he invited some of them to come to Czestochowa and take charge of the picture. By the side of the little wooden church they built their monastery and Opolski, who was both pious and rich, endowed it. Later he gave the money for this Gothic chapel. Sieges and fires have caused much rebuilding and remodeling of the rest of Jasna Gora, but this one room was never destroyed. (The last fire was in 1900—the west tower burned, but the damage was quickly repaired, for money poured in from every part of Poland.)

"The fortress part—the ramparts of earth, the moat, the bastions—was added in 1620, but the walls were twice as high as now. The Russians ordered them lowered. Did you know that Pulaski took shelter behind the walls of Czestochowa more than once, when he was hard pressed by the Russians? that this was the last refuge of the Confederation of Bar?"

"What is the picture like, under the 'dress'?" questioned Mrs. Sage.

"I'll show you a colored reproduction."

Against a green background the Virgin in a black

mantle lined with crimson and edged with gold, scattered over with golden fleur-de-lis—they came to light just a few years ago when the picture was cleaned. The Child's dress is red, with a small all-over pattern in gold, and a band of gold at neck and wrists and hem. Wide halos of gold, joined at one place—that's common in many paintings of the Siena school. The faces and hands are not white but brown, for this unknown artist followed the old Byzantine rule that in pictures of the Madonna and Child the flesh must be brown, like grain burned by the sun.

Across Mary's cheek are two parallel cuts—Swedish vandalism, Miss Interpreter thought, but Brother Wojciech corrected her; this damage was done, long before 1655, by Hussite troops who came to the monastery and carried away the picture. Half a kilometer away their horses stopped in front of a church and would go no farther. Angrily the soldiers slashed and stabbed at the canvas, tossed it away, and rode on. The back of the picture shows many mended places, but the most skilful restorers could not hide the two cuts on the cheek.

"And when did the miracles begin? you ask. No one knows," our monk went on with the story. "The picture was venerated in the fifteenth century and widely known. Why, there's a copy of it in a Krakow church, placed there the very year Opolski brought it to Czestochowa. But there came one miracle that made it famous everywhere. It was 1655—a crisis in Poland's history, when danger swept over the land like a flood; in fact, Sien-

kiewicz called his book about 1655 *The Deluge.* On the
east the Turks were attacking us. From the north came
the Swedes. The king fled from Warsaw. Danger, con-
fusion, fear on every hand.

"Ten thousand Swedes encamped before Jasna Gora.
Kordecki, the prior—you saw his statue outside?—had
a hundred and twenty monks and a handful of knights—
some books say thirty, some more; but take a larger figure, what were they against such an enemy? Day after
day the siege went on, for a week, two, three weeks—
five weeks and three days, and then—the miracle. The
Swedish cannon balls bounded back from the walls and
killed their own men. Amazed, afraid, they looked up
and there in the sky was the Madonna with the Child,
above the church, just as she is pictured in the chapel.
They were terror-stricken and marched away in the night.
The siege of Czestochowa was ended.

"That was the turning-point of Poland's crisis. The
people pulled themselves together, repulsed both Turks
and Swedes, the king returned to his throne and ac-
claimed the Madonna of Czestochowa as queen of Poland. The Pope sent her a crown of gold and jewels and
there was a great ceremony of coronation; no, not the
crown you saw to-day—this is a new one, given only a
few years ago, after the robbery."

"Stolen? Who would dare?" I demanded indignantly.

"Stolen by two Russians who pretended to be novices
and so got into the monastery. To avoid suspicion, they
did nothing for some weeks. Then one night they let

their accomplices in and fled with the two crowns—the Child had one also. Of course they couldn't sell them as they were. Probably they offered jewels and gold in various places. Then the Pope gave two new crowns, and on the day they were presented more than a million Poles came to Czestochowa.

"But to go back. Word of the siege and its dramatic ending went abroad and the fame of the picture grew and grew. Pilgrims came by hundreds, by thousands, to kneel before it and ask for what they desired; every one believed in the Madonna of Czestochowa. The crutches in the grill, the votive gifts on the walls, the objects you'll see in the treasury are but a few of the many, many that have been given by grateful suppliants here—we put out only as many as look well.

"And when Poland was partitioned, this Madonna came to mean even more to the people. Their religion was the one thing they had in common while they lived under czar and kaiser and emperor. Here they heard talks on patriotism; here they learned the music and the words of the patriotic hymn, and used to go away on foot, singing it. Here the power of the spirit seemed incarnate, almost tangible. The picture meant so much not only because it was religious, but because it was patriotic. Every Polish household has a copy; you see it in countless bedrooms, it stands for devotion plus patriotism. Why, Czestochowa is the heart of Poland!"

"There!" I exclaimed, "there's my chapter title—The Heart of Poland."

Brother Wojciech caught a word and turned to Miss Interpreter.

"A book? with a whole chapter on Jasna Gora? And will you put me into your book, please?"

As if a request from the bishop were nothing in comparison with having his name in print, he exerted himself to show us everything—the Swedish cannon balls, one, two, three, four, embedded in the wall; the door leading into the chapel, carved in rich brown wood, showing Ladislas Opolski coming with the picture; a piece of the true cross; a crucifix, famous in the annals of Czestochowa, because it once spoke to the brothers; and they say that sometimes even now blood comes out of the wound in the side, covered with a silver loin cloth.

He pointed out where the library was and regretted that ladies could not enter it; it has walnut chests, beautifully ornamented by one of the monks, and many treasures, old parchment books and records. Sienkiewicz pored over them to get the background for his book. We passed the refectory—alas! he could not take us inside.

"Have you never once in all these years had any women guests?"

"Only once, when a Polish king was married here. (It was Michael Korybut Wisniowiecki—to Eleanor of Austria.) The queen and her ladies in waiting came into the room then."

"Well, if you could do that for a queen, can't you give permission to an American?"

"Ah, yes," he answered quickly, "if you'd only let us

know you were coming. It means sending to Rome and getting a permit from the Pope. It would take a month or longer. The next time you come—but why don't you go across the courtyard and look in the refectory window? The curtain's pushed back at one of them.''

Not much to see after all—long, narrow tables, no cloths, benches without backs, a reading desk, a large crucifix at the end of the room.

We walked around the bastions of the fort and looked across the moat (now dry and used for flower-beds), at the stations of the cross; not pictures here, but bronze groups, the work of a noted Polish sculptor. The last one, Christ in the tomb, with the Roman soldiers standing on guard, was banked with flowers of white and red, the colors of the Polish flag.

''It's too bad,'' Brother Wojciech was grieved, ''too bad that you could not come earlier. The eighth of September is one of the special days at Czestochowa. The people come by thousands—this year over three hundred thousand. You'd see then what this place means to Poles. And you'd see, too, beautiful costumes from every part of our country.''

''I'm sorry to have missed that; but,'' I added cheerfully, ''you must make up for it. You'll have to tell me just how they come and what they do.''

We were walking near the open-air altar, with glass sides, built up high so that every one can see when mass is celebrated there. He pointed to a street with long lines of trees.

"This is the road they come by, marching along, sometimes with a band, sometimes without any music, but singing; and this is the song they sing, a very old song in honor of the Virgin."

He threw back his head and sang a stanza for us; then seeing the look on our faces, a second stanza. Easy to imagine it taken up by hundreds of voices. Easy to picture the pilgrims coming along that street, with their banners and flags.

"Yes," he repeated, "it's a shame you couldn't have seen some pilgrims. This is where the prior, or one of the monks, comes out to welcome them. I'm always glad when that falls to me. They dip their banners in reply, sing a hymn or two, and then they all go into the church to see the picture."

"Have there been any miracles recently?"

"There was one, a year ago. A paralyzed man was cured during mass. He rose and walked away without any help. The chapel was crowded with people, all so excited we could scarcely quiet them. The prior sent out and asked for the man's name and address. Later he wrote to the head of that village and received a statement, duly signed and witnessed, saying that this man had lived there all his life, had gone to Czestochowa a cripple, and returned cured, and was well at that date."

We started up the stairs to the treasury. Brother Wojciech and I happened to be ahead. He stopped and held up his hand.

"Listen! Don't you hear it? Music!"

He peered out of the little window on the landing, and beckoned for me to join him. I could hear music, faintly, far away. I gazed out. I looked up into his face. He smiled—a happy smile that lighted up his eyes.

"For you," he said in German, "for you, madam. It is"—he peered out again and nodded—"yes, it is pilgrims come to Czestochowa."

I clasped my hands excitedly.

"Oh, never mind the treasury now. It can wait. Can't we go down and see them? Ten minutes—five minutes even."

"Certainly," explained Miss Interpreter, "he says he can take us down to a place where we can see them coming along the avenue and up to Jasna Gora, and hear the prior welcome them."

Down the stairs we hurried, across a courtyard, through a passageway, and out on to one of the bastions. There they were—pilgrims! Pilgrims coming to Czestochowa, with a brass band at their head, and flags and banners.

"How many?" I asked.

"More than five hundred," he estimated, "between five and six hundred."

"And where do they come from—can you tell?"

Just then the first ones came into sight and we could see them plainly. Even I, a foreigner, knew they were from Lowicz.

"Oh, oh!" I cried, "why, if you'd planned it especially for to-day, it couldn't have worked out better. From Lowicz—Lowicz!"

On that wonderful Sunday I spent in Lowicz, I'd seen at the most a couple of hundred peasants, and that counted the ones in modern dress. Here every single one, even the leaders, all the men, all the women, the two dozen boys and girls in the front of the procession were clothed in Lowicz stripes. Think of it—nearly six hundred gorgeous costumes, every one a Sunday best.

We went nearer and I counted the banners—eleven, besides the large Polish flag, and the small ones the children carried. I counted the ribbons on some of the girls' head-dresses—six, ten, one had fourteen, each about a yard long, hanging straight down her back. And every girl and woman had five or six strings of beads. Four women carried on long poles a little red covered platform with a loom, another four had a spinning-wheel. Four men had a plow, and still another group had brought a pyramid of wheat and rye. These, Brother Wojciech told us, they would have blessed during their stay—symbols of their every-day work.

Many of them had suitcases—cheap, imitation-leather ones. Some had knapsacks, some baskets, some awkward bundles of food. They had come by train, not on foot, a journey of perhaps four hours; they'd marched only the few kilometers from the station. They didn't look tired out, but elated, happy; they'd reached their goal.

Presently a white-robed figure appeared and everybody crowded up to hear the welcome. All the banners dipped over, once, twice, three times. Then slowly they filed into the church. It was of course too late for a mass, but the picture was opened for them, the choir was summoned for a short service.

We went back to the treasury, a large room with glass cases for displaying the gifts given through the centuries to the Madonna of Czestochowa. Sometimes we would all stop, breathless over the beauty of a cross or chalice; again arrested by a name—Sobieski's silver trays and his sword, a piece Kosciuszko made. Objects of gold and silver and precious stones; paintings; vestments embroidered with jewels; ornaments for altars; reliquaries and rosaries; kings' scepters, swords of Polish marshals and hetmans; orders and honors; porcelains and tall candle-sticks; what dealers would call "museum pieces," the gifts of kings and bishops and noble families, till as Brother Wojciech read off the names it sounded like a *Who's Who* of Poland.

One piece he talked a long time about—a huge monstrance given by the people as a thank-offering after the Swedish siege; so many kilos it weighed, so many thousand emeralds and diamonds, so many rubies and pearls. Here too we saw another "dress" for the picture in the chapel—it has five or six.

Just after the war when Poland was suffering from hunger and the children dying for lack of food, it was proposed that the nation confiscate the treasury of Czestochowa and sell these gifts. I don't suppose any one's ever tried to put their value into dollars, but they must be worth millions. The "dress" and crowns that were stolen were worth more than half a million (dollars, not *zlotys*). But after I'd heard the music and seen the miraculous picture and talked with Brother Wojciech, I rejoiced that the Hoover Commission saved the lives of the Polish children without robbing the Virgin of Czestochowa. And yet—and yet, if America had not been willing to help, had not been able to send supplies, wouldn't the Madonna have nodded her head and said, "Take them—take all my treasures and sell them for my children's sake?" Wouldn't she perhaps have left her chapel and appeared again in the sky, to the terror and rout of modern enemies with such names as Hunger and Neglect and Famine?

Coming out from the treasury we went again up to the organ loft and looked down into the chapel, now crowded with Lowicz peasants—a sea of color. On every face a look of utter devotion. No whispering or laughing. Not a bit of levity among them all. They'd come on a pilgrimage. Here and there, attracting no attention from the others, I saw peasants lying prone, their arms stretched out so that their bodies made a cross. Even in Lowicz there were suppliants, come to Czestochowa to beg the Virgin to grant a boon.

"Well," said Mrs. Sage as we bade Brother Wojciech good-by and started toward the motor, "this is my sixth visit and never before did I have such an interesting time, or learn so much. I think, Miss Humphrey, your fairy godmother must have waved her wand again. We all owe her a vote of thanks."

Miss Interpreter touched my arm and I guessed she

wanted me to lag behind. I walked very slowly and leaned over to hear what she was saying.

"Mrs. Sage thinks it was all owing to your fairy godmother. But I think"—she stopped and looked up into my face—"I think it was the good God who planned this day at Czestochowa. He wants you to write that chapter in your book."

CHAPTER XI

For More Than Seven Hundred Years

"I've been thinking over what you said," began my Polish friend who thought America had no problems, "and I was wrong. You do have problems. But there's a difference. None of your questions seems unsolvable, for they're comparatively new ones that you'll work out in a generation or two. With patience and good will on both sides, I'll bank on the United States to find the right answer. But in Poland——"

"In Poland problems are gray-headed?"

"No wonder discussions start with a hopeless feeling, when both sides come to the table with inherited prejudices that make it hard to get together, hard to make concessions. Our problems are old, old, old. The struggle between Poles and Germans began in the tenth century, if indeed it doesn't go back to Wanda, the daughter of Duke Krakus, who drowned herself in the Vistula rather than marry a Teuton prince. On the east there's been a long contest with Russia, and whether it was really ended in 1920 only the future can tell. And another serious question—the relations between Poles and Jews—dates from the thirteenth century."

"Wasn't it Casimir the Great who invited the Jews to Poland, because he was in love with Esther, a beautiful Jewess?"

"No, it was several reigns earlier—Boleslas the Pious, in the twelve-sixties, who gave them many privileges. What Casimir the Great did was to confirm these special privileges and extend them to the whole of Poland. Our country was known as 'the paradise for Jews,' because in other parts of Europe they were persecuted or merely tolerated; here they were welcomed, for we needed business men and shopkeepers. But neither king admitted them to citizenship. They were a separate group, apart from the peasants, from the country gentry, from the nobles. They made their own laws, had their own courts, their own schools, their own district to live in; and of course complete religious freedom. That was where Poland made a mistake. To-day, more than seven centuries later, they are not Poles. Their presence is a real problem."

I started out with the same feeling this Pole had about American questions—that with patience and good will Jews and Poles could find some solution; but the longer I stayed in Poland the more I realized that it's a very serious problem, far more than is evident on the surface.

A friend asked on my return if I saw any Jews in Poland. She might as well have inquired if I'd been to Poland. I saw them everywhere. One person out of every nine is a Jew. They go about labeled—by their long, black coats that reach nearly to the ankle, by their little black caps with narrow visors, by their stiff, corkscrew curls hanging in front of their ears—if they're orthodox; the semi-orthodox screw this hair up into a tight little curl and tuck it around their ears, much as the Chinese wore their queues inside their hats. The women too have a label—a brown wig. On Saturday the long coat is black satin, the hat of velvet with brown fur; an elderly and wealthy Jew in this dress makes an attractive picture indeed. The poor Jew affects a fur-trimmed hat and satin coat, but the cheap satin is sleazy, spotted with grease, frayed in the back where his heels kick against it; the fur looks mangy and aged. But if cap and wig and coat and curls had all been absent, I could have picked out the Jews readily. Of course there are some exceptions, but most of them are slight, undersized, frequently stoop-shouldered, with heads that seem too large for their bodies, giving them a grotesque appearance.

"Are the Jews giving up their distinctive dress?" I asked a Jewish lawyer.

"It is lessening. But, you know, about seventy per cent. of our people in Poland are orthodox and they feel that this Essene costume is obligatory. The Talmud says they must show themselves distinct from the Christians in food and dress."

"Is this a town with ninety-some per cent. of the people Jewish?" I asked a man in Stanislawow.

"Why, no. Perhaps forty per cent. Why?"

"Well," I replied, "as I've been about to-day, it seemed to me the Jews must be a hundred and ten per cent. I've seen almost nobody else on the streets."

"That's because they carry on their business on the streets, and Poles in their shops and offices. They talk

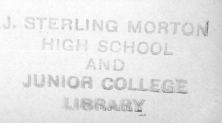

over things in public, they discuss and compare, quote prices and bargain; and the result is, they give the impression of being more numerous than they are."

Generally I went shopping with a Pole and of course went to Polish shops, but one day I happened to be with an Englishwoman who suggested looking for coat lining in a Jewish store. A pity to buy it then, she added, couldn't I wait till Monday?

"If you go very early, you can always get things for less on Monday morning. There's a tradition that if a Jew lets you leave on Monday without buying anything, he'll have bad luck all the week. You must say no decidedly and walk out; he comes running after you and says, 'At your price, lady.' "

I assured her I'd wait till Monday, to have the fun of such bargaining. She coached me as to what I was to do and say, but in the end went along to help; and it all worked out just as she'd said. His scissors were ready to cut off so many meters of my new lining when she stopped him. How much was it? He figured. Too much! The Amerikanka will give you this much. The bargaining began. At the right moment she turned to me, but I replied firmly, "No, no! So many *zlotys*—no more."

"But—lady——"

"No," and out I walked, very haughtily. We walked along slowly. She cautioned me not to turn around. If he shouldn't come, I thought regretfully, what a waste of time to go to another shop. My heart sank. We'd reached the deep archway opening from that courtyard to the street when she chuckled and whispered, "Here he comes!"

"*Prosze, pani—prosze, pani,*" (please, lady) he came running after us, breathless, hatless.

With sober faces, but laughing inside, we went back and made our purchase, with a saving of less than ten cents. He protested sadly that he was losing money.

"He isn't," she assured me when we were on the street again. "You paid enough. And if by any chance he is losing, the Jewish rule is to add the loss to the price you quote the next customer. That's why nothing is marked."

How much did I see of Jews and Jewish conditions in Poland? I lived a fortnight in Poznan, where the Jews are less than one per cent. of the population, I spent a day in Kazimierz where they're more than ninety-six per cent., and in towns in between. I went exploring in the ghettos. In Krakow and Warsaw I went to services in the synagogues, in other cities I hunted up old synagogues, interested in their architecture—the Goldene Rosa in Lwów is three hundred and forty-seven years old. Twice I went to Jewish cemeteries, and saw stone after stone with traditional emblems—the pitcher and bowl for a descendant of Levi, a crown (sometimes a crown with a pile of books) for a learned man.

In Warsaw, with a friend of the rabbi, I visited the Jewish museum (opened specially for me). I talked with the chairman at the O.R.T. headquarters, went to their technical schools and furniture factory. I went to public schools where all the boys (or all the girls) were

Jewish. I talked with teachers and principals, with lawyers and rabbis, with university professors and students. I made an honest effort to see all I could, to learn all I could; and yet I feel that I've only brushed the surface of what is a real problem for both Jews and Poles, separated by many barriers.

Perhaps this baffled feeling was due to the fact that I knew very few Poles with whom I could talk this over, or because I seldom talked more than once or twice with any Jews; or because of a little incident that came in my first month in Poland, and made me inclined to question every conclusion and doubt what I saw with my own eyes. How could I be sure that my impressions were half correct? For this is what happened in Warsaw:

One Friday I made an excuse to leave some Polish acquaintances, set off in a doroshka and went to the synagogue. I was early. A big crowd of men and boys in ordinary dress waited by the high gates that shut off the steps. I hung around on the outskirts and presently four Jews in long black coats and square hats unlocked the gates with huge keys. The crowd surged forward; some were admitted, others thrust back by the strong arms of the four. Much pushing and shoving—disorderly, undignified.

Two young men argued and tried to push by. A gatekeeper ran out and appealed to a policeman who shook his head and motioned with his stick. What a scene! I thought. Were these people Poles waiting till the gates were open, then rushing in to break up a Jewish service;

The rich Jew in a black satin coat and fur-trimmed velvet hat makes a
striking picture

Seventy per cent. of the Jews in Poland cling to their traditional costume,
which emphasizes their isolation

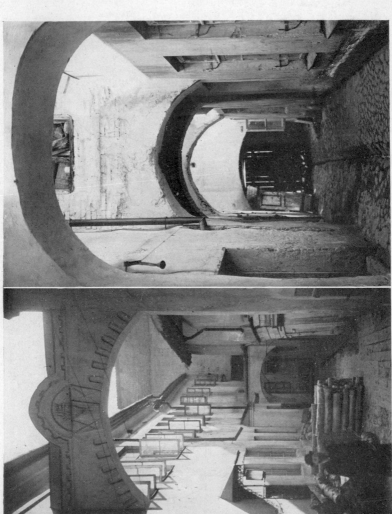

Photos by Jan Bułhak, Wilno

The ghetto, centuries old, with surface draining and congested housing

and the police, who are all Poles, would not interfere? Had I run into an anti-Semitic crowd that might quickly become a mob, with mob violence? Yet every one stood back respectfully for me.

"I have a letter to the rabbi, may I see him now or after the service?" I spoke in German to a man near the door. Afterward would be better. Then I asked about the crowd outside.

"It is always so—always so, every Friday," he replied sadly, but made no further comment.

I went into the synagogue—a huge room with round arches and barrel vaulting, with a narrow balcony on three sides. The pulpit was done in red; two seven-branched *menorah* (candelabra) with electric lights; seats marked with brass plates. No sooner had I sat down than some one came up and by gestures and a few words of Yiddish made me understand I must go up-stairs. Were all the seats on the floor reserved? Those in the balcony were labeled too. I hoped Sarah Rabinovitch wouldn't come, but I need not have felt anxious; only fifteen women appeared, scattered through the long balconies. I felt as if I were in the women's gallery of the House of Commons, only more so, for I could see nothing unless I stood up. Down-stairs the men—nine-tenths of them in ordinary clothes—walked about, shaking hands, taking off their hats to one another as if they were out-of-doors, and then putting them on again.

Every one rose. The four gatekeepers marched in, two rabbis in black robes and long white stoles embroidered in black, with square caps of black velvet; then two lay-men, as I thought, in Prince Alberts and silk hats, fine-looking and dignified. The service began—readings, chanting by a choir of about forty, unaccompanied; and all the time I was thinking, "Why, oh, why do the Poles want to interfere in a church service? A few did force their way in, but they aren't making any trouble. I can't even pick them out. Why? What does it mean?" and the more I thought, the more perplexed I was.

On Sunday I called on the rabbi and found him so pleasant that at last I screwed up my courage and asked him about the scene at the synagogue. His answer made me stare. The crowd I'd watched were not Poles but Jews, waiting for the gates to open so that they could go in to pray. It was a private synagogue, he added not without some pride, whose members buy their seats, and others are not admitted. Warsaw had other synagogues where they could go, and any number of little prayer-houses, each supported by a group of Jews.

"Those men want to come to the big fine synagogue, but they will pay nothing. No, no, madam, don't go back to America and report that you saw Poles forcing their way into a synagogue and the police looking on and doing noth-ing. Why, believe me, the Poles and the Jews are friends and get along very well together!"

The barrier between the two peoples is not a religious one. The Poles are tolerant in religious matters and have always been tolerant. Their country offered a refuge for the oppressed of all faiths. In the last few years there has been a marked improvement in the relations of the two groups. I think the Poles go out of their way now to avoid giving offense to the Jews. They do not hold either primaries or elections on Saturday. They have repealed all the old Russian laws that discriminated against the Jews, such as the one that required a special permission when a Jew wished to move from one city to another. There is no longer a fixed percentage of Jewish students in the universities, and already the results of this new regulation are marked—there are classes where the Jews outnumber the Poles!

When the priest goes twice a week to a public school for religious instruction, the Jewish children may go for a walk in the fresh air, or into another room to study; they do not remain, even as passive listeners. In public schools where most of the children are Jewish, the schedule provides time twice a week for religious instruction, given by the rabbis. In many cities school keeps six days a week, but Jewish children do not go on Saturday. They must do in five days what other groups do in six. In one school I visited, this is accomplished by cutting the lesson periods from fifty minutes to forty-five.

"Jewish children," commented the principal, "are gifted and learn very quickly. What they need isn't lessons, but training. As to holidays, we observe them all!"

The Poles are very strict about shops being closed on Sunday. The orthodox Jews are just as strict about closing Friday evening and Saturday. Many of them would be glad to sell on Sunday and argue that they're at a great disadvantage, in competition with storekeepers who have a six-day week; but this they are not allowed to do. Don't we do the same thing here in America?

Yet for all this tolerance in religious matters, the Jews say that anti-Semitism is always there and no one knows when it may break out (though they grant it is, in the last three or four years, less open and less sharp). To what is it due? Say some of the Jews, "It's a result of the old Russian laws that treated Jews and Poles differently. The Poles were encouraged to look down on us. And they still do. Unfriendliness is the outcome." Say some of the Poles, "What can you expect but unfriendliness? All the Jews trained in German or Russian schools learned a scorn of everything Polish. It'll take two or three generations to undo that teaching."

To what is it due? I think there are three causes. First, the social barrier between Poles and Jews. That exists in many countries, but it's unusually high in Poland because the Poles are exclusive. They're exclusive in the United States, even after they've lived here for years. There's no more social intercourse between Poles and Jews than between—well, between Poles and the German colonists that Bismarck planted in Poznan. Twice I met Poles in the seven Jewish homes I saw, never once Jews in perhaps fifty or sixty Polish homes. I can not tell whether my experience was the rule or the exception. I can only state what I myself noticed. But this is a matter of the personal equation, just as it is everywhere.

Second, it's a question of economics. The Jews were

invited into Poland and given special privileges because
they were business men, money-lenders, small shopkeepers. It was against the law for Poles to engage in trade.
The result was that Poles were on the land, Jews in the
towns. About 1850 the Poles set about creating a middle
class—nobles and gentry putting their sons into business,
the more intelligent of the peasants encouraged to start
stores for themselves. In large cities, in small towns and
villages they opened cooperative stores that sold a little of
everything. Putting capital into this movement was patriotic first and good business second: but the cooperatives
were so well managed that with part of the profits more
stores could be opened. But every new store meant loss of
trade for the Jews. Polish success with the cooperatives
meant in many cases Jewish bankruptcy. And they had
nothing else to turn to.

If the war had not come, if Poland were still divided into
three parts, a sharp business competition would have developed. To-day it's very keen, with all the world going
through a period of depression, with Russia not buying,
with farmers having a struggle to make ends meet. Where
the Jews have had the whole trade of a community for
generations, it's not surprising that they resent an association's opening a store and nursing it along till it gets
on its feet; and not surprising, either, that the Poles feel
it's patriotic to buy from Poles. This led to a wide-spread
boycott at the end of the war.

"No," Wanda would say when I'd stop before a window
that displayed something I wanted, "that's not a Polish

shop." Or, "I won't take you there—it's a Jewish store."

"How can I tell which are the Polish ones, since the names are no clue?" (For many of the Jews have changed their names and taken Polish ones, even the *ski* names which cost more.)

"Come Saturday. Stores open then are sure to be Polish."

With a few exceptions, Poland is a land of little shops. There are many tiny grocery stores, tiny dry-goods stores, small hardware stores, and so on—one room, always crowded. There are too many little shops for the amount of business done. How then can both Jews and Poles earn a living?

Nor are storekeepers the only group feeling a keen competition. A Katowice lawyer gave me this illustration: "Our town has too many lawyers. There's work enough, of the kind I do, to keep four men busy. How many do you think we are, Jews and Poles together?"

"Eight," I suggested, "each earning half a living?"

"Eight—eight wouldn't be so bad. There are twenty."

This overcrowded economic situation is true for both groups, but the Jew feels it more in the business world because storekeeping is born into him and it's comparatively new for the Pole. As in other countries of Europe, the land is overcrowded; there are too many little stores struggling along to support a large family, too many little farms, too many men, too few jobs; even in normal periods; when business depression comes and unemployment increases, the situation looks hopeless. Is there any sign of improvement in Poland?

Yes. Little by little, the Jews are getting into other lines of work than running shops. Jewish professional men—doctors, lawyers, engineers, executives—are increasing. Jews are professors in the universities, they're in the various ministries, in diplomatic posts. A Jew represents Poland at Geneva. One of the Polish ministers at Washington was a Jew. In Wilno and Warsaw I went to the trade schools where Jewish boys are being made into electricians and locksmiths and motion-picture operators as well as factory workmen. I thought the buildings crowded, inconvenient, old; the work done in them excellent.

"Are there jobs waiting for these boys when they've finished your course? Can you place them all?" I asked one of the instructors.

"That depends on what calls come in. Some Polish ladies would never let a Jewish workman repair a doorbell, no matter how good an electrician he might be. There's work for the majority of our boys and there'll be more when the school is better known. Already it is recognized by the Ministry of Education as coming up to standard."

And in the third place this undercurrent of hostility is partly a question of patriotism. To an American, used to seeing one or two generations change a group of foreigners into citizens, it is simply amazing that after seven hundred years in Poland the Jews are not Poles. Asked their nationality, they answer "Jewish" as unhesitatingly as the Poles who lived under the czar used to reply, "We are Poles," and never "We are Russians." In England and France, in the United States they have kept their religion and taken on a new citizenship; this has never been the case in Poland.

"After the Partitions," a Krakow Jew explained to me, "we were loyal to the existing governments. But often loyalty to Austria and loyalty to Poland didn't coincide. Every man had to choose. If a Jew sided with Austria, the Poles argued that he was therefore disloyal to Poland, and utterly unpatriotic. The same with Russia, with Germany. And that feeling lasts over now."

During the war both sides used the Polish Jews as interpreters. The Poles charge that some of them acted as spies and sold their information. Too many deaths they lay at the door of Jewish informers. In every land war breeds suspicion, and this is all too recent to be readily forgotten.

Again during the struggle with the Bolshevists, when the Poles were devoting every energy to self-defense, straining every nerve to save their country, they charge that the Jews were passive. To-day this counts against them.

But one of the most hopeful signs of the new Poland— hopeful for both sides—is the fact that now, for the first time in seven centuries, Jews are beginning to be proud of Poland. Not that it's come completely—that's too much to expect—but there are straws showing how the new wind is blowing. A university professor who had many Jewish students in his classes set himself to the task of getting them interested in Polish literature and Polish history, and of passing this on to the boys and girls who would be their pupils.

"I've just had a letter from one of my former students," he reported, "a young Jewess who's teaching in a boys' gymnasium in Wilno—nearly all Jewish boys. She's giving them generous doses of our literature till they're fired with enthusiasm, proud to belong to the nation that produced Mickiewicz and Sienkiewicz. She's making Poles of them!"

Nor is this an isolated instance. While I was in Krakow I went to a public school over in the Kazimierz—that's now a part of the city, but used to be a separate town; it was founded by Casimir the Great as a home for the Jews—that explains its name; all these many years it's been a Jewish district, and to-day practically no one else lives there. I had a note to the principal of a boys' school, but he did not know when I was coming; I am sure I saw just the every-day work, not dressed up to put on any "front" for an American visitor.

There were three hundred boys, from seven to fourteen, every one Jewish. Not one had on the long black coat. Not more than ten, said the principal, had side curls. At recess in the court I looked for them, but couldn't pick out a single lad with curls in front of his ears.

"I'll hunt around and find you a boy who has them," one of the teachers offered, and presently called three boys over to where we stood. Not regulation curls but a reminder of them, I thought, hair coming down in front of the ears about an inch, cut straight across at the bottom; on one lad it was wavy, on the others straight. "What will happen? By the time the boys are grown, say at twenty, their curls will be lost altogether. In the school nothing's ever said about them."

Every room in the building had Polish pictures, purchased from a fund raised by the boys themselves—those who can give a *zloty* a month. I saw a colored print of Kosciuszko enrolling peasants in his army, and asked if a boy would tell me the story. He might have been telling of Nathan Hale or Washington crossing the Delaware from his dramatic manner; the whole class listened and excitedly volunteered additions; of course I couldn't understand a word, but I could see how much the story meant to them. After seven years in that school they'll feel themselves half Poles—or at least a quarter. A few generations and why shouldn't they become as Polish as Jewish children are French in Paris and British in London?

"It is necessary also to change the attitude of some of the Polish children," the principal said when we discussed this point, "and I see little hints of this already. Not long ago I paid a visit to a Christian school and in one class a picture was being discussed—a woman in front of a cottage, wounded soldiers—Polish from their uniforms—a Jew in his black coat pointing, warning. 'What is he saying?' I asked. 'He's warning them—they must hide in the cottage—the enemy is coming.' And then the little girl added, 'A Jew also can be a good patriot!' I thanked the teacher and the child."

[270]

PRIVATE JEWISH SCHOOLS

Those boys were having all their lessons in Polish. Were they absolutely neglecting Hebrew, I asked. No, many of them were having regular instruction, but out of school hours—just as some children in America have French. Every one begins German in the fifth grade. Hebrew is not taught in the school.

The Polish Jews are divided into two groups, I learned: orthodox and Zionist; and each group maintains a school in Krakow. One of these private schools I saw; the boys go from nine to one and two to eight, and of this time they have Polish lessons for an hour and a half (that's required by the government) and all the rest in Hebrew. They all had long black coats and side curls. The rabbis might have stepped out of Rembrandt etchings, in their long robes, their fur-trimmed hats of velvet, with their long gray beards.

"The Zionists," they told me in answer to my questions, "insist on having their own schools. The Poles are tolerant and permit them. Some teachers and priests welcome the separate Jewish school, for they feel that Jewish boys and girls are not a good influence in the public school."

"Yes," said the principal of the boys' school, "occasionally boys come to us from one of those private schools. One this year—I'll point him out to you. He had to take examinations, of course, and I fancy he had a tutor; he was a bright lad and went into the class where, according to his years, he belonged. Ordinarily they lose at least a year in the transfer, for they've been taught by rote—not

[271]

the best mental training. What fraction of Jewish boys are now in public schools? About sixty per cent., and every year it is increasing."

I went also to a girls' school. Three hundred and sixty-five girls, and three hundred and sixty-four were Jewish; the one lone child was a Protestant! They were from six years old up to fifteen. In one room—the sixth grade, I think—the teacher asked for me how many were learning Hebrew in the afternoon; six of them; and this, she said, was about the proportion all through the school. Girls who finish here and want to go to the Zionist gymnasium must study Hebrew for several months.

Educating daughters is comparatively new, one teacher explained. Until recently the Jews paid little attention to them. A boy must be devout, and that meant going to school; beginning Hebrew at six or seven, sometimes at four, for three or four hours every day; from the time he was thirteen, a daily visit to the prayer-house; an enormous amount of religious instruction. A girl, on the contrary, must be merely good; must stay at home and learn a little from her mother; where the mother was a real teacher, well and good; where she wasn't, what did it matter? Girls were brought up with the idea of marrying early and having homes of their own; they seldom went to the synagogue; even now most of them go only a few times each year, for feast days—and always, added this teacher, with a perfectly sober face, always on Marshal Pilsudski's name-day.

"Is your school making Poles out of these girls?"

"A start," was her honest answer. "Perhaps one out of four will make a good citizen of Poland. The very poor are never good Poles, and as you can see for yourself we have in our school many more poor than rich."

This new attitude of Jews and Poles is not limited to Poland itself, but has spread to America. The Good Will Committee recently formed in New York has both Poles and Jews as members and has already begun to make cooperation wipe out the barriers of the past.

Interesting as I found the ghettos, as much fun as it was to go poking around in twisting medieval streets and alleys, peering into courts, walking slowly when I came to open doorways, sometimes I fear staring when I met some very rich or some very poor Jews, I found that half an hour was as long as I could stay. Now my sense of smell is subnormal. For the average tourist, ten minutes would be enough. Acute smellers had better get glimpses from the street-car and be content. For the ghettos I saw in Warsaw, in Wilno, Lublin, Krakow are not only ugly and dreary, they're smelly—an ancient, medieval odor plus a sour odor. The streets are dirty (even in Warsaw), they're crowded too, and with people who are not always clean. Not that the houses are small or poorly built; but they're discolored, squalid, neglected—unattractive to the maximum degree.

I've heard it said that the Jews in Poland dress in black because it doesn't show the dirt. Any woman who's ever been in mourning knows how false an idea that is. But the Jews don't seem to mind spots on their black coats.

[273]

"This is how he eats," said a Jew, describing his grandfather in the Warsaw ghetto, "with his fingers mostly—no napkin—wiping his mouth and his dripping chin on his left sleeve. And he never washes the sleeve!"

Oh, I know there's much to be said on the other side. Cleanliness is ninety per cent. a matter of economics and adequate income. I can not wonder at their condition when I think how much physical care and beauty cost. I know that the Jews in Poland are nearly all wretchedly poor, facing a terrible struggle just to exist. I know that nearly all of them live in very crowded rooms, without baths; that they must carry up many flights of stairs every drop of water for cooking, laundry, bathing. But many Poles live under the same conditions, yet give no such impression of permanent dirt as do the Jews. If one of these Jews sat down by me in the street-car I would move or stand up; what with the dirt, the smell, the fear that something would crawl over on to me, I couldn't ride next them, but cringed and drew away as I never do from negroes. There's something sinister about them.

If I had a mint of money to use for Polish Jews, I'd put some into the new trade schools and special text-books, and all the rest into better housing. New apartment-houses, and remodel the old ones, with running water everywhere. And now I learn that Poland is planning this very thing—a plan which may take years to work out, that will banish the ghetto, save for a bit of picturesque architecture here and there, and provide adequate housing for the Jews, who will be on the way to becoming Poles.

[274]

CHAPTER XII

I Wish We Could Borrow from Poland——

Some things we Americans do better than the Poles. Often and often the tourist finds himself longing for them. But in some things they're far ahead of us. If we could only borrow these ideas and put them into daily practise.

What things?

Here are a few I chanced to notice.

I wish we'd borrow the clever way streets are marked in the city of Poznan. At every intersection you see the name of the street, clearly posted in blue letters on white enamel, and underneath the numbers in that block, with an arrow. Like this:

Ulica Klasztorna   and opposite,   Ulica Klasztorna
80—72 ←≪   ≫→ 68—54

Think how often you come to a corner on a cold day, or a sizzling hot day, or a busy day when every minute counts. No one in sight to ask. Is 247 to right or left? The Poznan street-sign answers your question.

And speaking of numbers, there's a Polish custom of lighting house numbers at night. Poles aren't particularly proud of it, for it's a hangover from the old Russian police regulations. When I spoke of it Jadwiga exclaimed, "Ah, but your streets are so much better lighted than ours! You don't need special lights for your house numbers." But don't we? How many streets do you know

[275]

in your home town, where the numbers are plain at dusk?

Just how are Polish numbers arranged, you want to ask. The most common way is a triangle of glass, with an electric light inside, with the figures painted on two sides so that they show in both directions, and the name of the street in small letters below.

"What is this? Does it tell about Valery Lukasinski?" I never could pass a Polish tablet. That morning in Zamosc I stopped before a notice on the brick wall of the Russian prison. We'd been talking of the great patriot who spent more than fifty years in prisons, all over Poland, who lived here for a year and a half.

"No, it's only a warning—what you call a no-trespassing sign. This building's under the protection of the National Commission. After the war the people would gladly have torn down every brick and stone, but the Commission stepped in and said this wing was historic and must be saved. Fifty, a hundred years from now it'll be very precious."

I heard more of this National Commission with a name I couldn't pronounce. On the excursion from Wilno to Troki we rowed out to an island in a lake, to see the ruins of a castle and fort, built in the fourteenth century before Lithuania was united with Poland. I was amazed at the tidiness of this isolated spot, at the care with which each chimney and archway was looked after; yet we'd paid an admission of less than three cents.

"Why, it's under the Commission," explained the

[276]

ancient caretaker. "No one would dare touch a stone, there's a big fine for the least destruction."

This was the case, I found, in every part of the country. Under its sheltering wings the National Commission for Preserving the Antiquities of Poland takes palaces, forts, and city walls, or their ruins, battle-fields and places with some historic interest, buildings remarkable for architecture, or even for some rare detail of their architecture—like the house in Lwów where they showed me kitchen windows with three steps up and deep stone frames carved by a master hand; and a country house where I slept under an old-style Polish roof, nowadays as rare as a white eagle; and the granary on the M.'s farm near Krakow.

"The special thing about it is the roof," said Pani M. "Hand-made shingles, probably made right here on the estate some centuries ago; but not to be had to-day except in one distant village in the mountains, where one or two old men know how to cut them. A new roof'll cost us six thousand *zlotys*, and we could buy ordinary shingles for one thousand. But—the Commission has issued an order that we can't put a modern roof on a medieval granary. They've listed it as one of the antiquities of Poland."

What a to-do we make when one of our historic spots is threatened! With a frantic rush, because some one's eager to tear it down and build a sky-scraper or an addition to a factory, we get a special bill introduced into Congress, patriotic organizations are stirred to action, the mails are flooded with letters begging senators to save a house or a site; or we try raising the money by subscription, which means that the same interested persons pay time after time; more than once valiant efforts have failed and precious buildings been lost for ever. Private initiative is slow and sometimes ineffective.

Once Mount Vernon was in danger, saved by the energetic action of a group of women. How much would Massachusetts give to-day, if the John Hancock house hadn't been torn down to make room for a publishing plant? It took years to collect the money for Betsy Ross's little house in Philadelphia. The big trees in California were rescued at the eleventh hour. There are no funds to furnish Alexander Hamilton's country house, now that it's safe from destruction.

But in Poland all such matters are cared for by this National Commission. It has a regular budget to work with, and when special needs arise it asks for an increased amount, meanwhile notifying the owners of a threatened site that palace or field or ruin must not be desecrated.

Think how often a hurried appeal goes out: Rally to save this! We must not lose that! Think of all we have lost through indifference and neglect. Before it's too late, why can't we have a National Commission to save what will some day be our antiquities?

That's not a practical scheme, you argue, for a country as huge as the U.S.A. Then borrow again from the Poles, for their Commission divides its field into twelve districts, each looking after local antiquities. Why not forty-eight state commissions to preserve our treasures?

I wish our mail service would borrow some details from Poland's. Watch the man collecting mail from our letter boxes—so many motions to go through as he unlocks the box, takes out handful after handful of letters, and at last reaches up to make sure none are caught in the box. The Polish collector rides up on his motorcycle, snaps open his bag and fits it to the bottom of the box; a gentle push, the bottom slides back, all the mail falls into the bag; a pull, and he is off. No chance for letters to fall out. No getting wet in a storm.

But before he starts, the Pole slips into its frame on the front of the box a white enamel disk telling the hour of the next collection. You don't have to consult a long table of hours for week-days and hours for Sundays, to decide if you must go to the post-office with important mail. One glance at the disk, which is rain-proof, as well as always legible.

Have you ever been so unfortunate as to have some one steal part of a package, sent by parcel post? In Poland you go to the post-office with a valuable something, taking along scissors, twine, sealing wax and matches. You open the package for inspection; then across the room at a long table you wrap, tie and seal it. Impossible to add anything to its contents, impossible for anything to be taken out of your box, for you put on as many seals as you like. (My suitcase came, unlocked, with no less than eight huge red seals; and came intact.) If you tip the man, say two cents, he'll do this for you.

This wouldn't do in America? You're thinking of the

afternoon rush with parcel post? Well, limit such packages to the forenoon.

I wish the clerks who sell stamps passed out with the stamps a moistened sponge in a glass bowl, as is done in Poland. How shocked bystanders were when I licked mine! They gestured to the wet sponge and cried "Unhygienic!" in three languages. I laughed to myself at the idea of getting a hygiene lesson from Poles, who never wrap their bread and never—oh, heaps of things! But their sponge for stamps is a good scheme.

And one more thing in the Polish post-office. When two holidays come in succession—Sunday and Monday, say—letters are delivered on the second day.

One February day I was walking in the Planty in Krakow—the Planty's a long and narrow boulevard that encircles the old town, where once stood the city walls—and coming to a cross-street I started over when suddenly, out of nowhere, appeared a taxi, almost on top of me. I threw up my arm, stepped back, and just as the dexterous chauffeur swerved to the left, missing me by the narrowest of margins, I lost my balance and went down in the snow and slush.

The chauffeur came running back, very white and scared, to ask if I were hurt. His middle-aged passenger climbed out to reassure himself that they hadn't struck me.

"Thank you, I'm all right—just a bit wet and spattered."

Off they drove. But the crowd of spectators grew and grew, all talking at once. What was the trouble? The taxi knocked you down? Where does the lady live? What does she speak—no Polish? French? German? Ah, the lady speaks English; who can interpret for the lady? Ask her where she lives.

Mechanically I repeated the address, refused a cab some one had summoned, and had walked a block or two when a voice at my elbow said, "Please, madam, this officer is a special policeman. Will you write your name in his note-book?" I answered his questions as I scribbled my name—no, I wasn't hurt, it was my fault far more than the chauffeur's, I wasn't English but American— walked back to my pension, tidied myself, and dismissed the matter from my mind.

Not so that special policeman, whom some spectator had sent for as soon as they learned I was not a Pole. A week later an imposing official of Krakow called on me. Alas! I wasn't in.

"You never told us you'd been knocked down by a taxi!" my landlady said reproachfully. "But we heard about it this morning. The city has taken the matter up. I was to tell you this particularly: already that chauffeur has been severely reprimanded, officially reprimanded, for not tooting his horn. Now, what do you want to do— bring suit against him or against the taxi company, and get damages? The city of Krakow offers you a lawyer. Here's the card of the man you're to consult. They wish you to know everything will be done for you, and with no charge. There is," she finished proudly, "a special department for the protection of foreigners."

"But if I don't wish to bring suit—if I wasn't really hurt—if the chauffeur wasn't to blame?"

"Oh, in that case," with a Polish shrug of her shoulders, "you do nothing at all. The matter will drop."

But it didn't drop. A few weeks later I received a summons to appear in court, spent an hour listening to other cases, heard the chauffeur and his passenger tell their stories, and added my testimony, exonerating the man and proving to the judge that I was alive and well. The special policeman lost his case and in the corridor outside the courtroom the anxious taxi-driver kissed my hand as it had never been kissed before. And all the time I was thinking, "A special department for the protection of foreigners. What it would mean if we had that in America!"

I wish we could borrow the old Polish custom of having a President of the City, who is the social head of the government. This is a very great honor—and it should be. The President is usually an elderly, white-haired gentleman, very dignified, who knows how to wear a frock-coat and gray gloves in the morning, or evening dress, who makes an excellent impression when he speaks or presides. The position is for life, though if the people are displeased there is a way to get rid of him and choose another. The actual supervision of city affairs is in the hands of a group of vice-presidents serving a few years.

THE NATIONAL COAT OF ARMS

How many times, at banquets, at important public meetings, our good citizens have hung their heads in shame at the impression made by some politician! You remember the tale of the mayor's wife who turned to Elizabeth of Belgium with "Queen, you've said a mouthful!" New York City has indeed recognized this need and has a Committee for the Reception of Distinguished Visitors. Why not go one step farther and have a social head, a President of the City?

Why don't we use our national coat of arms? In Poland whatever belongs to the national government is labeled with the white eagle. Every postman has it on his cap, every railroad employee, the customs officials, and many others. It's used for all sorts of decorations— on banners, in processions.

I wish too our cities had emblems and used them. Is there a special celebration? Torun puts out the city flag with its coat of arms, Warsaw displays a siren, Krakow the three towers, Lwów a lion. You see it in shop windows, on private houses and city buildings—the symbol of the city; and the citizens are immensely proud of it— and well they may be, for many of them are centuries old and each detail has a story.

But, protests some eagle-screamer, we don't have heraldry in America, it isn't democratic. Why shouldn't we have city emblems, without calling them coats of arms? Something democratic, local, distinctly American. New York's flag, with beavers and windmill, sailor and Indian,

[283]

shows history at a glance. Why not small towns as well?

I wish all our City Halls had beautiful assembly-rooms, as is the case everywhere in Poland. (I know of only one in the United States and it isn't used by the people.) The room belongs to the citizens, not to the mayor and council only; and under certain restrictions they are free to use it—and they do. For what kind of meetings? In Krakow the speeches on the hundred-and-fiftieth anniversary of Pulaski's death were given in the Town Hall. In Warsaw the Polish-American Club had a celebration on the Fourth of July. If in neither case could I follow the speeches, it was worth going to see the paneled walls and the portraits of famous Poles, a fitting background for the robe of the archbishop and the Polish officers with all their decorations. Why don't our people use our City Halls? But first, we must make the room beautiful.

I wish we had in many states, in many cities, tombs of Unknown Soldiers. Poland has hers in Warsaw—not far away in a military cemetery, as we buried our man at Arlington, but as in Paris, in the very heart of the city where thousands are passing every day, the men always taking off their hats, the women stopping for a moment by the flickering flame, where a sentinel paces slowly up and down. Wilno too has an Unknown Soldier, and Krakow, and Lwów, and I don't know how many other places. For every patriotic event it gives a special place for the people to gather, a tangible something that embodies their sacrifices. It seems a comfort to them to put flowers and wreaths there, and candles. Is one Unknown Soldier sufficient for the whole United States?

Last year a Polish city asked the Ministry of the Interior for a loan of six millions—dollars, not *zlotys*. (Perhaps you'd like to know what it was for? A sewer. Three times the citizens had collected money for this purpose, and three times the Russian governor took the money, went to St. Petersburg, and bought himself a title and honors.) The Ministry sent a committee to study the situation, and this was their report:

"You need a modern sewerage system, it's true. But you're spending too much money. You have too many city employees. For the work of a city this size, you should have seventeen hundred; and how many have you on the pay-roll? Two thousand, three hundred. Get rid of six hundred and then we'll take the matter up with you again."

An American city takes its bond issue to a syndicate. Do they ever study the local situation and point out that the city's wasting its cash in padded pay-rolls, and they must cut down expenses before they can get new bonds marketed? Why not?

I wish it was as easy to find the way around in our railroad stations as in Polish ones. Theirs are much larger than ours, for they have waiting-rooms for three classes, many ticket windows, and at least two restaurants—everybody eats and drinks while he waits for a train. I seldom had to ask my way in a station; arrows and Roman numerals directed me to a certain platform, through a passage and up this stairway. Cars are labeled on the outside and also in the corridor. Trains use the same tracks day after day, so the signs are permanent. And by the way, why don't our railroad tickets have price and distance printed on them?

I liked too the Polish scheme for marking street-car stops. Experts in traffic say our cars waste time by stopping too often. Polish busses and trams have regular stations, almost too far apart, I thought sometimes, for comfort. And how much a station tells you. There's an arrow at the top showing the direction for cars on that side of the street; and a list of all the cars that stop there, with their itineraries; in some places they're marked with numbers, in others with letters, but any tourist can understand "Tram M" or "Tram 7." Wouldn't that be easier than explaining to a stranger in the New York subway, "Your train is marked 'Broadway—Van Cortlandt Park' "? What a help it would be in Boston or Chicago or St. Louis!

A tourist who hasn't learned any Polish can consult his map and see if bus H will take him out to Lazienki or to the Place of the Three Crosses, near the house where he's invited for tea, or to the Stare Miasto. And some of these signs in Warsaw are actually revenue-producing; triangles perhaps five feet high, the three surfaces divided into oblongs for advertisements, the tramway using one or two spaces; under the list of trams you find cigarettes or soap or furniture, shown in colors on glass, with electric lights inside. No, they don't take up valuable space, they're not in the street, but up on the sidewalk.

Warsaw's clean streets amazed me. They're cleaned at night by machines, I learned, the men I saw working in the daytime were just doing the extras—of course the main streets in a city of a million people couldn't go for twenty-four hours without attention. Why were some men in uniform and others not? Those in ordinary clothes are the unemployed; the city must take care of them anyway, why shouldn't they do something in return?

"But away from the business center the streets are just as tidy, and the parks too. How do you manage there?"

"The janitor in every house is responsible for the street in front. He must keep it as clean as he finds it in the morning—pick up papers, and so on. If he is slack, the policeman speaks to him. And in the park, if you drop a piece of paper—a tram ticket or a wrapping from a sweet—you must pay a fine of one *zloty,* and in Poland one *zloty* is quite a sum! The people have been educated to save their papers—you'll often see them holding them till they come to a basket; and the baskets are more numerous than I saw in your American parks, and better-looking too."

Going along the street in Krakow, on our way to an

eleventh-century church, I spied a sign on a small house and stopped my companion to ask, "What does it say, please? I can make out one word—school. Surely this isn't a school, this little house?"

"No, it's just an office. The sign says, 'Advice given here about schools in Krakow.' There are nowadays so many schools," she explained when I looked very puzzled, "elementary schools and gymnasiums, technical schools, special schools for art and commerce and trades, for this and for that. Many parents don't know about them. They can come here and ask where to send a boy, or a girl, who has some problem to be worked out."

A good idea for us?

I wish some of our private schools in cities could borrow something from the Zamoyski Gymnasium in Warsaw, a private day-school with a thousand city boys. Some miles out in the country it owns a plot of ground. A man with three sons in the school gave them the house. Little by little they've equipped it with beds and blankets, tables and chairs. The boys go out in groups with their masters, sometimes staying for two or three days. They dig and plant and harvest in the garden and fields, they have botany lessons and nature study at different seasons of the year.

All the schools in Krakow, where space was limited by the city walls, are built flush with the sidewalk and have only small courts, crowded at recess. There is no adequate playground space. Why not, suggested Dr. Jordan, a park for games and sports on the edge of town? It

Photo by Jan Bułhak, Wilno

The ghetto may look intriguing with its dark winding ways, but it is smelly with a sour medieval smell

Photo by Jan Bulhak, Wilno

The Poles have a plan—it may take years to work it out—to banish the ghetto, save for a bit of picturesque architecture here and there

took time to convert people to his idea, but to-day the Dr. Jordan Park is a reality. There are football and basketball spaces, for this game and that, a central building for supplies. Most of the youngsters can't afford street-car fare, but meet at school and march out, singing part of the way.

- The bell rings. Boys line up—and girls—and answer to roll-call. The teacher signs for so many balls or bats, rackets or bean-bags, and two youngsters proudly carry them at the head of the line. Off they march to their assigned plot. Some teachers are specials, working from four to seven, with a different group each day; some, particularly with the younger children, are the regular teachers from their schools. It isn't voluntary, it's required twice a week. I watched a third grade playing a merry game where they tried to hit a boy with a large soft ball; then a Polish version of prisoners' base; then volley ball, tag in various forms, sheep and wolf. I looked at the flushed faces of those young women and thought Jordan Park was as good for them as for the children.

Where adequate space for athletics is too costly in our city schools, why couldn't our Boards of Education and of Parks cooperate and give us Jordan Parks?

The close of school in Poland marks the beginning of pupils' excursions. With one or two teachers thirty, forty, fifty of them start off on a trip of four days or a week, to see another section of their country. The three partitioning powers didn't want the Poles traveling back and forth and made it extremely difficult; they refused

[289]

passports or delayed giving them, or charged exorbitantly. It's not to be wondered at that many Poles said to me, "Why, you've seen far more of Poland than I have!" But this generation of boys and girls can't grow up ignorant of their country. All summer long I met groups of them listening to a teacher, taking notes in a museum, eating in an outdoor restaurant, waiting in a station, walking two by two through a medieval marketplace toward their lodgings.

How can they afford it, I wondered. They travel amazingly cheaply. The railroad gives them a third-class car and they pack themselves in. Sometimes two boarding schools exchange and the children sleep in each other's dormitory; or barracks are offered if the soldiers are away on field service; or a monastery or convent takes them in—for two cents a night. A trip may cost as much as five dollars, many cost far less. Museums are free or half price.

The Ministry of Education has worked out a scheme for these excursions, dividing Poland into seven districts. Each year a class visits one and at the end of their elementary schooling they will have seen practically all of Poland. And what a good time they have—singing often as they march along, window-gazing from the train, seeing the very places they've learned about in history lessons, getting to know their own country. Incidentally the teachers too are learning by this traveling.

A fine plan, but not practical at all, you argue, in our land where distances are so great and cost of living so high. Why not try it out? Some railroads would co-operate, with the idea that boy and girl travelers will make a greater traveling public in a few years. In proportion American parents have more to spend for such a luxury than Polish parents. Many children I saw in Poland had saved up the money, one *zloty* at a time.

There are little things I wish we could borrow, too—the uniform of Girl Scouts in Poland, gray; it's far more becoming than khaki, and looks well with a tie of green, red, orange or blue.

—the little circles of glass behind their electric-light switches; easier to clean than metal, more attractive whether the wall is papered or painted.

—the shower baths in the basement of a public school; that part of the building had a separate entrance and was open all summer long for the children of that school and their parents.

—the list of tenants, posted at the entrance of every apartment-house, with the number of the apartment. In one city the address of the nearest telegraph office was posted here also.

—what the newest Polish houses have in their bathrooms—hot and cold water running into the tub through one faucet, with a thermometer.

—linen napkin cases in a Polish pension (or are there no boarding-houses left in America?); more sanitary than rings; between meals nothing touches your napkin.

I wish—oh, I wish——

CHAPTER XIII

STRAIGHTENING OUT POLISH HISTORY

FOR all my reading up before I sailed, I found out on the voyage that my acquaintance with Polish history was hazy and mixed. The only things that stood out in my mind were the things I'd known before—what most Americans know: Sobieski at Vienna, plotting and intriguing at the election of every king, the Partitions, Kosciuszko, Countess Potocka writing of Napoleon at Warsaw, the hopeless insurrections. All the rest was vague, dateless.

Now in Italy, France, England, tourists lose out if they haven't a pretty clear idea of the history; and it's easy enough to get it, for there are books galore. How would I get along in Poland?

Strange to say, I had no trouble at all with the geography. Shaped something like a frying-pan with a short handle, Poland has four terraces from west to east: the seacoast—sand, marsh, many lakes; the wide plain ("the land of the plain" is the translation of the name Poland); plateaus; mountains, with oil-fields and salt mines; and in every part forests. Warsaw, the capital, about in the center; an important city in each corner—Wilno, Lwów, Krakow, Torun. Add to these Gdynia on the Baltic, Lodz, Poznan and Katowice, and the lesson was over. Not difficult to fix in my mind.

As to the history, there was no cause to worry. It didn't matter an iota whether I knew kings, battles, treaties, marriages, dates or not. Poland teaches you her history on the spot, in the most fascinating way imaginable! People, places, events began to fit themselves into a framework and stayed there unforgettably. It came gradually, a touch here, a fortnight later more in another city, a third bit in a museum or from some children, and behold! one day I saw the model for a *Procession to the Wawel* in which the sculptor gave a résumé of Polish history— kings and queens, priests, university men, the Polish folk, led by Destiny; to my surprise and delight, I found I knew them all. Order out of chaos in my mind. What had been hazy and mixed was now as clear as crystal. The story was no less wonderful and romantic, but no longer intricate beyond understanding.

"It was an old Polish custom," my university student explained the frescoes in the Poznan cathedral, "to cut a boy's hair on his seventh birthday. Here you see the lad standing shyly by his mother; the father greets two guests and offers them bread; one blesses it, the other holds up a cross—they are angels. This boy is Piast, the first of the long line of Piast princes. A few miles from Warsaw you'll see the ruined towers of one of their castles.

"And on this side is Mieczyslaw, the first king of Poland, accepting Christianity. His wife, a princess from Bohemia, is kneeling and the bishop is laying the first stone of this church. He was the fifth of the Piasts, I think; anyway I'm sure of the date—963. Now jump to the year 1000. Otto III—yes, the Holy Roman Emperor—kneels at the tomb of St. Wojciech (St. Adalbert you call him in English), the patron saint of Poland. From Poznan to Gniezno it's fifty kilometers, and the emperor went all that way on foot, like a pilgrim, for the great love he bore to Wojciech, his friend.''

Wojciech became a very real person instead of a misty, far-away saint, when I spent a day in Gniezno. The verger took me into every chapel—about two dozen!—and made me look at monuments and tombs galore; but if he hadn't been so thorough I might have missed the doors at a side entrance, and they alone were worth the trip. Roman work, he announced proudly, from the early thirteenth century, the most beautiful specimen in Poland; the panels tell the story of the good St. Wojciech—his baptism, at prayer, made a priest, crossing in a ship to East Prussia, preaching to the heathen, here they put him to death, the king offers for the body its weight in gold, they weigh the gold (notice, lady, the primitive scales) and put in more and more—always too little, till at last a poor woman approaches and throws in one *grosz* (that's a tenth of a cent) and it balances exactly, then the funeral procession and the burial in this church.

''Wojciech was bishop of Prague,'' he went on as we walked to the center of the nave where lies the body of this missionary-martyr, ''and carried the new faith into Hungary, then into Poland and East Prussia. His death made a great furore in Europe—the world was aghast.

The king of Poland ransomed the body. The emperor came to pray at his tomb. Who are the silver figures holding up the casket? Priest, peasant, nobleman, merchant—that you can tell from the fur on his dress—every class does honor to Poland's patron saint."

In the market-place in Krakow is the tiny little church of St. Wojciech, built on the spot where he preached; a very old building, I could tell, for I had to go down five or six steps; the level of the market-place is to-day so much higher than in medieval times.

Months later I was invited to tea at a country house a few miles from Krakow and the daughter of my hostess asked, "Are you interested in old stories? Every village in Poland has one, and this is ours. Did you ever hear of St. Wojciech? Here in our village he preached his last sermon to Poles, just before he started to East Prussia. He asked the people what they wanted most. Some said, 'Water—a spring,' and some said, 'Oh, to get rid of the snakes!' for there were so many snakes the peasants were in great danger. When the mass was over, Wojciech knelt down and prayed, and lo! a spring of water—the people get their water from it to-day, and from that time to this the village has had no more trouble with snakes. On the old maps—I mean, the German maps, the village is called Gebetsort—the praying-place."

Some things in Polish history I understood after I'd traveled back and forth, here and there and yonder. It is part of the great central plain of Europe and has no natural boundaries—save for a few miles on the Baltic and the mountains on the south. It merges into Germany, Lithuania, Russia as Indiana merges into Illinois.

"Look, there's the frontier," the son of Szemetoszczyzna said and pointed to the horizon. "Beyond is Lithuania." To my eyes it was no boundary at all, just an arbitrary line set up by a group of men at Versailles.

"See, here are the boundary stones." Adam and Marya called my attention when we floated down the Dunajec River on a raft—a stream so narrow that at many places I could have tossed a stone across. "They're marked P on one side and CS on the other. And there are the sentinels pacing up and down. We'll be challenged in a moment." And we were.

"Do you see that line of trees?" a man asked as we stood on the top of the Union of Lublin mound near the heroic city of Lwów. "It used to mark the frontier— Austria here, Russia just across."

And again, from Katowice we motored out to the Three Kaisers' Corner, where two insignificant streams meet and flow on as one; here met the domains of the czar, the emperor of Austria, the German kaiser. And not many miles away is the modern Three Republics' Corner where to-day Poland and Czechoslovakia and Germany meet.

The point is just this: Poland is flat and level, with no efficient boundaries made by nature, nothing permanent. Across these plains the frontiers have shifted and changed, back and forth, for nine centuries, according to wars or marriages or a child's inheritance. Once upon a time one king ruled over Poland and Bohemia, again over Hungary and Poland. For more than a century the Hohenzollerns were vassals of a Polish king. (In the market-place in Krakow they showed me the steps where Albrecht of Brandenburg knelt before Sigismund I to pay homage and swear loyalty, and then Matejko's painting of that scene, in the National Museum.) Vassals they remained till the sixteen-fifties when the Swedes invaded Poland, and the Poles, hard pressed well-nigh to the breaking point, granted independence to Brandenburg in return for help in this emergency. Once too Sweden and Poland had the same king—Sigismund Vasa, who combined historic names of both countries. And there was a time when the Russians chose as their czar the son of a Polish king, and only his father's objections on religious grounds prevented his being crowned at Moscow. With such neighbors and such boundaries it's not surprising that much of Poland's history is concerned with wars and battles, with invasions and repelling of invasions. Czechs, Swedes and Tartars were her occasional enemies; Germans and Russians her permanent foes. But there is one great difference between the story of Poland and of her neighbors: she fought to defend herself, not for aggression.

Of the early kings I made friends with two—Ladislas Lokietek (the elbow high, his name means) and his son, Casimir the Great. I remembered Ladislas the Short because I saw his portrait in the Town Hall in Torun; then his tomb in the cathedral in Krakow, where the sculptor put a console beneath his feet to make him a little taller;

and the Franciscan cloisters where he hid and later escaped in a monk's robe—the early fourteenth century, that was, when three times the German citizens of Krakow combined against him and drove him from the throne. And at Ojcow (you pronounce that Oy'-sof!), a beauty spot in the mountains an hour away from the city, the guide who was taking us through a cave put down his candle and told a story:

"This is where Ladislas Lokietek lay hidden—once for six weeks, again for three, the last time for only a few days. The soldiers pursuing him searched all the countryside, after they'd tracked him this far, but found no king, no cave. The peasants were loyal and covered over the entrance with plants and trees, coming at night to let food down on a rope. Now if you'll come farther in, I'll show you the rock that served as the royal council table, where the king and his knights made their plans, and the great flat rock where Ladislas Lokietek slept—surely a royal bedroom, for there's a crown in the wall above it."

In Krakow I was told about their famous Cloth Hall, built by Casimir the Great. He planned it to replace an unsightly row of little shacks and booths, and all these years it's been a place for merchants. Done by Casimir the Great, they exclaim when they excavate in Krakow and nine or ten feet down come on traces of old water pipes. His name is spelled with a K in Polish, that's why each little square of the cathedral doors at the Wawel bears a K, crowned; and tradition says these were the first things made of iron in Poland. Our cathedral isn't new, they said in Lwów, the cornerstone was laid by Casimir the Great. And in a church in the oil-fields I saw his portrait in an old fresco. Ruins of his castles I found in no less than five cities, not to mention his palace on the Wawel, part of which was good enough for the Italian architects to utilize when they were building the new one for Sigismund I.

And if I couldn't remember his long reign for its few wars and its quantity of building, I'd not forget his tomb at the Wawel. Under an elaborate canopy, added long afterward, lies his noble figure, the head crowned, with long curled beard.

"Notice," said one of my Polish friends, "he has side curls and a long tunic, and of course this was his costume in the thirteen hundreds. Do you suppose the Jews are to-day wearing the identical dress of their ancestors who were invited here by Casimir the Great? Quite a stopover for the wandering Jew—more than six centuries!"

Then we come to one of my favorites, the girl queen, Jadwiga. The Poles love her and speak of her as if they'd known her, as if she were an aunt or a cousin. It seemed as if I touched her story at every turn in Krakow. One day we were motoring out to a farmhouse and stopped at the brow of a hill, to get the first view of the city and the Wawel that Jadwiga had when she came from Hungary to be crowned.

She used to come here, Marya told me when we went to the Franciscan cloisters, to meet her lover—you know, he was Wilhelm, the Archduke of Austria. Evidently the monks loved her as much as the people did, for they let the two meet here—more than once. They were betrothed as children, she five or six, with the understanding that if, when they grew up, they didn't like each other, the match would be broken off. But when Wilhelm presented himself in Krakow, she loved him at first sight, for he was tall, strong and very handsome. There was every reason for the marriage.

But the Polish nobles had other plans. To the north was Lithuania which ought to be their ally against the Teutonic Knights. Why not make sure of that friendship and cement the alliance by marrying their queen to the grand duke? To be sure, he was a great deal older than she, he was crude and cruel and savage, a ruler with no background of culture; moreover he was a pagan.

"Fly with me!" urged Wilhelm. "Come, this very night! I will have horses waiting just beyond the Wawel walls. We will ride through the night and to-morrow you shall be my bride. Come!"

And she consented.

Which stairs did she go down? I asked the guide at the palace. But he was conscientious and replied cautiously, "We're not sure. There's a legend that one stairway used to go down two hundred steps and came out near the Vistula—an emergency exit."

Wasn't it an emergency that night? The queen stole down—she was fifteen years old—but at the foot of the stairs she was stopped by one of the Polish nobles.

(Marya told me his name, but I don't remember it; but this is all a matter of history, not a legend.) He pleaded with her not to go, to give up Wilhelm and wed Ladislas Jagello. (His second name is a simplified form of the Lithuanian James.) Against her love and her youth, everything else, he put up two arguments: the good of Poland, and what was perhaps the strongest possible argument in medieval times, the benefit to the Church— for they would make it a condition that all Lithuania accept Christianity. Jadwiga listened. In the end she yielded and slowly climbed the stairs back to her room. But, added Marya emphatically, she yielded of her own free will, they did not force her into this marriage—not in Poland.

As a special favor to the Amerikanka, we went into Jadwiga's suite in the palace. To-day these two rooms are in the part of the building reserved for the President of Poland, and are generally not open to visitors. They're built out at an angle from the straight wall of the palace, and supported by three piers that have given rise to the name "the hen's foot." And they do suggest a hen's foot—after somebody explains it to you.

"Can you understand me?" Marya turned to me anxiously. "I mean—the lady of the cock. And see, there are windows on three sides, and Jadwiga's coat of arms, and Jagello's, above them. When these rooms were being restored, the workmen found under the floor the remains of furnace pipes, installed for Jadwiga who was very delicate and suffered greatly from the cold."

Jagello came to Krakow from his home in the north and was baptized here in the choir of the cathedral, the story went on when we'd crossed to the church, and three days later they were married here—the beginning of the famous Jagellonian dynasty that ruled Poland for almost two hundred years. Not without a struggle on the bride's part. Near the high altar is a large crucifix made of black stone—very, very old; legend says it was found in the Vistula, early in the fourteenth century, and it's been here in the cathedral ever since. On the night before her marriage Jadwiga knelt before it and prayed for guidance; was it God's will that she give up the man she loved and marry the Lithuanian? All during the long hours of that night she knelt there till the image of Christ turned to her and spoke: "Marry Jagello—for the good of Poland, for the good of the church." When she left at dawn, she hung over the crucifix a piece of black net as an expression of the grief and sorrow in her heart. And ever since the priests have kept black net over it, and it's always called Jadwiga's altar. As many times as I went into the cathedral, at any hour of the day, I never walked past it without seeing people kneeling there—not always women, many men pray at the crucifix of Queen Jadwiga.

Jagello survived her by many years and is buried in the nave—a tomb that's interesting because it was made immediately after his death, the figure done by a sculptor who knew him, so that it's a real likeness. I stood looking down at his face, stern and severe, not handsome; I thought of the attractive, young archduke, in love with her and she with him; I sighed for the happiness Jadwiga gave up—for Poland. Then I walked back into the choir and stood a long time by her tomb—a perfectly plain, black marble tomb, in this place of greatest honor, because it was nearest the high altar. A few feet distant, just outside the choir, is her monument, to my mind the most beautiful thing in the cathedral. The figure is of Carrara marble on a base of yellow, with the Polish eagle and some words in Latin. She lies there, a long slight figure, not dead but sleeping, with her hands together in prayer.

One morning I was taking a walk in Krakow, by myself, and saw a sort of corner-stone in the wall of a church, protected by a screening. There were some marks on it and the words "Stopa Jadwigi." What could it be? I copied down that brief inscription and carried it to my landlady.

"Oh, yes," she explained in German, "you've been to the Carmelite church. It says 'Jadwiga's footprint.'"

And with her son's help, for he spoke some English, and with the pictures in her little girl's book, I finally got the story: The queen and some of the court went one day beyond the city walls to see how this church was progressing. A stone-cutter sat there disconsolate, looking very sad and sorrowful. What was the trouble? Abashed at Jadwiga's noticing him, the man stammered out that his wife was very sick and his children were almost starving. Her heart was touched, but she had not expected to do any errands of mercy and had not brought her purse. Yet she could not walk away and do nothing at all. She glanced about; nothing offered.

The queen leaned down and took from her slipper the golden buckle. Silently she handed it to the stone-cutter. Some of the courtiers tossed the fellow some coins as they left. With tears in his eyes the man turned back to take up his tools, and lo! there in the stone was the imprint of Jadwiga's foot! The monks called it a miracle and carefully kept the stone and built it into the corner wall; and in every rebuilding during these five centuries that stone has always been preserved.

This is only one of many, many stories of Jadwiga. Her husband I remembered because of his victory at Grunwald. Did you ever hear of the Teutonic Knights? I never had, but I ran into them in Poland frequently. In Torun there's a leaning tower, a square tower built of brick, with a story less prosaic than Pisa's: Long ago, said the princess who was my hostess there, a wicked Teutonic Knight lived here, very wicked—so wicked that at last he could not endure the thought of all his sins and he committed suicide by hanging himself from the top of the tower. And so great was the weight of his sins that they pulled the tower over, just as you see it to-day.

Who were the Teutonic Knights? she repeated my question, and I could feel how surprised she was that I had to ask. A military order founded in the Holy Land—I believe it was the end of the twelfth century. The members were to fight for Christianity, but hold no property, no land. They lived in what is now Germany and one of their campaigns was against the heathen Prussi of the north. They went and conquered, and then settled down to stay, taking both the land and the name of the Prussi. Soon they wanted more land and seized it. The struggle with the Poles went on, victory now with one side, now with the other, till 1410 when Ladislas Jagello gave them a crushing defeat in the battle of Grunwald. Matejko painted a large picture—I must see it in the Art Museum in Warsaw—the grand master of the Knights in a white robe, on a white horse, the Polish nobles, Jagello and his brother, and in the clouds the image of St. Stanislas, Poland's patron saint. Battle axes, halberds, swords, a marvelous, fighting picture; you can almost hear the shouting and tumult. (That was what it meant then, when Poles referred to a possible war over the Corridor, and said grimly, "If war should come, it will be another Grunwald, for every man, woman and child would go to take part.")

I skipped the rest of the Jagellonian kings till I came to the last two—Sigismund I (Sigismund Stary—the Old, the Poles often call him) and his son, Sigismund August, their reigns marking the zenith of Poland's greatness in politics, in wealth, in the arts. The first Sigismund spent his childhood at the Hungarian court, and there while he was still crown prince, he made a plan to rebuild the royal palace in Krakow in the new fashion (Italian Renaissance) and asked an Italian architect to design it for him. It's one of the most perfect examples of Renaissance work in all Europe, with some details as fine as any I've seen in Italy (the carved doorways and the oriel window on the third floor), and withal some details distinctly and definitely Polish (the "under the heads room," where each compartment made by the deep beams of the ceiling had a carved head, about life-size. The Austrian soldiers left only a few in place, but the Tartar chieftain and the talkative woman with the bandaged mouth still gaze down on the room where ambassadors were received by the kings of Poland.) People say Sigismund Stary had one extravagance—architecture.

His wife was Bona Sforza, a princess of the famous family in Milan, and she brought with her into Poland many Italian artists—sculptors, architects, goldsmiths, painters, who found here a ready market for their work and appreciative patrons. Over the gateway of the palace on the Wawel are three coats of arms—the eagle of Poland, the knight of Lithuania with his sword raised to strike, and a serpent swallowing a tiny man—the arms of the Sforzas, I learned after much asking.

There's a portrait of Queen Bona in the palace, and I saw her again in Matejko's *Prussian Homage,* the seated figure in green, for which Pani Matejko was the model. Before the war, an Englishman told me, he'd often seen Poles stop in front of that canvas and gaze and gaze at it, as if they found some crumb of comfort in the fact that the partitioners have not always been their masters. What a regal figure Sigismund Stary is as he returns the banner to Albrecht of Brandenburg and gives his hand to be kissed!

His tomb is in the crypt of the Krakow cathedral, in a
room quite by itself, away from the other kings, away
even from his children, placed here directly under his
chapel. Some of these royal tombs are ornate and fussy,
with elaborate decorations of silver-gilt. His is as severely plain as early Renaissance architecture, with no
more trimming than a medallion, with his profile and a
brief Latin inscription. His real monument is the chapel
just above. There I got the "feel" of Sigismund I—the
red marble seat where he heard mass, the two tall candle-
sticks, marked with his name and the date, the altar-piece
he carried about with him wherever he went—even to war;
it was made by craftsmen in Nuremburg, and as many
times as I looked at it I could never decide which was the
lovelier—the outside panels with Durer's paintings or the
reliefs in silver on the inside. And opposite are the full-
length figures of the two Sigismunds, made by Italian
sculptors, one over the other, making that panel of the
wall an architectural unit, though the truth is more than
forty years passed between its start and finish.

What a beautiful chapel! I shut my eyes now and
try to recall it. The rich decoration of the wall panels
isn't made of stucco, as I thought at first, but of stone.
Eighty rosettes, also of stone, in the cupola, and no two
of them alike. And at the highest point the name of
Berecci, the architect from Florence. The roof too was
beautiful—a kind of shingle with a curved edge, made of
copper heavily gilt. Here and there I saw black marks
and streaks, left by the tar with which the Poles covered

it at the last Partition, to save it from the Austrians.

Even more interesting, according to some of my Polish friends, is the second Sigismund. I met him first with his tutor, a child of five or six, in a long red dress, standing back of his father in *Prussian Homage*. He went on with the plans for the royal palace, which was over sixty years in building. Part of it was burned and had to be entirely redone. There were changes in the plans. The courtyard was doubled in size—that's why the entrance seems to be in a queer place. The arcades were repeated on all three floors, even along the side where there are no rooms—just a three-story wall to give the same effect.

Sigismund August's was one of the most brilliant courts in Europe, and fittingly he housed it. Instead of the red tile that I saw, the roofs were porcelain and gleamed in the sun. Foreigners used to write about it in their letters home. The balconies were hung with tapestries. The courtyard was gay with color and life. And for the inside walls the king ordered the gorgeous tapestries that are still called by his name. A great patron of art—that you feel constantly in the palace on the Wawel.

But it was in Wilno, to my surprise, that I came even closer to Sigismund August. He liked that city in the north and spent perhaps half his time there. He had fallen in love—madly in love with Barbara, a princess of the Radziwill family; but the Polish nobles strenuously opposed this marriage on the ground that it would make the Radziwills too powerful and upset the carefully maintained balance of power within the state. Bluntly they put the matter to the young prince: "Become the next king of Poland—or marry Barbara. You may not do both. Now, take your choice."

"I choose," he made unhesitating answer, "I choose to live with this lady to whom I've pledged my word." Then with withering scorn he turned on those men. "What sort of king would I be if now I preferred to be the king of Poland? What would my word be worth if, in order to win the throne, I broke it without scruple? Could you ever trust me then?"

They were married secretly. I hunted up the chapel where the wedding took place. It's in the Wilno cathedral and probably looks much as it did then (in the fifteen-forties), for though the church was built over in another style of architecture this room was left unchanged. Why? I asked. Because the architect found an old inscription warning every one that ill luck would follow if anything was altered there.

In another chapel, at the opposite end of the cathedral, Barbara lies buried, with a plain tomb of black marble. Sigismund August ordered in Italy a splendid Renaissance monument, which was made and shipped north. It was extremely heavy and had to travel in the winter when sledges could be used; en route it crossed a river on the ice, but its weight was so great that the ice gave way and down it fell to the river bed, and could never be recovered.

"But," said my Wilno professor, "see the inscription here. Who'd want a splendid tomb from Italy in exchange for this? You read medieval Latin at sight, madam? I will translate—only roughly.

> Barbara, the beloved, wife of Sigismund August. She died too early, but had she lived to be very— ancient (is that the word? or is old better?) he would still say, she died too soon.

"There's an ugly story," he went on, "that the beloved Barbara was heartily disliked by her mother-in-law, Bona Sforza, who summoned one of her Italians, a noted poisoner, and bade him put her out of the way. She died after a sudden, short illness that no one understood. One of my medical friends studied the old records and says that nowadays we'd think she had appendicitis. Sigismund August was inconsolable, but for reasons of state he must needs marry again—indeed, twice more. In the Czartoryski Museum in Krakow you'll see a series of portraits by Cranach—the whole family."

A love story—sad because it was so brief. What other crown prince, out of the fairy stories, gave up being king to keep his word to the lady of his heart? Who else said of his bride, if she had lived to be very ancient, I would still say that she died too soon?

Then began the election of kings in Poland. The first was Henry of Valois, a son of that arch-plotter and schemer, Catherine de Medici, who after a few months in Krakow learned of his brother's death and the vacant throne of France, and ran away at night to claim it. They showed me the palace stairs where he slipped down, rid-

ing all night long to get to the frontier, so afraid was he
that the Poles would try to keep him by force. Did I
remember, they asked me, the impression made in Paris
by the committee who went to offer Henry the crown of
Poland—their magnificent clothes, their speaking in
Latin, their courtly manners?

His successor was the Transylvanian, Stephen Batory—
one of the greatest and wisest of Polish sovereigns. A
great statesman as well as a great warrior. I saw his
portrait in a Krakow church, in a long yellow robe and
yellow shoes. I saw a large Matejko canvas in the royal
castle in Warsaw, showing the Russians kneeling to pay
tribute after one of his great victories. I went into his
chapel in the Wawel cathedral, with his throne and his
monument, and saw from the outside the overhead passage joining his rooms in the palace with the balcony of
this chapel. But mostly I remember Batory for his chancellor, Jan Zamoyski.

And then, for about eighty years, the Vasa kings, so
named because they belonged to the royal house of
Sweden. The first of them inherited the Swedish throne
through his mother. He it was who set the Krakow palace
on fire, during an experiment to make gold out of iron
(for he was by way of being an amateur alchemist) and
then, because nearly all the splendid furnishings were
ruined, he moved the capital to Warsaw. He it was who
sat in the great hall in his castle there and had brought
before him in chains a prisoner of war—the Russian czar.
He it was who refused to let his son be crowned at Moscow,

because Poles and Russians could not agree on some question of religion. And it is he who stands high up on a column, in the heart of Warsaw, holding cross and sword and looking out over the city, looking down on the castle where now lives the President of Poland.

The next king I met was Sobieski, the savior of Vienna (and of the whole of Europe) when it was besieged by the Turks—a fact I couldn't forget in Poland, for in city after city they showed me booty he sent back. One church in Lwów has vestments made of Turkish embroidery. Their tents I saw in the Lubomirski Museum and in the Czartoryski collection, along with curved scimitars and flags with crescents.

And if the booty hadn't interested me, there was Wilanow, a summer palace Sobieski built near Warsaw, using the labor of his Turkish prisoners. He was a military man first and foremost, and the entrance gate has military emblems, while the façade has a row of reliefs showing scenes in Vienna: the city walls, Turks in turbans and Poles with crests of eagles' feathers, the meeting of emperor and king, the thanksgiving service where the *Te Deum* was sung and the text of the sermon was, "There was a man sent from God whose name was John," returning with the spoils of war—all this told in sculpture, with a quaint touch in one panel where the canopy over the bishop is not modeled, but made of actual cloth.

All over Poland I saw Sobieski portraits; his house in Lwów, now a museum; his house in Lublin, which I guessed must have had a special owner, for it has five windows; in Danzig a palace and church erected for him, when he went there once for a week; and his statue in the grounds at Lazienki, placed at the very end of the walk at the back of the palace, because the Russians wouldn't allow it a prominent site. He was buried in a little chapel in the church of the Capuchins in Warsaw, because he was very friendly to the good brothers of that order; when later it was determined to take the body to Krakow, the monks kept the heart of Sobieski. And after the Partitions a Russian czar built in that chapel a splendid monument, where I puzzled out a long, pompous Latin inscription in which Nicholas I proudly names himself as the successor of the great Sobieski.

No Pole is proud of the next group—the Electors of Saxony, August II and III, absentees who neither governed nor defended the country, but exploited Poland for the benefit of Saxony. I had only a bowing acquaintance with their fat faces, when I met them near the Saxon palace in the center of Warsaw, or in its beautiful garden, now a public park. A sad period of decadence. Just a minute for them, let's go on quickly.

One of my great favorites was Stanislas August, the last king of Poland, chosen at the dictation of Catherine the Great, whose favorite he had been, with fifteen thousand Russian troops watching over the election. He had a long reign—over thirty years, marked by attempts at reform (the valiant efforts of the Confederation of Bar, the Constitution of the third of May) and by the tragic Partitions. A handsome man he was, to judge by his many portraits. Handsome too in the great Matejko painting I saw in the Warsaw castle—my first Matejko.

"Which is the king?" I asked, "and what is the story?"

"They are starting into the next room to sign the papers for the first Partition. This patriotic Lithuanian, Reytan, throws himself on the floor, tears back his coat to bare his breast, and calls out dramatically, 'Kill me, but do not sign!' Later he went insane from grief for Poland. These are all portraits—the Primate, Czartoryski, Potocki, the Russian ambassador in the balcony, the picture of Catherine on the wall, and Stanislas August—the one with the wide blue ribbon of an order."

The castle is furnished—as far as it can be said to be furnished, thanks to the Russians—with things of this period. He was contemporary with Louis XV and XVI and was a great lover of French things. Some of the frescoes were done by Le Brun. There are French clocks and French bronzes and chairs. In one room I came suddenly on a bust of Benjamin Franklin.

"An American," stated the guide, "Washington."

"No, no!" I cried, "not Washington."

"Ah, madam is right. I have the names mixed. It is Franklin—right?"

"But—but how in the world does it happen to be here—in a royal palace in Poland?"

The explanation seemed to him the most natural thing in the world. The king had his agents in Paris and gave them instructions to send him all the most fashionable things. Franklin was in France, representing the American colonies, a favorite of Marie Antoinette, his picture sold on the city streets, his wise sayings quoted. What was it they called him? Poor—poor Something.

"Poor Richard," I supplied.

And so, this marble bust was purchased for Stanislas August.

But it was at Lazienki (Wa-zen'key) I got to know him intimately. That's the most delightful and charming palace I've ever seen—bar none. Nowadays it's on the edge of the capital city, it used to be out in the country. Think of Versailles, of Schönbrunn at Vienna, on a smaller scale, with fewer rooms, far more homelike, far more beautiful, and you'll be somewhere near having Lazienki. Indeed, art experts say it's the most beautiful building of this period in all Europe. And one joy about it—it's just as the king left it—yes, completely furnished; for the czars kept it for their own use and never took its treasures away. I felt as if Stanislas August and his friends had gone away for a few hours, as if any moment a major-domo might throw open the door and announce, "His Majesty!"

It's not a large building. The street floor has reception-rooms, a picture gallery, the Solomon room with frescoes where that wise king has the face of Stanislas, the green room hung with portraits of the beauties of his court—he was a connoisseur in beautiful women! and up-stairs the charming rooms where the king lived: the blue and silver bedroom, a writing-room, the china room where the royal dishes were kept. A porcelain caricature of Franklin, facing one of Voltaire, showed that his agents did buy all the Paris novelties.

"No guest rooms?" I asked.

"Yes, separate little buildings, scattered over the palace grounds. We'll pass some of them. There's the White House where the king's morganatic wife lived; and the hunting lodge of Jozef Poniatowski (the king's nephew—yes, it's his statue you saw near the Unknown Soldier), with his initials over the door; and the orangery where the first oranges in Poland were grown—under glass. We mustn't fail to see the little open-air theater where performances used to be given for the court—and occasionally now, for some very special visitors, they give a play or dances. The stage and orchestra are on a little island. It's a fairy spot—all it needs is Stanislas August and his friends in their lovely costumes.

"For a long, long while," Zofia went on, "Poles were inclined to belittle our last king. They called him weak and cowardly when the times demanded a strong ruler—especially if you remember that his contemporaries stand out in European history as ruthless, powerful sovereigns—Maria Theresa, Frederick the Great, Catherine of Russia. But now that Poland is free again, when we have a truer perspective and can judge him with less bitterness and prejudice, there's come a marked change; we see him as a great patron of the arts, a real connoisseur and lover of beauty. He drew to his court painters and sculptors and architects from all Europe. His Thursday dinners—did you see the Thursday room in the palace?—

led directly to a flowering of Polish literature; he would have perhaps two dozen guests, writers and artists, and many of them owed their inspiration and encouragement to the talks around that dinner table.''

The next day an official in the Ministry of Foreign Affairs asked what he could do for me, and I was prompt to reply, ''There's just one thing to make my cup run over. If you could arrange it? I want to take a nap in the blue and silver room at Lazienki, and wake up to see the swans on the lake, have tea in the gardens, and watch Polish dances in the little theater.'' Except for the nap, it all came true.

And after Stanislas August what? The last Partition; Napoleon's rise and the Poles enlisting by thousands, lured by his vague promises. ''God is with Napoleon, Napoleon is with us,'' was one of their watchwords. How their hopes flamed up when he created the Duchy of Warsaw! It would be the nucleus of a new Poland.

Here enters the fascinating Jozef Poniatowski, one of the most popular of Polish heroes, who became my hero too. Often I stopped on my way through a great square in Warsaw, to look up at his statue. Did I know about his death? asked a young Pole, and the story of this monument?

''At the battle of Leipzig he was sorely wounded. When he saw that all was lost, that he could not carry out Napoleon's orders, he refused to live defeated, spurred his horse into the river and was drowned. 'God gave me the honor of Poland to defend,' were his last words, 'and to Him alone can I surrender it.'

"He had been the idol of Warsaw," my Pole went on, "brave, handsome, charming, with all the ladies in love with him. The Russians were loath to give their consent for this monument, saying it would foster our national pride; but finally they gave the permission on condition that Thorwaldsen should dress him like a Roman and not a Polish general. The statue came to Warsaw, but before it could be erected the insurrection of 1830 broke out. The Russian general Paskevich found it in a warehouse here, after his entry into the city. Now Paskevich"—he hesitated—"Paskevich is not a name we Poles love, but this one thing he did—he respected the statue as a work of art and took it, still in the packing cases, off to his estate.

"There it was set up in a splendid site on the bridge over the moat—I've seen pictures of it—and there it stayed in exile for nearly a century. The Poles would say, 'Poniatowski prefers exile to slavery. He will come back when we are free.' More than once the czar ordered it sent to St. Petersburg to be made into cannon, but each time Paskevich persuaded him to allow it to stay.

"When the war with the Bolshevists ended, the treaty of peace said—just the opposite of Napoleon's conditions!—that certain treasures of Poland's should be given back: the Sigismund August tapestries that you'll see at Krakow, the University of Warsaw library, and so on, and this Poniatowski statue. A committee of distinguished men escorted it—on flat cars, gaily decorated, and people all along the way greeted it with cheers. It was set up here in the Plac Pilsudski and dedicated with a brilliant ceremony. Foch, the modern marshal of France, came to pay tribute to our former marshal. There—I almost forgot to tell you something; it came back minus one item, and there followed reams of diplomatic correspondence over the return of Poniatowski's horse's tail! Now, you appreciate why it's called the most romantic statue in Europe.''

To go back a little and pick up my thread. Napoleon's Duchy of Warsaw lasted only till the Congress of Vienna could make a new map of Europe—but without a Poland, the partitioning was to be permanent. There were three insurrections, the last one coming during our Civil War. Then a period of hopelessness and apathy till the Versailles treaty brought about the birth of a new Poland.

Most of this romantic story of a nation that would not die I learned on the spot, from my many Polish friends; but some I got from Matejko's pictures—a second delightful way to have a history lesson. He must have been an indefatigable worker and a very rapid worker as well, for he did more than two hundred large canvases, to say nothing of portraits and sketches and smaller pictures; and how he ever managed to live and support his family was a puzzle, for he never sold the huge historical paintings, but gave them away to this gallery and to that museum. And he was nearsighted besides!

For his models and his backgrounds he needed numerous objects—armor and rich fabrics, jewels and lace, crowns, sandals, halberds. Sometimes he could borrow, often he bought with a sketch, till he got together a unique collection of costumes and accessories for servants and sovereigns and courtiers and soldiers for every period— not a higgledy-piggledy lot, but each thing carefully chosen. On his death his house in Krakow was immediately made into a Matejko museum, before these precious things could be scattered and lost. The rooms are full of atmosphere, with the artist's furniture, his palette and paint tubes, photographs of his work, and hundreds, hundreds of sketches—a page of sleeves, of shoes, a medieval room, a quaint doorway or window, faces, head-dresses, priests' robes and jeweled crosses.

I climbed the stairs to his studio on the top floor—a very small room for a studio, I thought; even for portraits a man needs to stand away from his canvas and from his sitter; how did he manage a picture fifty or sixty feet long? He worked on only one part at a time, they told me, and kept the rest rolled up. He was a Pole through and through, though he exhibited in many cities and won a prize at Paris—the highest honor France has ever given to a foreigner. He spoke Polish and nothing more; when the Austrian emperor went to call on him they had to talk through an interpreter.

He did an inestimable service for his country. He lived at a time when Poland needed him sorely. After the last insurrection came a long period of utter discouragement and disillusion. There grew up a school of historians, some of them educated in Germany, some indirectly swayed by Prussian or Russian influence, who by lectures

and writing spread abroad a new conception of Poland—
that she fell from internal weakness and not from outside interference; that had she deserved to live Europe
would have prevented the Partitions by some concerted
effort; that her past was only a sham greatness covered
with a tinsel of glory that concealed the rotten core; that
there was no possible future for such a nation. And many
Poles read and heard this till they actually began to believe it, or at least to doubt and question.

Just when this idea was gaining ground appeared
Sienkiewicz and Matejko, and like trumpeters announced
to the new generation of Poles and to the world what a
splendid and glorious past they had. One in the pages of
his novels, the other in pictures, they told of thrilling mo-
ments in Poland's story—of Grunwald and Sobieski, of
Reytan's protest, of Stephen Batory and the Sigismunds,
of Kosciuszko with his peasant soldiers. And thousands
of young Poles made answer, "Poland is not yet dead!"

It was Matejko who introduced me to my favorite priest
in Poland. I'd gone to an art gallery in Warsaw to see
his famous *Grunwald*. No one had told me there were
other things I must see, so I used all the time I had on
Jagello and the Teutonic Knights; then as I turned to
leave the room I saw another Matejko—that I knew at a
glance. Was it something important in Polish history?
What? I found a guard who spoke some French and
pointed to the picture's title; he repeated it in Polish, but
couldn't say it in French. I pointed to various figures;
he caught my meaning and began naming them: Skarga—

Sigismund III in black velvet with a wide lace collar—the queen and her daughter—a cardinal—all portraits. That was as much as I could make out.

" 'The Prophecy of Peter Skarga,' " my hostess at tea translated the words I'd copied down. "Tell you of him? He was a Jesuit priest living at the time of Stephen Batory and Sigismund III—the end of the sixteenth century; a combination of priest and prophet like the men in the Old Testament. He preached sermon after sermon—to-day every school child studies them, for they're remarkable as literature—pointing out fearlessly the sins and the weaknesses of Poland, foretelling the nation's downfall unless king and nobles changed their ways. And two hundred years later all that he prophesied came true, exactly as he'd said. Our country was partitioned—and lost——"

I could not forget that stern lined face with the ascetic look, the thin hands held up in denunciation. Weeks later in Wilno I was taken to see the university and walked through the court of Skarga. I understood why there was a Mickiewicz court, but what connection did this school in the far corner of Poland have with my prophet-priest?

"Why, he was the first rector here. He made the university. You must ask at the cathedral and they'll show you his toga—the Wilno rector to-day wears one made like his; it's a peculiar color, between red and purple— amaranth."

More than a month later I was exploring all by myself in Krakow and finding St. Peter's church open, I went in.

[322]

Without any warning, I came on the tomb of Skarga and his statue near by. Think of a guide-book giving two paragraphs to that church and never mentioning the fact that Skarga is buried there—my Peter Skarga!

On my last day in Poland a friend took me for a last look at the Stare Miasto—Warsaw's medieval market-place, whose fine old houses have been restored, after a long period of neglect and abuse, and painted with beautiful designs and gay colors. Helena pointed out a famous old wineshop, one house that belonged to the Piast princes, another that's been made into a museum.

"And that one on the corner was Peter Skarga's. He lived part of the time in Warsaw, as he was court chaplain and preacher to king and Diet. No, the house hasn't a tablet to mark it—but it has a story. The Poles believed that in times of great stress and need Peter Skarga came out on to the balcony, as if——"

Helena stopped and looked at me intently, as if to make sure that I would understand. I looked up at the balcony and slowly nodded my head.

"As if he were trying to speak to them again, as if he wanted desperately to warn them—as in days of old. Many persons thought they saw him on the balcony—in 1914."

We turned to go. The late afternoon shadows stretched across the cobblestones of the old market-place. At the corner I stopped for a last long look. I was sailing the next day. A ray of sunlight touched the house with the balcony.

Was it a wish that came to my lips—or a prayer?

"Skarga," I called silently to my priest across the many years, "oh, Peter Skarga! Don't let anything happen now to Poland that will bring you out on the balcony again!"

THE END

INDEX

INDEX

[327]

INDEX

INDEX